Intellectual Property Law and Plant Protection

This book is the first to provide a detailed and critical account of the emergence, development, and implementation of plant variety protection laws in Asian countries. Each chapter undertakes a critical socio-legal analysis of one or more legal frameworks to understand, evaluate, and explore the concerns of diverse national stakeholders, the histories and dynamics of law-making, and the ways in which plant variety protection and seed certification laws interact with local agricultural systems.

The book also assesses how Asian countries can capitalise on the 'unused policy space' in international agreements such as the *Agreement on Trade-Related Aspects of Intellectual Property Rights* and the *International Convention for the Protection of New Varieties of Plants*, as well as international obligations beyond these, such as those contained in the *Convention on Biological Diversity* and the Plant Treaty. It also highlights the many ways in which Asian experiences can offer new insights into the relationship between intellectual property and plants, and how relevant laws might be re-imagined in other regions, including Africa, Europe, and the Americas.

By adding an important new perspective to the ongoing debate on intellectual property and plants, this book will appeal to academics, practitioners, and policy-makers engaged in work surrounding intellectual property laws, agricultural biodiversity, and plant breeding.

Kamalesh Adhikari is AIBE Research Fellow in Food Security and a Member of the Australian Research Council (ARC) Laureate Project *Harnessing Intellectual Property to Build Food Security* in the TC Beirne School of Law at the University of Queensland, Australia.

David J. Jefferson is a Research Fellow and Member of the Australian Research Council (ARC) Laureate Project *Harnessing Intellectual Property to Build Food Security* in the TC Beirne School of Law at the University of Queensland, Australia.

Routledge Research in Intellectual Property

Available:

Annotated Leading Trademark Cases in Major Asian Jurisdictions
Edited by Kung-Chung Liu

Cultivating Copyright
How Creators and Creative Industries Can Harness IP to Survive the Digital Age
Bhamati Viswanathan

Biotechnology, Patents and Morality
A Deliberative and Participatory Paradigm for Reform
Maureen O'Sullivan

Internet Intermediaries and Trade Mark Rights
Althaf Marsoof

Intellectual Property and Access to Medicines in Africa
A Regional Framework for Access
Olasupo Owoeye

Intellectual Property Branding in the Developing World
A New Approach to Non-Technological Innovations
Tshimanga Kongolo

The Patentability of Software
Software as Mathematics
Anton Hughes

For more information about this series, please visit www.routledge.com/Routledge-Research-in-Intellectual-Property/book-series/INTELLPROP

Intellectual Property Law and Plant Protection

Challenges and Developments in Asia

Edited by
Kamalesh Adhikari and David J. Jefferson

Routledge
Taylor & Francis Group
LONDON AND NEW YORK

First published 2020
by Routledge
2 Park Square, Milton Park, Abingdon, Oxon OX14 4RN

and by Routledge
52 Vanderbilt Avenue, New York, NY 10017

Routledge is an imprint of the Taylor & Francis Group, an informa business

British Library Cataloguing in Publication Data
A catalogue record for this book is available from the British Library

Library of Congress Cataloging-in-Publication Data
A catalog record has been requested for this book

ISBN: 978-0-367-18099-7 (hbk)
ISBN: 978-0-429-05952-0 (ebk)

Typeset in Galliard
by Taylor & Francis Books

Intellectual Property Law and Plant Protection

Challenges and Developments in Asia

Edited by
Kamalesh Adhikari and David J. Jefferson

Routledge
Taylor & Francis Group
LONDON AND NEW YORK

First published 2020
by Routledge
2 Park Square, Milton Park, Abingdon, Oxon OX14 4RN

and by Routledge
52 Vanderbilt Avenue, New York, NY 10017

Routledge is an imprint of the Taylor & Francis Group, an informa business

British Library Cataloguing in Publication Data
A catalogue record for this book is available from the British Library

Library of Congress Cataloging-in-Publication Data
A catalog record has been requested for this book

ISBN: 978-0-367-18099-7 (hbk)
ISBN: 978-0-429-05952-0 (ebk)

Typeset in Galliard
by Taylor & Francis Books

Contents

Illustrations

Figure

Tables

Contributors

Kamalesh Adhikari is Australian Institute of Business and Economics (AIBE) Research Fellow in Food Security and Member of the Australian Research Council (ARC) Laureate Project *Harnessing Intellectual Property to Build Food Security* in the TC Beirne School of Law at the University of Queensland, Australia. He is also a research partner in the Research Council of Norway and the Fridtjof Nansen Institute's 'Suitable Seeds Project.' His current research focusses on developing access and benefit sharing models for the Australian native food industry and exploring the role of networks, informality and community seed banks in shaping seed regulation across developing and least-developed countries. Kamalesh is also undertaking a critical account of the concept of farmers' rights in intellectual property law.

R. C. Agrawal is an Agricultural Research Services Scientist who has spent 20 years working with the Indian Council of Agricultural Research – National Bureau of Plant Genetic Resources. Presently, as the Registrar General of the Protection of Plant Varieties and Farmers Rights Authority of the Government of India, he is directly responsible for the implementation of the *Protection of Plant Varieties and Farmers Rights Act 2001.* He has published more than 35 research papers, authored two books, published 15 technical bulletins, and has participated in more than 100 conferences and workshops to deliver invited talks. Recently, Dr Agrawal was elected by the Secretariat of the Plant Treaty to lead a group to develop strategies for the implementation of Farmers' Rights.

David J. Jefferson is a Research Fellow and Member of the Australian Research Council (ARC) Laureate Project *Harnessing Intellectual Property to Build Food Security* in the TC Beirne School of Law at the University of Queensland, Australia. He is also the Law and Policy Analyst at the Public Intellectual Property Resource for Agriculture, a non-profit organisation based at the University of California, Davis, and in this role he serves as the Program Director of the *Licensing Academy: Intellectual Property and Technology Transfer* professional certificate course. David's academic work focusses on how intellectual property laws structure relationships between people, institutions, and plants, and on the circulation and commercialisation of native plant genetic resources. His primary research sites are located in Latin America and Australia.

Rajeswari Kanniah holds a doctorate in law from the University of Malaya. She has served as the Dean of the School of Law of two private universities in Malaysia and a part-time lecturer in law at Heriot Watt University, Malaysia. Her recent appointments include Honorary Fellow of the School of Law, Deakin University, and Conjoint Senior Lecturer, Law School, University of Newcastle, Australia. She has published widely on intellectual property rights and consumer protection.

Charles Lawson is a Professor in the Griffith Law School, Griffith University. He studied science and law at The Australian National University (ANU) and holds a Bachelor of Science with Honours in biochemistry and genetics and a Bachelor of Laws. He also holds a Doctor of Philosophy from the ANU's Research School of Biological Sciences in molecular biology and biochemistry and a Master of Laws from Queensland University of Technology for research into gene patenting and competition. Before joining the university sector he worked as a lawyer in both the private and public sectors, including at the Australian Government Solicitor and the Commonwealth Department of Finance and Deregulation. His research focus is on patents, plant breeders' rights and public administration law.

Pawarit Lertdhamtewe is at the Faculty of Law, Ramkhamhaeng University, Thailand. He holds a PhD in law from the University of London where he was a Herchel Smith Scholar.

Asanka Perera is a Lecturer at the Monash Business School. At Monash, she teaches Business Law and Australian Company Law. Her area of interest is intellectual property law, and at present, she is completing a PhD in law. Her PhD thesis undertakes an exploratory study of how different types of intellectual property regimes could complement or complicate the economic development of Sri Lanka. Asanka has authored several scholarly articles on plant breeders' rights, farmers' rights, patents, innovation, and economic development. She also has presented papers in a number of international conferences.

Muhammad Ahsan Rana is an Associate Professor of Agricultural and Social Policy at the Lahore University of Management Sciences, Pakistan. He has worked extensively with public and private sector institutions in Pakistan. As a former member of the Pakistan Administrative Service, he has held senior policy assignments in the governments of Sindh and Punjab. He also has worked with a number of national and international organisations. Ahsan has authored several articles and chapters in academic journals and books. He is best known for his work on the seed sector, intellectual property, and agricultural trade in Pakistan.

Pratap Shrestha is a Programme Specialist for seed systems and plant genetic resources, and Coordinator of the scientific advisory team at USC Canada in Ottawa. Previously, he served as the Executive Director at the Nepal-based Local Initiatives for Biodiversity, Research and Development (LIBIRD), a non-governmental organisation.

Acknowledgements

This volume is based in part on content that was presented and discussed during a workshop entitled *Reimagining the Governance of Genetic Resources and Intellectual Property for Agriculture and Food Security in Asia*. This event was co-hosted on August 2–3 2017 in Kathmandu, Nepal by the Australian Research Council (ARC) Laureate Project *Harnessing Intellectual Property to Build Food Security* at the University of Queensland, South Asia Watch on Trade, Economics and Environment (SAWTEE), and the Fridtjof Nansen Institute (FNI).

The aim of the workshop was to bring together leading scholars and policymakers with expertise in intellectual property law and the governance of plant genetic resources, and to engage these individuals in a collegial academic forum. The invited experts were required to submit and make presentations on draft chapters that were aimed specifically at addressing the issues and concerns of Asian countries in relation to intellectual property for plant varieties. We would like to thank all of the authors for revising their draft chapters based on the comments that they received at the workshop, and from the editors during subsequent rounds of revision. We also would like to thank FNI and SAWTEE for their financial support, and Pragati Koirala and other colleagues at SAWTEE for their logistical support in organising the workshop in Kathmandu.

In compiling this edited collection, we also acknowledge the generous support of the ARC Laureate Fellowship scheme (project number FL150100104). Led by Professor Brad Sherman (the Laureate Fellow) at the University of Queensland, the Laureate Project aims to approach the subject of intellectual property and agriculture through a range of interconnected projects that enhance the understanding of the impact of the law on our contemporary global food and seed systems. We are grateful for the comments that our colleagues in the Laureate Project provided for draft versions of several of the key chapters of the volume. We would like to thank especially Dr Tad Brown, Dr Susannah Chapman, Dr Xan Chacko, Professor Brad Sherman, and Dr Andrew Ventimiglia for their feedback. Lastly, we appreciate the comments that Dr Mathilde Pavis of the University of Exeter Law School provided while serving as a visiting scholar at the University of Queensland.

Abbreviations

1976 Seed Act	*Seed Act 1976* of Pakistan
2015 Seed Act	*2015 Seed (Amendment) Act* of Pakistan
AFLP	Amplified Fragment Length Polymorphism
AIBE	Australian Institute of Business and Economics
ANU	Australian National University
ARC	Australian Research Council
ASEAN	Association of South East Asian Nations
ASPA	Asia and Pacific Seed Association
ASSINSEL	International Association of Plant Breeders
CBD	*Convention on Biological Diversity* of the United Nations
CGIAR	Consultative Group for International Agricultural Research
CPTPP	*Comprehensive and Progressive Agreement for Trans-Pacific Partnership*
DUS	Distinctness, Uniformity, and Stability
EAPVPF	East Asia Plant Variety Protection Forum
EDVs	Essentially Derived Varieties
FAO	Food and Agriculture Organization of the United Nations
FNI	Fridtjof Nansen Institute
FSC&RD	Federal Seed Certification and Registration Department of Pakistan
GRAIN	Genetic Resources Action International
IFPRI	International Food Policy Research Institute
Indonesian PVP Act	*Plant Variety Protection Act No. 29 of 2000* of Indonesia
IPO	Intellectual Property Organisation of Pakistan
LIBIRD	Local Initiatives for Biodiversity, Research and Development
Malaysian PVP Act	*Protection of New Plant Varieties Act 2004 (Act 634)* of Malaysia
MoAC	Ministry of Agriculture and Cooperatives of Thailand
MoC	Ministry of Commerce of Thailand

Nagoya Protocol	*Nagoya Protocol on Access to Genetic Resources and the Fair and Equitable Sharing of Benefits Arising from their Utilization to the Convention on Biological Diversity*
NDPP	National Directorate of Policy and Planning of Timor Leste
Philippines PVP Act	*Plant Variety Protection Act of 2002 (Republic Act No. 9168)* of the Philippines
Plant Treaty	*International Treaty on Plant Genetic Resources for Food and Agriculture* of the Food and Agriculture Organization of the United Nations
PPV&FR	Protection of Plant Varieties and Farmers' Rights
PPV&FRA	Protection of Plant Varieties and Farmers' Rights Authority of India
PVP	Plant Variety Protection
PVP Bill	*Draft Bill on the Protection of Plant Varieties (Breeder's Rights)* of Sri Lanka
RAEBIA	Resilient Agriculture and Economy through Biodiversity in Action
RCEP	*Regional Comprehensive Economic Partnership*
SAWTEE	South Asia Watch on Trade, Economics and Environment
Thai PVP Act	*Plant Variety Protection Act B.E.2542 (1999)* of Thailand
TPP	*Trans-Pacific Partnership*
TRIPS	*Agreement on Trade-Related Aspects of Intellectual Property Rights* of the World Trade Organization
UPOV	International Union for the Protection of New Varieties of Plants
UPOV Convention	*International Convention for the Protection of New Varieties of Plants* of the International Union for the Protection of New Varieties of Plants
UPOV 1978	1978 Act of the UPOV Convention
UPOV 1991	1991 Act of the UPOV Convention
USDA	United States Department of Agriculture

Foreword

Over the last decade or so, a rising global population, a comparative decline in arable land, and growing evidence of the negative impact that climate change is having on agricultural production have elicited widespread concerns about our ability to feed the world in the future. Given the important role that intellectual property laws play across the food chain – from accessing genetic materials and protecting breeding and on-farm innovations, through to the processing, packaging, storage, transportation, and consumption of food – it is not surprising that there has been a growing interest in the role that intellectual property laws play, for better or worse, in responding to the problem of food security.

Focussing on intellectual property protection for plants in 12 Asian countries, *Intellectual Property Law and Plant Protection: Challenges and Developments in Asia* makes a valuable and timely contribution to this important ongoing debate. There are a number of notable things about this edited collection, which built upon a workshop that was held in Nepal in August 2017. One of which is that the collection provides a comprehensive account of the emergence and implementation of plant intellectual property laws, or plans there for, in a range of different Asian countries. As well as including up-to-date chapters on countries such as India and Thailand, which have already attracted some scholarly attention, the collection also includes chapters on Cambodia, Laos, Nepal, Myanmar, Pakistan, and Timor-Leste, which have largely been neglected in the literature. In so doing, the volume not only provides readers with an opportunity to appreciate the different ways that different Asian countries have implemented, or plan to implement, intellectual property laws for plants, but also provides a unique opportunity to understand how countries in different stages of economic development and with different social, cultural, and physical environments have responded to the challenge of protecting biological innovations.

Another notable feature of the collection is that it was motivated by a desire to move beyond a top-down approach to intellectual property law to one that explores the socio-legal dynamics associated with the regulation of plant varieties as intellectual property. This is reflected in many of the chapters in an examination of the experiences that diverse stakeholders, such as public and private seed entities and farmers' groups, have had in the development and implementation of plant-based intellectual property laws in their respective countries.

The volume grew out of the Australian Research Council's Laureate Project, *Harnessing Intellectual Property to Build Food Security*, which is based at the University of Queensland. This project approaches intellectual property and its engagement with agriculture through a range of interconnected studies in order to understand the impact that the law has on the contemporary global food system. By moving beyond the logic of intellectual property doctrine to consider how the law orders relationships between people and plants, this volume allows us to better understand how intellectual property and related legal frameworks are able to address challenges related to food security, climate change, and agricultural change, both in Asia and throughout the world more generally.

Professor Brad Sherman
Australian Laureate Fellow
The University of Queensland

Chapter 1

Intellectual property law for plant varieties

Challenges and developments in Asia

Kamalesh Adhikari and David J. Jefferson

The creation of legal regimes that grant exclusive proprietary rights to produce, circulate, and market novel plant varieties is not a recent phenomenon. Laws that enable plant breeders to obtain intellectual property for the new varieties that they develop originated decades ago in North America and Europe. The first of these took the form of a specialised 'plant patent' regime, which the United States enacted in 1930. Subsequently, an international framework to grant plant breeders' rights was conceived through a collaboration between several European governments in the 1960s.[1] As we discuss throughout the volume, since especially the mid-1990s, also an increasing number of Asian countries have begun either to draft or to implement national legislation to create systems of intellectual property for plant varieties.

The Asian countries that we include as case studies in this volume can be grouped according to the size and sophistication of their economies. Thus, certain chapters analyse the cases of a group of developing countries (India, Indonesia, Malaysia, Pakistan, Thailand, the Philippines, and Sri Lanka), while other chapters focus on lawmaking in least-developed countries (Cambodia, Laos, Myanmar, Nepal, and Timor-Leste). Agricultural systems and plant breeding differ in certain ways in developing versus least-developed Asian countries. Nevertheless, the volume demonstrates that all of the countries studied must confront similar challenges when they draft and implement national regimes to protect plant varieties as intellectual property. One reason for this shared experience is that all of the case study countries are subject to internal and external pressures to end hunger,

1 The 1930 *Plant Patent Act* of the United States is the first specialised patent law designed for the sole purpose of granting patent protection for plants. Subsequently, as an alternative to the plant patent system, the plant breeders' rights model was formalised following the enactment of the 1961 *International Convention for the Protection of New Varieties of Plants* (UPOV Convention). For a comprehensive review of the *Plant Patent Act*, see Pottage, A. and B. Sherman. 2007. 'Organisms and Manufactures: On the History of Plant Inventions.' *Melbourne University Law Review* 31 (2): 539–568. For a detailed analysis of the UPOV Convention, see Sanderson, J. 2017. *Plants, People and Practices: The Nature and History of the UPOV Convention*. Cambridge: Cambridge University Press.

ensure food security, promote sustainable agriculture, and achieve a number of other *Sustainable Development Goals* by 2030.[2]

Furthermore, developing and least-developed Asian countries must address a diverse set of more specific economic, social, and environmental priorities when they draft and implement intellectual property laws for plant varieties. The volume demonstrates that these priorities include the need to incentivise the breeding of new varieties by public and private institutions as a means to improve crop yields and to provide better resilience to pests, diseases, and climate change impacts. Likewise, lawmakers in these countries also aspire to transcend the conventional logic of intellectual property in their efforts to identify ways to conserve and sustainably use native plant genetic diversity, and to protect the rights of farmers. Of especial importance is the need to ensure that farmers may continue to rely on customary agricultural practices, including the use and circulation of plant varieties that either are native or have been introduced and adapted to local growing conditions.

Another major common challenge that developing and least-developed Asian countries face is the need to design systems of intellectual property for plant varieties that would simultaneously protect domestic interests and fulfil multiple obligations under several relevant international laws. The treaties that require countries in Asia and other world regions to uphold diverse commitments related to the governance of plant varieties – albeit in different ways – include the 1995 *Agreement on Trade-Related Aspects of Intellectual Property Rights* (TRIPS) of the World Trade Organization, the 1991 Act (UPOV 1991) of the *International Convention for the Protection of New Varieties of Plants* (UPOV Convention),[3] the 1992 *Convention on Biological Diversity* (CBD) of the United Nations, the 2010 *Nagoya Protocol on Access to Genetic Resources and the Fair and Equitable Sharing of Benefits Arising from their Utilization to the Convention on Biological Diversity* (Nagoya Protocol), and the 2001 *International Treaty on Plant Genetic Resources for Food and Agriculture* (the Plant Treaty) of the Food and Agriculture Organization of the United Nations.

2 For further information about the *Sustainable Development Goals* and challenges surrounding the realisation thereof for Asian countries, see ESCAP. 2018. *Asia and the Pacific SDG Progress Report 2017*. Bangkok: United Nations Economic and Social Commission for Asia and the Pacific. Accessed May 22 2019. www.unescap.org/sites/default/files/Asia-Pacific-SDG-Progress-Report-2017.pdf

3 The first Act of the UPOV Convention was signed in 1961. Since then, the Convention has been revised in 1972, 1978 and 1991. Because the 1978 Act formally ceased to accept new members in April 1999, over the past two decades, UPOV 1991 has emerged as the dominant international model of intellectual property for plant varieties. As of May 2019, 75 territories, including the European Union and the African Intellectual Property Organization, had joined the UPOV Convention. See International Union for the Protection of New Varieties of Plants. 'Members of the International Union for the Protection of New Varieties of Plants.' Accessed May 29 2019. www.upov.int/export/sites/upov/members/en/pdf/pub423.pdf

Among these regimes, the TRIPS Agreement forms the baseline for the governance of plant varieties as intellectual property, because it obligates all members of the World Trade Organization to protect this subject matter through either patents, or an 'effective *sui generis* system,' or a combination of both.[4] As we discuss in several chapters of the volume, the meaning of 'effective *sui generis* system' according to the terms of TRIPS is often interpreted to refer exclusively to the plant breeders' rights model that the UPOV Convention embodies. Notably, both patent laws and systems of plant breeders' rights modelled on the UPOV Convention are designed to grant exclusive rights for the commercial exploitation of new plant varieties. Thus, both types of frameworks bestow upon plant breeders the exclusive ability to produce, reproduce, sell, export, and import the seeds and other propagating material of the plant varieties over which they obtain protection.[5]

In contrast to TRIPS and the UPOV Convention, the CBD and the Nagoya Protocol are treaties that obligate their members to enable native and other types of genetic resources that fall under national jurisdiction to be easily accessed and used for diverse purposes, including plant breeding and crop varietal development.[6] Thus, signatories to the CBD and the Nagoya Protocol are required to establish legal frameworks to facilitate access to plant genetic resources based on prior informed consent, and to ensure that mutually agreed terms – including in relation to the equitable sharing of benefits – are negotiated between the providers and users of plant genetic resources. Furthermore, these regimes require their members to enact national legislation to protect the interests of local, indigenous, and farming communities. This obligation is based on the recognition that these groups often act as conservers and holders of plant genetic resources, and possess important traditional knowledge associated with the use of these resources.

The system to govern the access and use of plant genetic resources for food and agriculture that the Plant Treaty envisages differs from that of the CBD and the Nagoya Protocol. For its part, the Plant Treaty promotes access and benefit sharing in relation to these resources through the mobilisation of a 'Multilateral System.'[7] Major objectives of the Multilateral System that the Plant Treaty establishes include facilitating access to a predetermined set of 64 species of food and forage crops,[8] and ensuring that benefit sharing is brokered through a multilateral fund, created for this purpose.

The Plant Treaty also aims to protect 'farmers' rights' in relation to the conservation and sustainable use of plant genetic resources for food and agriculture.

4 TRIPS. Article 27.3(b).
5 See, for example, UPOV Convention. Article 14.
6 See CBD. Articles 1 and 15; Nagoya Protocol. Articles 1, 5, and 6.
7 Plant Treaty. Articles 10, 11, 12, and 13.
8 A list of these crops is included in Annex 1 of the Plant Treaty. See Food and Agriculture Organization of the United Nations (FAO). 2009. *International Treaty on Plant Genetic Resources for Food and Agriculture*. Rome: FAO. Accessed May 22 2019. www.fao.org/3/a-i0510e.pdf

For example, the conceptualisation of farmers' rights under the Plant Treaty includes protections for traditional knowledge associated with plant genetic resources for food and agriculture.[9] The Plant Treaty also aims to encourage members to protect, among other subject matter, the rights of farmers to save, use, exchange, and sell the farm-saved seed of all types of plant varieties. However, it is notable that this latter right is circumscribed by the limitation 'subject to national law and as appropriate.'[10] This means that Plant Treaty member countries may effectively limit the protection of certain categories of native plant varieties, depending on how the relevant national intellectual property, seed, or biodiversity law is formulated to recognise the rights of farmers. In such situations, there is often tension between the intellectual property rights of plant breeders and the realisation of farmers' rights as imagined in the Plant Treaty.

Because many Asian countries have joined several of the international agreements described above, it is fundamental that lawmakers in these countries understand how to reconcile treaty obligations that may sometimes conflict with one another. The existence of tension and ambiguity between the various legal frameworks that relate to the governance of plant varieties has incited numerous debates over how to protect plant varieties as intellectual property in Asia and other world regions. Initially, discussions centred on the need of developing and least-developed countries to introduce a national law to protect plant varieties as intellectual property, as a means to comply with TRIPS. One of the major outcomes of these debates was the recommendation that developing and least-developing countries – where the majority of farmers rely on traditional agricultural systems and native plant genetic diversity for seed and food security – should design *sui generis* plant variety protection legislation.[11] Such laws would be distinct from systems that grant plant breeders' rights, including those that are modelled on the UPOV Convention, or which have been developed primarily to address the needs of industrial agriculture.

As we explore in detail in several chapters of the volume, the argument in favour of adopting *sui generis* systems is based on the assumption that UPOV

9 Plant Treaty. Article 9.
10 Plant Treaty. Article 9.3.
11 See, for example, Dhar, B. 2002. *Sui Generis Systems for Plant Variety Protection: Options under TRIPS.* Geneva: Quaker United Nations Office; Robinson, D. 2008. 'Sui Generis Plant Variety Protection Systems: Liability Rules and Non-UPOV Systems of Protection.' *Journal of Intellectual Property Law & Practice* 3 (10): 659–665; Correa, C. M., with contributions from S. Shashikant and F. Meienberg. 2015. *Plant Variety Protection in Developing Countries. A Tool for Designing a Sui Generis Plant Variety Protection System: An Alternative to UPOV 1991.* Bonn: Association for Plant Breeding for the Benefit of Society (APBREBES). Accessed May 24 2019. www.apbrebes.org/files/seeds/ToolEnglishcompleteDez15.pdf; Ravishankar, A. and S. Archak. 1999. 'Searching for Policy Options: Is CoFaB a Suitable Alternative to UPOV?' *Economic and Political Weekly* 34 (52): 3661–3667; and De Jonge, B. and P. Munyi. 2016. 'A Differentiated Approach to Plant Variety Protection in Africa.' *The Journal of World Intellectual Property* 19 (1–2): 28–52.

Convention-compatible plant breeders' rights frameworks reward only the inventive activity and the labour of professional plant breeders who develop varieties that are new, distinct, uniform, and stable. Thus, opponents of the plant breeders' rights model contend that UPOV Convention-based systems do not consider how to protect the rights of communities and individual farmers who historically have maintained and developed plant genetic diversity. A related concern is that unlike the CBD, the Nagoya Protocol, and the Plant Treaty, UPOV Convention-compliant plant breeders' rights laws do not require users (i.e., plant breeders) to share any benefits that they derive from the commercial exploitation of protected varieties with the providers of the source breeding material. Lastly, critics allege that UPOV Convention-compliant plant breeders' rights regimes restrict farmers' customary practices of saving, using, exchanging, and selling the seeds or other propagating material of protected breeders' varieties.

Although the initial focus of the debates about intellectual property for plant varieties centred on how to comply with the obligations that different international agreements contain, recent debates have advanced to consider other pertinent issues and concerns. In an attempt to address these issues and concerns, this volume explores a series of questions, including: What challenges have developing and least-developed Asian countries experienced when they have drafted and implemented *sui generis* plant variety protection laws? Have these countries perceived any benefits from their *sui generis* regimes? What would joining the UPOV Convention imply for the legal systems, agricultural sectors, and customary farming practices of Asian countries that have enacted *sui generis* legislation? How do other national legal frameworks – such as seed laws or policies – complement or complicate the implementation of *sui generis* plant variety protection laws in Asian countries? Lastly, what are the opportunities and challenges associated with establishing systems of intellectual property for different categories of plant varieties, which may include farmers' varieties, traditional varieties, wild plants, and varieties that are 'essentially derived' from intellectual property-protected plant varieties?

This volume provides detailed and critical responses to these questions and a number of other issues and concerns that Asian countries should address in order to improve the governance of plant varieties as intellectual property within their borders. However, the utility of the volume is not limited to Asia. Instead, the analyses and findings also are relevant for developing and least-developed countries located in other world regions. Furthermore, the findings that the volume presents could inspire lawmakers in developed and developing countries alike, where the use of intellectual property law and related legal regimes has been conceived as a vehicle to support the conservation, use, and development of native plant genetic resources.

The volume is comprised of ten chapters. Each chapter focusses on one or a group of Asian countries, which serve as case studies to evaluate issues and concerns associated with the origin, development, and implementation of intellectual property laws for plant varieties. In its analysis, the volume conceptualises the notion 'intellectual property for plant varieties' broadly, to include systems that grant plant breeders' rights according to the terms of the UPOV Convention, the *sui generis* plant variety protection legislation that several Asian countries have established, and national seed laws and policies.

The contributors to this volume include experts with experience of working in academic institutions, government agencies, and non-governmental organisations. Most of the chapter authors are citizens of Asian countries, and thus they possess intimate knowledge of the political, social, economic, and environmental dynamics of the places about which they write. Some of the authors have also served actively on government committees that were formed to draft or implement national plant variety protection laws in the countries that they study. Such is the case for the chapters that focus on the experiences of Timor-Leste, Nepal, and India.

Furthermore, many of the stories that the chapters recount are based on field-work that the authors conducted in the countries whose laws they analyse. Examples of this socio-legal approach may be found in the chapters that cover Indonesia, Malaysia, Nepal, Pakistan, the Philippines, Sri Lanka, Thailand, and Timor-Leste. Below, we briefly summarise each of the remaining chapters, high-lighting how we have structured the volume to focus on numerous issues and concerns that lawmakers in Asian countries and beyond may consider when they develop, implement, or reformulate intellectual property laws for plant varieties.

In Chapter 2, 'Plant breeders' rights proliferate in Asia: The spread of the UPOV Convention model,' David J. Jefferson provides a detailed analysis of the influence of the UPOV Convention model of plant breeders' rights in several mainland Southeast Asian countries, namely Cambodia, Laos, Myanmar, Malaysia, and Thailand. In doing so, the author offers a critical account of how a number of factors have impelled these countries towards membership of the UPOV Convention. On the one hand are 'hard' factors, which are primarily embodied in the formal legal obligations that various bilateral, regional, and trans-regional free trade agreements contain. On the other hand are 'soft' factors, evidenced in the pressure that various actors, including representatives of private industry and government institutions, have exerted on lawmakers in mainland Southeast Asian countries.

Following an analysis of the 'hard' and 'soft' factors that have influenced the decisions of Southeast Asian lawmakers surrounding the desirability of the UPOV Convention model to govern plant varieties as intellectual property, Jefferson recommends that these countries should consider a strategy of 'compliance with resistance.' The author argues that this approach would enable governments to comply with the UPOV Convention and simultaneously to experiment with alternative legislative and regulatory imaginaries. Doing so would address diverse national priorities, including those related to protecting customary farming practices, assuring sustainable food production, and conserving agricultural biodiversity.

In Chapter 3, 'Essentially derived varieties: A workable compromise against free riding breeders?,' Charles Lawson explores a number of issues and concerns that could be relevant for countries in Asia and other world regions to address when they incorporate protections for essentially derived varieties (EDVs) into their domestic intellectual property laws. In so doing, Lawson first notes that the extension of plant breeders' rights to cover EDVs was intended to limit the possibility that later plant breeders could unfairly free ride on the time and investments of another, earlier breeder. However, the author contends that one of the flaws in the UPOV 1991 conceptualisation of EDVs is the lack of clarity in relation to certain key terms. Thus, Lawson substantiates the meaning of these terms through an exploration of the UPOV Convention guidance documents, towards the aim of understanding what EDVs are, and the possible implications that protecting these varieties as intellectual property could have for plant breeding, varietal innovation, and the rights of concerned stakeholders.

Furthermore, Lawson critically analyses a series of judicial decisions that have considered the scope of protections for EDVs in countries that have implemented UPOV 1991-based plant breeders' rights laws. The author observes that while these cases provide some clarity about the meaning of EDVs, the question of how to determine whether a particular plant variety is essentially derived remains contested. Nevertheless, Lawson argues that despite enduring ambiguities in finding essential derivation, it is possible that the introduction of the EDV standard into legal frameworks based on UPOV 1991 effectively has achieved its purpose of preventing unfair free riding. This conclusion is based on the lack of recent cases in any international jurisdiction that would adjudicate questions related to essential derivation, which suggests that breeders may have heeded the decisions analysed in the chapter. Lawson's findings are relevant to Asian countries because they may enable lawmakers to better understand the nature of EDVs when drafting and implementing both *sui generis* regimes and UPOV 1991-based systems.

In Chapter 4, 'Implementation of the plant variety protection laws of Indonesia, Malaysia, and the Philippines: Trends and future prospects,' Rajeswari Kanniah discusses how the governments of these three countries developed innovative *sui generis* laws that are distinct from the plant breeders' rights model that the UPOV Convention embodies. Furthermore, Kanniah provides a thorough analysis of the implementation of the Indonesian, Malaysian, and Filipino *sui generis* regimes, by discussing trends associated with the registration and protection of different types of plant varieties as intellectual property in these countries.

Kanniah recognises that the Indonesian, Malaysian, and Filipino plant variety protection laws, which already have been in force for several years, aim to promote the breeding and commercialisation of new plant varieties and their seeds. Nevertheless, the author's findings demonstrate that in these countries, farmers' seed systems – in which farmers save, use, exchange, and sell farm-saved seeds – remain vibrant and vital. Thus, public and private sector-driven seed systems on the one hand, and farmers' seed systems on the other hand, continue to coexist in these countries, collectively meeting the needs of plant breeding, seed security, and food production. However, as Kanniah notes, it is likely that Indonesia, Malaysia, and the Philippines will eventually join the UPOV Convention. The author observes that it is uncertain how the alignment of these countries' intellectual property laws with the UPOV Convention standard would affect farmers' seed systems.

In Chapter 5, 'Opportunities and challenges created by the *Plant Variety Protection and Farmers' Rights Act* in India,' R. C. Agrawal offers a critical assessment of the *sui generis* intellectual property law for plant varieties that has received the most scholarly attention to date. Similar to prior studies of the Indian regime, Agrawal explores the different types of protection available for different categories of plant varieties, including those developed by farmers and by professional plant breeders. However, the chapter departs from, and builds upon, previous research by focussing on the impact of the Indian law in practice. This impact is evidenced partially in the thousands of plant variety rights certificates that the Plant Variety Protection and Farmers' Rights Authority has granted to public research organisations, private seed companies, and farmers.

Furthermore, Agrawal demonstrates how the Act has generated a number of additional opportunities for Indian stakeholders, for example, through the mobilisation of the National Gene Fund and the various institutional programmes that the government has devised to reward farmers for their roles as conservers, developers, and owners of plant genetic resources. However, the author also contends that several challenges continue to impede the full realisation of the goals of the Indian system of intellectual property for plant varieties. Thus, Agrawal suggests that in the future, lawmakers should take measures to address the various challenges that the Indian Plant Variety Protection and Farmers' Rights Authority continues to face. These include the need to encourage the use of protected farmers' varieties for breeding and benefit sharing purposes, to enable farmers to commercialise their protected plant varieties, and to harmonise the *Plant Variety Protection and Farmers' Rights Act* with the Indian *Seed Act*.

In Chapter 6, 'Policy, politics, and implications of Pakistan's *Plant Breeders' Rights Act*,' Muhammad Ahsan Rana and Kamalesh Adhikari unpack the historical, political, and social dynamics surrounding the development of a new plant breeders' rights law in Pakistan. In this chapter, the authors recount how the roles of the various actors in the national seed sector have changed over the course of the past 50 years. In so doing, Rana and Adhikari also discuss the emergence of large-scale public and private seed-provisioning entities and the role of customary practices and unsanctioned seed transactions in Pakistan. The authors also analyse how conflicts between private seed enterprises and civil society groups – in addition to certain political factors – delayed the enactment of the Pakistani *Plant Breeders' Rights Act* for nearly 17 years.

Rana and Adhikari argue that the Pakistani plant breeders' rights law could have important implications for diverse actors in the national agricultural sector, including private companies, public institutions, and farmers. While exploring these potential repercussions, the authors outline areas of convergence and divergence between the Pakistani *Plant Breeders' Rights Act* and the UPOV Convention, and between the Act and the national Seed Act. Rana and Adhikari argue that the tensions between these regimes should be resolved through the formulation of rules and regulations that the Pakistani government should implement to realise the goals of the *Plant Breeders' Rights Act.*

In Chapter 7, 'The *National Seed Policy* of Timor-Leste: Laying the foundation for the regulation of plant varieties as intellectual property,' Pratap Shrestha tells the story of the development of a national system of plant variety protection in an unlikely place, namely the Timorese *National Seed Policy.* In his analysis, Shrestha describes how a series of domestic issues and factors led the National Seed Policy Working Group to imbue the *National Seed Policy* with a comprehensive scope. Thus, the Policy encompasses provisions whose purpose is to foment the conservation and sustainable use of plant genetic resources, the registration of local plant varieties, and the protection of breeders' and farmers' plant varieties as intellectual property.

As of May 2019, the Timorese *Seed Policy* was not yet binding. Shrestha argues that Timor-Leste should take advantage of the draft nature of the framework by continuing to experiment with strategies that would best safeguard the interests of farmers. The author contends that it is important to do so because farmers' customary practices form an integral part of the cropping and seed systems that characterise Timorese agriculture. According to Shrestha, the national government, local farming communities, and civil society organisations should collaborate actively to ensure that the *National Seed Policy* is implemented in a way that would ensure the vitality of Timorese agriculture, while simultaneously protecting the interests of plant breeders and farmers alike.

In Chapter 8, 'A fresh look at the protection of "domestic" and "wild" plant varieties in Thailand,' Pawarit Lertdhamtewe and David J. Jefferson explore a number of issues related to the protection of 'local domestic,' 'general domestic,' and 'wild' plant varieties in Thailand. After describing how diverse social actors participated in the lawmaking process that created the *sui generis* Thai *Plant Variety Protection Act B.E.2542 (1999)*, the authors summarise how this regime converges with and diverges from the UPOV Convention model. Subsequently, Lertdhamtewe and Jefferson critically examine how the categories of 'local domestic,' 'general domestic,' and 'wild' plant varieties have been conceptualised in the Thai law, while revealing ambiguities and inconsistencies in these framings.

For instance, the authors speculate about why no local domestic plant varieties have obtained legal protection in Thailand, despite the fact that the law has been in force for approximately two decades. Lertdhamtewe and Jefferson argue that Thai lawmakers should address this and other issues related to the protection of domestic and wild plant varieties in the country. One way that this could be done would be to foment the registration of local domestic varieties by creating separate criteria for protection that would be easier for farmers to meet. Lastly, the authors contend that Thailand should avoid aligning the national plant variety protection framework with the UPOV Convention, unless the government also enacts parallel reforms that more effectively would protect 'domestic' and 'wild' plants, and the associated knowledge and practices of the peoples who historically have used them.

In Chapter 9, 'From neglect to protection: Recognising the importance of farmers' varieties in Sri Lanka,' Asanka Perera and Kamalesh Adhikari argue that Sri Lanka should create opportunities for farmers to obtain legal protections for the plant varieties that they have been conserving, cultivating, and developing for generations. After discussing the evolution of the Sri Lankan *Draft Bill on the Protection of Plant Varieties (Breeder's Rights)* and its major provisions, Perera and Adhikari describe how lawmakers in Sri Lanka have failed to take advantage of the different options that are available in the context of international legal obligations to protect farmers' varieties.

To address this situation, the authors offer two potential approaches that Sri Lanka could follow to protect farmers' plant varieties in a revised version of the *Draft Bill on the Protection of Plant Varieties (Breeder's Rights)*. The first approach would be to create a 'dual system' that would recognise protections for both breeders' and farmers' plant varieties according to the logic of intellectual property. The second approach would involve retaining the intellectual property model for breeders' varieties, while creating protections for farmers' varieties based on non-proprietary principles. According to this latter approach, farmers' plant varieties would be safeguarded in a way that would prevent misappropriation by third parties; however, the law would not grant exclusive rights surrounding the use of these varieties. This non-proprietary approach to the protection of farmers' varieties could be based on access and benefit sharing principles, such as those articulated in the CBD and the Nagoya Protocol.

Chapter 10, the final and concluding chapter, authored by Kamalesh Adhikari and entitled 'What does it mean to protect farmers' varieties as intellectual property?,' begins by exploring how and why the concept of the 'farmers' variety' evolved as a legal construct. This materialisation is evident in what the author terms 'UPOV-plus' plant variety rights laws, including those that India, Thailand, and Malaysia have enacted. Adhikari then examines how the approach to protecting farmers' varieties as intellectual property in Nepal differs from the Indian, Thai, and Malaysian systems. The author also describes how farmers' understandings of different categories of native, local, traditional, and indigenous plant varieties were discussed by various actors during the making of the Nepali *Draft Bill on Plant Variety Protection and Farmers' Rights*. This process effectively converted the notion of farmers' varieties into a new legal concept in Nepal.

Using a case study of a participatory plant breeding programme, Adhikari recounts the story of how *Jethobudho* – a rice cultivar that traditionally is grown by farmers in the Pokhara Valley of Nepal – evolved to obtain legal protection as *Pokhareli Jethobudho*. The author invokes this case study to analyse a series of questions and concerns related to the conceptualisation of farmers' varieties as intellectual property in Nepal. These questions and concerns range from whether farmers have the ability to protect their varieties as intellectual property, to the implications that participatory plant breeding programmes operating as collaborations between farmers and non-farmer entities may have for obtaining exclusive rights over locally bred varieties. Adhikari's chapter also addresses other important questions and concerns, such as: Should farmers' varieties be subject to any protection period, or should these varieties be in the public domain? What kinds of exclusive rights do farmers need to commercialise their varieties? And, what are the access and benefit sharing obligations of the owners of farmers' varieties in cases where they use other farmers' local varieties as source germplasm?

We hope that this volume will advance the knowledge of scholars in an array of disciplines, who study the relationship between intellectual property law and plants. Furthermore, our aim is to provide a useful tool for other actors, including policymakers, local community leaders, development practitioners, commercial enterprises, and international institutions, when they engage with questions related to the governance of plant genetic resources. The chapters of this volume are intended to contribute to global and national debates about intellectual property, agriculture, and food security, and we hope that readers will find the volume to be an accessible resource to inform their perspectives.

Chapter 2

Plant breeders' rights proliferate in Asia

The spread of the UPOV Convention model

David J. Jefferson

2.1 Introduction

Since the formation of the World Trade Organization and the entry into force of its *Agreement on Trade-Related Aspects of Intellectual Property Rights* (TRIPS), much has been written on what compliance with this treaty might imply for member countries.[1] One particularly provocative area of analysis may be summarised by concerns over 'ultracompliance.' This is the idea that TRIPS might 'have normative effects that are greater or more powerful or different than what may be desired or consistent with the values or intentionality that might plausibly be attributed to the 'creators' of this framework.[2] Many actors – including scholars, representatives of the governments of developing countries, and civil society activists – have attempted to combat the threat of ultracompliance with strategies for exploiting the exceptions and lacunae that TRIPS contains, to ensure that States remain able to make laws that are responsive to local needs. For the purposes of the present chapter, these strategies are termed 'compliance with resistance.'

The foundational purpose of TRIPS was to establish minimum standards for intellectual property protections that World Trade Organization members are obligated to incorporate into their respective national laws. An exploration of the compliance with resistance notion may be especially productive in relation to one of the essential requirements that the Agreement institutes, namely the mandate that all member countries must offer a system through which plant varieties[3] can

1 Comprehensive works on the TRIPS Agreement and the effect of this treaty on national-level lawmaking include Correa, C. M. 2000. *Intellectual Property Rights, the WTO and Developing Countries: The TRIPS Agreement and Policy Options*. New York: Zed Books; Matthews, D. 2003. *Globalising Intellectual Property Rights: The TRIPS Agreement*. New York: Routledge; and Deere, C. 2009. *The Implementation Game: The TRIPS Agreement and the Global Politics of Intellectual Property Reform in Developing Countries*. Oxford: Oxford University Press.

2 Howse, R. and R. Teitel. 2010. 'Beyond Compliance: Rethinking Why International Law Really Matters.' *Global Policy* 1 (2): 127–136, 133.

3 TRIPS does not define the term 'plant variety.' According to the *International Convention for the Protection of New Varieties of Plants* (UPOV Convention), a variety may be understood as:

be protected as intellectual property. The pertinent provision of TRIPS – Article 27.3(b) – states that intellectual property for plant varieties may take the form of patents, an 'effective *sui generis*[4] system,' or any combination thereof.

The TRIPS Agreement was not the first international effort to harmonise national standards for intellectual property lawmaking. Notable initiatives date to at least the end of the nineteenth century.[5] However, TRIPS represents the most comprehensive multilateral agreement to require the enactment of systems to protect plant varieties as intellectual property,[6] and the treaty is striking especially because World Trade Organization members who do not adhere to its terms could face trade sanctions.[7] Given the perceived importance of compliance with TRIPS, since its entry into force on January 1 1995, the meaning of 'effective *sui generis* system' for plant variety protection has been frequently debated.[8] Another major point of contention has been how the Article 27.3(b) requirement affects the ability of countries to balance the interests of diverse national stakeholders, who may include plant breeders, scientific researchers, agricultural enterprises, and farmers.

Overall, critics have contended that TRIPS and the World Trade Organization more generally function as structures through which wealthy, industrialised nations can dominate the economic and legal systems of developing

> a plant grouping within a single botanical taxon of the lowest known rank, which...can be defined by the expression of the characteristics resulting from a given genotype or combination of genotypes; distinguished from any other plant grouping by the expression of at least one of the said characteristics and; considered as a unit with regard to its suitability for being propagated unchanged.

See 1991 Act of the *International Convention for the Protection of New Varieties of Plants* (UPOV 1991). Article 1(vi).

4 From the Latin *sui generis*, which may be translated as 'of its own kind.' In the context of the making of plant variety protection laws and against the backdrop of TRIPS, *sui generis* means an alternative to the provision of patent protection for new plant varieties.

5 For instance, the *Paris Convention for the Protection of Industrial Property* is a multilateral agreement adopted in 1883. This Convention applies to patents, trademarks, industrial designs, utility models, service marks, trade names, geographical indications, and the repression of unfair competition. Similarly, the *Berne Convention for the Protection of Literary and Artistic Works* is a multilateral agreement adopted in 1886, dealing with the protection of creative works and the rights of their authors.

6 However, it should be noted that least-developed member countries of the World Trade Organization are not required to be TRIPS-compliant until July 1 2021.

7 Kennedy, M. 2016. *WTO Dispute Settlement and the TRIPS Agreement: Applying Intellectual Property Standards in a Trade Law Framework*. Cambridge: Cambridge University Press.

8 See, for example, Dhar, B. 2002. *Sui Generis Systems for Plant Variety Protection: Options under TRIPS*. Geneva: Quaker United Nations Office; and Robinson, D. 2008. 'Sui Generis Plant Variety Protection Systems: Liability Rules and Non-UPOV Systems of Protection.' *Journal of Intellectual Property Law & Practice* 3 (10): 659–665.

countries.[9] While such reproaches may still have merit today, since the finalisation of TRIPS, the globalisation of intellectual property norms has continued to proliferate. This means that national-level lawmaking now requires a nuanced understanding of how the various international obligations that a given country has assumed intersect and diverge. In the specific context of intellectual property for plant varieties, numerous bilateral, regional, and transregional free trade agreements have recapitulated the TRIPS Article 27.3(b) requirement, while also frequently increasing the minimum standards to which countries must adhere.[10] Typically, these free trade agreements require that signatories ratify another international regime, the 1991 Act of the *International Convention for the Protection of New Varieties of Plants* (UPOV 1991) as a means to provide a *sui generis* system of intellectual property for plant varieties.[11]

As with the TRIPS Agreement, UPOV 1991 has been criticised by a diverse array of actors, including scholars, policymakers, and advocates for farmers, peasants, and indigenous groups.[12] One of the most significant critiques of UPOV 1991 argues that its model of granting exclusive rights to professional plant breeders is inappropriate for the forms of agriculture typically practiced outside of wealthy industrialised economies.[13] Additional concerns include the potential impediment of traditional agricultural systems, including customary practices of seed saving, exchange, and sale by farmers.[14] Governments of developing countries that have considered joining UPOV 1991 as a means to implement a *sui generis* system of intellectual property for plant varieties in some cases have been met with fierce opposition from advocacy groups.[15] Based on

9 Correa, C. M. 2000. *Intellectual Property Rights, the WTO and Developing Countries: The TRIPS Agreement and Policy Options*. New York: Zed Books.

10 Drahos, P. 2001. 'BITs and BIPs.' *The Journal of World Intellectual Property* 4 (6): 791–808.

11 Dutfield, G. 2011. *Food, Biological Diversity and Intellectual Property: The Role of the International Union for the Protection of New Varieties of Plants (UPOV)*. Global Economic Issue Publications. Intellectual Property Issue Paper No. 9. Geneva: Quaker United Nations Office.

12 For a discussion of the various lines of criticisms that have been launched against the UPOV Convention, see Sanderson, J. 2017. *Plants, People and Practices: The Nature and History of the UPOV Convention*. Cambridge: Cambridge University Press, pages 8–9.

13 GRAIN. 1998. 'Ten Reasons Not to Join UPOV.' *Global Trade and Biodiversity in Conflict*, Issue 2, No. 2.

14 Braunschweig, T., F. Meienberg, C. Pionetti, and S. Shashikant. 2014. *Owning Seeds, Accessing Food. A Human Rights Impact Assessment of UPOV 1991 Based on Case Studies in Kenya, Peru and the Philippines*. The Berne Declaration. Accessed May 16 2019. www.publiceye.ch/fileadmin/files/documents/Saatgut/2014_07_10_Owning_Seed_-_Accessing_Food_report_def.pdf

15 Such was the case with the 'No to UPOV' campaign organised in Nepal beginning in 2003. Winge, T., K. Adhikari, and R. Andersen. 2013. 'Advocacy for Farmers' Rights in Nepal.' In *Realising Farmers' Rights to Crop Genetic Resources: Success Stories and Best Practices*, edited by R. Andersen and T. Winge. Abingdon: Routledge, pages 181–194. A similar protest campaign was organised to oppose the proposed '*Ley Monsanto*'

concerns about the need to balance the interests of plant breeders with those of other important stakeholders, numerous scholars and civil society actors have launched proposals for an alternative to the model that UPOV 1991 embodies.[16]

Meanwhile, some of the most prominent real-world examples of non-UPOV Convention systems have been implemented successfully in Asian countries. As described in other chapters of this volume, *sui generis* plant variety protection legislation has been in force since 2001 in India, in the form of the *Protection of Plant Varieties and Farmers' Rights Act.* Other Asian countries such as Indonesia,[17] Malaysia,[18] the Philippines,[19] and Thailand[20] have also enacted *sui generis* laws to balance the aim to protect the intellectual property of plant breeders with other national priorities, which have included the safeguarding of customary farming practices, the conservation of plant genetic diversity, and the promotion of food security or food sovereignty. As other chapters of this volume discuss, additional Asian nations, including Sri Lanka[21] and Nepal[22] have drafted non-UPOV Convention *sui generis* plant variety protection bills, which as of May 2019 were still under consideration by these countries' national legislatures.

Scholars have touted the legislation developed by these Asian countries as successful examples of how World Trade Organization members can comply with international legal obligations and simultaneously resist undue external pressures. In other words, the Asian examples of *sui generis* forms of intellectual property for plant varieties demonstrate how to fulfil the TRIPS mandate while also safeguarding the interests of diverse actors in the national agricultural sector.[23] Notwithstanding the generally positive reception of these *sui*

which would implement a UPOV 1991-based law in Chile. Jefferson, D. J. 2014. 'Development, Farmers' Rights, and the Ley Monsanto: The Struggle Over the Ratification of UPOV 91 in Chile.' *IDEA – The Intellectual Property Law Review* 55 (1): 31–104.

16 See, for example, Correa, C. M., with contributions from S. Shashikant, and F. Meienberg. 2015. *Plant Variety Protection in Developing Countries. A Tool for Designing a Sui Generis Plant Variety Protection System: An Alternative to UPOV 1991.* Bonn: Association for Plant Breeding for the Benefit of Society (APBREBES). Accessed May 24 2019. www.apbrebes.org/files/seeds/ToolEnglishcompleteDez15.pdf; Ravishankar, A. and S. Archak. 1999. 'Searching for Policy Options: Is CoFaB a Suitable Alternative to UPOV?' *Economic and Political Weekly* 34 (52): 3661–3667; and De Jonge, B. and P. Munyi. 2016. 'A Differentiated Approach to Plant Variety Protection in Africa.' *The Journal of World Intellectual Property* 19 (1–2): 28–52.

17 *Laws of the Republic of Indonesia, No. 29 of 2000 on Plant Variety Protection.*

18 *Protection of New Plant Varieties Act of Malaysia, Act 634 (2004).*

19 Philippine *Plant Variety Protection Act of 2002 (Republic Act No. 9168).*

20 *Plant Varieties Protection Act of Thailand, B.E. 2542 (1999).*

21 Perera, A. 2011. 'Plant Variety Protection in Sri Lanka and its Impact on Sri Lanka's Agricultural Economy: A Critical Analysis.' *The Journal of World Intellectual Property* 14 (3–4): 301–333.

22 See Adhikari, K. 2019. This volume.

23 Robinson, D. 2007. *Exploring Components and Elements of Sui Generis Systems for Plant Variety Protection and Traditional Knowledge in Asia.* Geneva: International Centre for Trade and Sustainable Development (ICTSD).

generis regimes, in recent years an increasing number of Asian countries have elected to follow the UPOV 1991 model of intellectual property for plant varieties. In some instances, proposals for UPOV Convention-based laws have been newly introduced, while in others, reforms have been proposed to develop *sui generis* systems that would align these frameworks with UPOV 1991.

The present chapter maps the influence of UPOV 1991 in Asia, with a particular focus on the Southeast Asian subregion. The discussion is structured as follows: section 2.2 describes how bilateral, regional, and trans-regional free trade agreements have proliferated following the entry into force of the TRIPS Agreement. This section focuses on 'hard' influences, which are understood as formal legal obligations that countries in different Asian subregions have assumed to implement UPOV Convention-compliant national laws. Section 2.3 complements section 2.2 by focusing on 'soft' factors that in some instances have swayed government officials towards UPOV Convention-style legislation. These soft influences include the various means through which the seed industry has endeavoured to shape domestic policy across Asia, as well as pressures exerted by other actors both within and outside the countries' borders.

Section 2.4 focuses specifically on the growing tendency to adopt UPOV 1991-based legislation in mainland Southeast Asian countries. This section reviews the recently enacted plant breeders' rights laws in Cambodia and Laos, and the draft framework that as of May 2019 was still under review in Myanmar. It also highlights how Southeast Asian nations that had previously developed independent *sui generis* intellectual property laws for plants are now taking actions to conform to UPOV 1991. Such is the case in Malaysia and Thailand, which are currently weighing reforms to their extant plant variety protection regimes.

Section 2.5 concludes the chapter by arguing that in the context of this Asian turn towards UPOV 1991, it is paramount that countries endeavour to counterbalance laws that encapsulate the plant breeders' rights model with policies designed to advance other national priorities related to customary agricultural practices, food production, and biodiversity conservation. In so doing, countries might consider a strategy of compliance with resistance. This approach would offset the UPOV 1991 template for governing relationships between human actors and plants, by experimenting with alternative legislative and regulatory regimes.

2.2 Hard influences: The post-TRIPS proliferation of free trade agreements

In the years since the TRIPS Agreement was adopted, many countries have entered into bilateral, regional, or trans-regional free trade agreements, the terms of which frequently include minimum criteria for intellectual property protection to which parties must adhere. Opponents have labelled these treaties 'TRIPS-plus' regimes, because they essentially mandate ultracompliance with TRIPS. Thus, relatively wealthier territories have often required that their developing country partners implement standards for intellectual property protection that exceed those found in

TRIPS, in exchange for enhanced market access.[24] One common provision that many free trade agreements contain is the obligation that parties join the UPOV Convention, which either implicitly or explicitly means UPOV 1991. The reason for this is that even where a trade agreement is ambiguous as to which version of the UPOV Convention the parties should recognise, the older 1978 Act of the Convention (UPOV 1978) ceased to accept new members in April 1999.[25]

Numerous analyses have argued that UPOV 1991 contains provisions that could negatively impact the agricultural practices on which farmers in many developing countries rely. For instance, UPOV 1991 may restrict customary seed management techniques including saving, exchange, and non-branded sale in local markets; jeopardise the internationally recognised right to food in countries that rely on production by smallholder farmers; and hinder the implementation of farmers' rights in countries that have acceded to the 2001 *International Treaty on Plant Genetic Resources for Food and Agriculture.*[26] Nevertheless, developing country membership in UPOV 1991 has increased significantly in recent years. In December 2004, 31 parties had acceded to UPOV 1991.[27] This number burgeoned to 75 territories that had joined UPOV 1991 as of May 2019, a nearly twofold increase.[28] Moreover, from 2013 to 2019, all of the new signatories to the UPOV Convention were classified as developing countries or transition economies.[29]

One of the more recent accessions to UPOV 1991 was the African Intellectual Property Organization, an intergovernmental group comprised of 17 sovereign States, all of which are either developing or least-developed countries. Meanwhile, in 2014, the UPOV Council evaluated the draft protocol of another African intergovernmental

24 Helfer, L. R. 2009. 'Regime Shifting in the International Intellectual Property System.' *Perspectives on Politics* 7 (1): 39–44.

25 Deere, C. 2009. *The Implementation Game: The TRIPS Agreement and the Global Politics of Intellectual Property Reform in Developing Countries.* Oxford: Oxford University Press, page 109.

26 Braunschweig, Meienberg, Pionetti, and Shashikant, note 14; De Schutter, O. 2009. *Seed Policies and the Right to Food: Enhancing Agrobiodiversity, Encouraging Innovation.* Report by the UN Special Rapporteur on the Right to Food (A/64/170). Presented at the 64th Session of the UN General Assembly, October 21 2009; and Christinck, A., and M. W. Tvedt. 2015. *The UPOV Convention, Farmers' Rights and Human Rights: An Integrated Assessment of Potentially Conflicting Legal Frameworks.* Bonn: Deutsche Gesellschaft für Internationale Zusammenarbeit (GIZ) GmbH. Accessed May 29 2019. www.zukunftsstiftung-landwirtschaft.de/media/Dokumente_Lesenswertes/giz2015-en-upov-convention.pdf

27 Jordens, R. 2005. 'Progress of Plant Variety Protection Based on the International Convention for the Protection of New Varieties of Plants (UPOV Convention).' *World Patent Information* 27 (2005): 232–243, 236.

28 International Union for the Protection of New Varieties of Plants (UPOV). 2019. *Members of the International Union for the Protection of New Varieties of Plants, Status on February 14, 2019.* UPOV Pub. No. 423. Geneva: UPOV. Accessed May 29 2019. www.upov.int/export/sites/upov/members/en/pdf/pub423.pdf

29 Since 2013, the territories that have joined the UPOV Convention are the African Intellectual Property Organization, Bosnia and Herzegovina, Montenegro, Kenya, Serbia, and Tanzania. Ibid.

body – the African Regional Intellectual Property Organization – and concluded that the framework complied with all major provisions of UPOV 1991.[30] Members of other regional groups, including the Southern Africa Development Community, the Common Market for Eastern and Southern Africa, and the East African Community currently are working to harmonise their national laws with UPOV 1991.[31]

In contrast to the situation in Africa, to date most Asian territories have elected not to ratify the UPOV Convention, although in some instances these countries developed *sui generis* national legislation to comply with TRIPS. This means that until recently, 'patchiness' has characterised the landscape of intellectual property laws for plant varieties in Asia. As of May 2019, the only Asian members of the UPOV Convention were China (a signatory to UPOV 1978), and Japan, South Korea, and Vietnam (adhering to UPOV 1991).[32] Nevertheless, recently other countries in the region have begun to bring their national plant variety protection laws into conformity with UPOV 1991. For instance, in October 2017, the UPOV Council reviewed the frameworks of Brunei Darussalam and Myanmar, finding both to be compliant with UPOV 1991.[33] Other States throughout Central, South, and Southeast Asia, including Cambodia, Indonesia, Laos, Mongolia, Pakistan, and Thailand have communicated with UPOV Convention administrators to request assistance towards the development of laws based on UPOV 1991.[34]

One predominant reason for the escalating interest in UPOV 1991 is that ratification of the UPOV Convention is required regularly under the terms of bilateral, regional, or trans-regional free trade agreements. For their part, bilateral treaties are frequently executed between wealthy, industrialised governments on the one hand, and countries with relatively smaller economies on the other hand. The two territories that to date have acted as the most prolific protagonists of bilateral trade agreements are the United States and the European Union, though other wealthy countries such as Australia and Japan also have negotiated commercial treaties with developing nations in the Asian region.

In the United States, bilateral trade agreements have centred mostly on reducing barriers to commerce with the country's geographic neighbours in Latin

30 International Union for the Protection of New Varieties of Plants (UPOV). 2014. *Examination of the Conformity of the Draft ARIPO Protocol for the Protection of new Varieties of Plants with the 1991 Act of the UPOV Convention*. UPOV Document C (Extr.)/31/2. Geneva: UPOV. Accessed May 29 2019. www.upov.int/edocs/mdocs/upov/en/c_extr_31/c_extr_31_2.pdf
31 Correa, note 16, page 29.
32 UPOV, note 29.
33 International Union for the Protection of New Varieties of Plants (UPOV). 2017. *UPOV Council Holds its Fifty-First Ordinary Session*. UPOV Pub. No. C/51/19 Rev. Geneva: UPOV. Accessed May 29 2019. www.upov.int/edocs/mdocs/upov/en/c_51/c_51_19.pdf
34 International Union for the Protection of New Varieties of Plants (UPOV). 2018. *Overview of UPOV*. UPOV Pub. No. 437. Geneva: UPOV. Accessed May 29 2019. www.upov.int/export/sites/upov/about/en/pdf/pub437.pdf

America,[35] and with territories in the Middle East that are strategic military allies.[36] However, the United States has also negotiated trade agreements with several countries in Asia. These include Cambodia,[37] Laos,[38] South Korea,[39] Singapore,[40] and Vietnam.[41] Some of these agreements obligate the parties to give effect to either UPOV 1978 or UPOV 1991, while others specifically require ratification of UPOV 1991. For instance, the *United States – Vietnam Agreement on Trade Relations* stipulates that each party must follow either of the two active versions of the UPOV Convention.[42] In contrast, the United States – South Korea free trade agreement mandates adherence to UPOV 1991.[43]

Similarly, over the past two decades, the European Union has executed various kinds of trade agreements with Asian countries whose terms require adopting the UPOV 1991 model to protect plant varieties as intellectual property. One example is embodied in a proposed region-to-region free trade agreement between the European Union and the Association of South East Asian Nations (ASEAN). Negotiations towards the execution of this treaty began in 2007 but stalled in 2009. At that point, the European Union shifted its focus to dealing with ASEAN countries on a bilateral basis.[44] Since then, commercial treaties have been executed separately with the Philippines,[45] Singapore,[46]

35 These countries include Costa Rica, Dominican Republic, El Salvador, Guatemala, Honduras, Mexico, Nicaragua, and Panama.

36 These countries include Bahrain, Jordan, Morocco, and Oman.

37 *Agreement between the United States of America and the Kingdom of Cambodia on Trade Relations and Intellectual Property Rights Protection*. 2006. Article XI(1)(D).

38 *Agreement between the United States of America and the Lao People's Democratic Republic on Trade Relations*. 2003. Article 13.2(d).

39 *Free Trade Agreement between the Republic of Korea and the United States of America*. 2007. Article 18.1(3)(g).

40 *United States – Singapore Free Trade Agreement*. 2003. Article 16.1(2)(a)(ii).

41 *Agreement between the United States of America and the Socialist Republic of Vietnam on Trade Relations*. 2000. Article 1(3)(D).

42 Ibid.

43 *Free Trade Agreement between the Republic of Korea and the United States of America*, note 40.

44 European Commission. 2019. *Countries and Regions: Association of South East Asian Nations (ASEAN)*. European Commission. Accessed May 16 2019. http://ec.europa.eu/trade/policy/countries-and-regions/regions/asean/

45 *Framework Agreement on Partnership and Cooperation between the European Union and its Member States, of the one part, and the Republic of the Philippines on the other part*. 2011 (Article 19.3 of this Agreement states '[t]he Parties agree to enhance cooperation…in the area of protection of plant varieties, bearing in mind others, and where appropriate, the role of [the UPOV Convention].').

46 *Free Trade Agreement between the European Union and the Republic of Singapore*. 2014 (Article 10.35 of this Agreement reaffirms the parties' obligations under UPOV 1991, including their ability to implement the optional exception to the breeder's right).

and Vietnam,[47] and talks are ongoing with Indonesia, Malaysia, Myanmar, and Thailand.

Outside the ASEAN group, the European Union has signed trade treaties with countries in other Asian subregions, including Bangladesh,[48] Japan,[49] Kazakhstan,[50] Kyrgyzstan,[51] South Korea,[52] Tajikistan,[53] and Uzbekistan.[54] Meanwhile, the European Trade Commission continues to pursue new bilateral agreements with China, India, and Pakistan. All of the accords that the European Union has executed to date with Central, South, and East Asian nations contain terms related to the implementation of laws to grant intellectual property for plant varieties that conform to the UPOV 1991 model for plant breeders' rights.

While the United States and the European Union are the territories that in recent history have been the greatest protagonists of the execution of free trade agreements with developing countries, other wealthy nations have followed suit. For instance, Australia has finalised free trade treaties with

47 *Free Trade Agreement between the European Union and the Socialist Republic of Vietnam.* 2016 (Chapter 12, Article 11 of this Agreement states that the parties 'shall protect plant varieties rights, in accordance with [UPOV 1991], including the exceptions to the breeder's right.').

48 *Cooperation Agreement between the European Community and the People's Republic of Bangladesh on Partnership and Development.* 2001 (Article 4(5)(c) of this Agreement requires accession to UPOV 1991).

49 *Annex to the Proposal for a Council Decision on the signing, on behalf of the European Union, of the Economic Partnership Agreement between the European Union and Japan.* 2018 (Article 14.3(h) of this Annex affirms the parties' commitment to comply with obligations set forth under UPOV 1991).

50 *The European Union and the Republic of Kazakhstan Partnership and Cooperation Agreement.* 1995 (Article 42 of this Agreement requires accession to UPOV 1991 by the end of the fifth year after the entry into force of the Agreement. The treaty entered into force in 1999).

51 *Partnership and Cooperation Agreement establishing a partnership between the European Communities and their Member States, of the one part, and the Kyrgyz Republic, of the other part.* 1999 (Article 43 of this Agreement states that by the end of the fifth year after entry into force of the Agreement, the Parties shall accede to UPOV 1991. The treaty entered into force in 1999).

52 *Free Trade Agreement between the European Union and its Member States, of the one part, and the Republic of Korea, of the other part.* 2010 (Article 10.39 of this Agreement states '[e]ach Party shall provide for the protection of plant varieties and comply with [UPOV 1991].').

53 *Partnership and Cooperation Agreement between the European Communities and their Member States, of the one part, and the Republic of Tajikistan, of the other part.* 2009 (Article 39 states that by the end of the fifth year after entry into force of the Agreement, the Parties shall accede to UPOV 1991. The treaty entered into force in 2010).

54 *Partnership and Cooperation Agreement between the European Communities and their Member States, of the one part, and the Republic of Uzbekistan, of the other part.* 1996 (Article 41 states that by the end of the fifth year after entry into force of the Agreement, the Parties shall accede to UPOV 1991. The treaty entered into force in 1999).

Japan[55] and Singapore,[56] the provisions of which require adherence to UPOV 1991. The Australian Department of Foreign Affairs and Trade is currently negotiating agreements with Hong Kong, India, and Indonesia, which when finalised could contain similar terms. Furthermore, the pursuit of commercial treaties has not been the exclusive purview of Western democracies. For instance, Japan has free trade agreements in place with Indonesia[57] and Vietnam[58] that mandate the protection of plant varieties pursuant to frameworks that comply with UPOV 1991.

In addition to these bilateral trade accords, regional and trans-regional agreements have become increasingly relevant vehicles for the spread of the UPOV 1991 model in recent years. Among the most prominent of these was the *Trans-Pacific Partnership* (TPP), a proposed trade agreement that included as parties Australia, Brunei, Canada, Chile, Japan, Malaysia, Mexico, New Zealand, Peru, Singapore, Vietnam, and the United States. Although the TPP was signed in February 2016, the treaty was unable to be ratified after the United States withdrew its signature in January 2017. Subsequently, the agreement morphed into the *Comprehensive and Progressive Agreement for Trans-Pacific Partnership* (CPTPP), which included all of the original parties to the TPP, minus the United States.

The CPTPP incorporated most of the essential provisions that had been set forth in the text of the TPP, including the obligation that each party will accede to UPOV 1991 by the date on which the agreement becomes binding, which was set to occur 60 days after ratification by 50 percent of the signatories.[59] The CPTPP was executed by all 11 signatories in March 2018, and it entered into force between Australia, Canada, Japan, Mexico, New Zealand, and Singapore in December 2018. For most of the CPTPP members, the requirement to implement domestic legislation based on UPOV 1991 is inconsequential. That is, Australia, Canada, Japan, New Zealand, Peru, Singapore, and Vietnam already had UPOV 1991-compliant national laws in place at the time when the CPTPP was signed.

Nevertheless, several of the parties will be required to reform their domestic intellectual property laws for plant varieties once they ratify the CPTPP. These countries include Chile and Mexico, whose domestic regimes currently are based

55 *Japan – Australia Economic Partnership Agreement.* 2005 (Article 16.11 of this Agreement provides that '[e]ach Party shall, in accordance with its rights and obligations under the UPOV Convention, provide for protection of plant varieties....').

56 *Singapore – Australia Free Trade Agreement.* 2003 (Chapter 13, Article 2.2(d) of this Agreement states that the parties affirm that they have ratified or acceded to UPOV 1991).

57 *Japan – Indonesia Economic Partnership Agreement.* 2007. Article 116.

58 *Japan – Vietnam Economic Partnership Agreement.* 2008. Article 90.

59 *Comprehensive and Progressive Agreement for Trans-Pacific Partnership, incorporating the provisions of the Trans-Pacific Partnership Agreement* (TPP). 2016. Article 18.7(2)(d).

on UPOV 1978, and Brunei Darussalam and Malaysia, which are not members of the UPOV Convention. As discussed above, the UPOV Council has reviewed the 2015 *Plant Varieties Protection Order* of Brunei and determined that the law conforms to UPOV 1991, paving the way for the country to join the Union. In contrast, when the UPOV Council evaluated the *Protection of New Varieties of Plants Act* of Malaysia in 2004, the Council noted several areas of discrepancy between this framework and UPOV 1991.[60]

Issues that the UPOV Council flagged included the creation in the Malaysian legislation of a separate system of protection for plant varieties that are bred, or are discovered and developed by a farmer, local community, or indigenous group;[61] the prohibition on the grant of plant breeders' rights where there is reasonable ground to believe that the cultivation, reproduction, or any other use of the variety in question may produce a negative impact on the environment;[62] and the inclusion of an exception to the breeder's right for the exchange of protected propagating material among small farmers.[63] The review of the Malaysian plant variety protection law by the UPOV Council indicates that Malaysia may need to institute substantial reforms to its national system of intellectual property for plant varieties upon ratification of the CPTPP. Doing so could detrimentally affect customary agriculture in the country, for instance by eroding the possibility that small-scale farmers might protect the plant varieties that they develop, or by restricting farmers' ability to exchange the seeds of protected breeders' varieties.

Meanwhile, another multilateral trade agreement that could further expand the influence of the UPOV 1991 model in Asia remained in negotiation at the time of writing of this chapter. The *Regional Comprehensive Economic Partnership* (RCEP) is a proposed treaty that has been touted as an alternative to or rival of the CPTPP. Current parties to the RCEP negotiations include the ten member countries of ASEAN, in addition to Australia, China, India, Japan, New Zealand, and South Korea. Similar to the CPTPP and the bilateral agreements discussed earlier, the draft intellectual property chapter of the RCEP contains language that requires signatories to adhere to UPOV 1991.[64] If this provision were included in the final version of the RCEP, the treaty would obligate several countries either to adopt new plant breeders' rights legislation, or to reform their current regimes to meet the standards of UPOV 1991. The countries that would be affected include

60 International Union for the Protection of New Varieties of Plants (UPOV). 2005. *Examination of the Conformity of the Protection of New Plant Varieties Act 2004 of Malaysia with the 1991 Act of the UPOV Convention.* UPOV Pub. No. C(Extr.)/22/2. Geneva: UPOV. Accessed May 29 2019. www.upov.int/edocs/mdocs/upov/en/c_extr/22/c_extr_22_2.pdf

61 Ibid, paragraph 10.

62 Ibid, paragraph 15.

63 Ibid, paragraph 26.

64 *Single Working Document on the Intellectual Property Chapter Regional Comprehensive Economic Partnership (RCEP) Free Trade Agreement.* 2015. Article 1.7(2)(j).

all of the ASEAN members other than Singapore and Vietnam, in addition to China and India.

Although China is already a UPOV member with a national framework based on UPOV 1978, India represents the most prominent example worldwide of a country that has developed non-UPOV Convention *sui generis* plant variety protection legislation. While the original version of India's Plant Variety Bill was modelled on UPOV 1978,[65] prior to enactment, the Bill was modified to incorporate a chapter on farmers' rights. After the Indian Parliament approved the 2001 *Protection of Plant Varieties and Farmers' Rights Act*, the government made a formal request to join the UPOV Convention in 2002. At that time, the UPOV Secretariat apparently extended an oral offer to open an exception that would allow India to ratify UPOV 1978, which had formally ceased to accept new members in April 1999.[66]

An initial examination of the Indian legislation by the UPOV Consultative Committee began in October 2002, and it resulted in a number of observations on the compliance of the law with UPOV 1978. The communications between the Indian government and the Consultative Committee were never made public, and ultimately negotiations between India and the UPOV Secretariat ceased in 2003. At that time, the prospect that the country might join the UPOV Convention provoked significant civil society unrest, culminating in a public interest lawsuit that challenged the government's intention to adhere to the Convention.[67] It is likely that any future attempt to join UPOV 1991 would be similarly opposed if India were required under the terms of the RCEP to reform its *Protection of Plant Varieties and Farmers' Rights Act.*

As the numerous bilateral, regional, and trans-regional trade agreements reviewed in this chapter demonstrate, in recent years Asian countries have increasingly assumed obligations to model their domestic intellectual property laws for plant varieties on UPOV 1991. The hard influence of these treaties may already have impacted the development of UPOV Convention-based plant breeders' rights legislation in certain countries, including Brunei, Cambodia, Laos, and Myanmar. However, it also must be recognised that soft factors, such as the influence of actors representing industrial and governmental interests, were also instrumental in occasioning this regional turn towards UPOV 1991.

2.3 Soft influences: How commercial interests shape lawmaking

As described in section 2.2, over the past two decades, free trade agreements have operated to harmonise trade relations between sovereign States, with spill-over

65 Ranjan, P. 2009. 'Recent Developments in India's Plant Variety Protection, Seed Regulation and Linkages with UPOV's Proposed Membership.' *The Journal of World Intellectual Property* 12 (3): 219–243, 231.

66 Peschard, K. 2014. 'Farmers' Rights and Food Sovereignty: Critical Insights from India.' *The Journal of Peasant Studies* 41 (6): 1085–1108, 1095.

67 Ibid.

effects on member countries' national legal systems. Regimes whose purpose is to protect plant varieties as intellectual property have been particularly affected by these formal international influences. However, on some occasions the reforms to Asian intellectual property laws in recent years may be attributed to other, subtler factors, including threatened trade sanctions by wealthy countries or lobbying by business groups.[68] Thus, the actors that have promoted the UPOV 1991 model in Asian countries range from industry representatives – including multinational seed companies and regional trade associations – to foreign governmental entities.

Activist organisations have argued against the recommendation advanced by agricultural corporations predominantly based in North America and Europe that Asian countries should look to UPOV 1991 as a means to harmonise plant breeders' rights legislation throughout the region. One international non-governmental organisation, Genetic Resources Action International (GRAIN), contends that the reason why multinational agricultural firms have pushed for local adoption of the UPOV 1991 model is to enable the commercialisation of their plant varieties in Asian markets, and to obtain exclusive control over the sale of hybrid and genetically modified seeds.[69] GRAIN further claims that 'the seed industry and its allies have aggressively promoted [...] UPOV as the appropriate system' for countries to comply with the TRIPS obligation to provide intellectual property for plant varieties.[70]

The influence of private commercial interests on lawmaking in Asia has, in some instances, been consolidated by the governments of the countries in which several major multinational agricultural firms are based. For instance, the United States Department of Agriculture (USDA) oversees a Foreign Agricultural Service that promotes international agricultural development, which is driven by the goal to enhance the capacity of countries to participate in international trade. Pragmatically, this approach to development has manifested in the Asian context through USDA-funded projects that aim to introduce new commercial crop varieties into local agricultural economies.[71] Typically, these varieties are conceptualised as economic goods that multinational firms have developed, and which they seek to protect with exclusive exploitation rights. Thus, agribusiness actors have a direct interest in lobbying for the establishment of UPOV 1991-based plant breeders' rights regimes in their target markets.

68 Kuanpoth, J. 2008. 'Intellectual Property Protection after TRIPS: An Asian Experience.' In *Interpreting and Implementing the TRIPS Agreement: Is it Fair?*, edited by J. Malbon and C. Lawson. Cheltenham: Edward Elgar, pages 72–73.

69 Kuyek, D., GRAIN, MASIPAG, PAN Indonesia, Philippine Greens, UBINIG, R. Quijano, and O. B. Zamora. 2001. *Intellectual Property Rights: Ultimate Control of Agricultural R&D in Asia*. GRAIN Reports. Accessed May 29 2019. www.grain.org/article/entries/30-intellectual-property-rights-ultimate-control-of-agricultural-r-d-in-asia

70 Ibid, page 6.

71 Bhutani, S. 2013. *Re-Searching Agriculture in South Asia: The Law and Policy Context for Agricultural Research and Development and its Impact on Smallholder Farmers*. London: International Institute for Environment and Development, pages 6–7.

While the influence of multinational seed companies that are predominantly based in North America and Europe is important, these are not the only actors that have promoted the UPOV 1991 model in Asia. In recent years, some of the pressure to accede to UPOV 1991 has come from influences internal to the region. For instance, the Asia and Pacific Seed Association – whose members include national seed associations, governmental agencies, and public and private seed companies – has advocated for the adoption of harmonised plant breeders' rights legislation in the Asia and Pacific region. A recent position paper published by the Association 'recognises the UPOV Convention and the Act of 1991 as the best system of plant variety protection.'[72] Further, the paper expressly 'encourages countries in the region to ratify and implement the 1991 Act of the UPOV Convention.'[73]

Actors from Asian governments also have played an instrumental role in promoting the UPOV 1991 model in the region. Among the most prominent organisations to involve governmental participants is the East Asia Plant Variety Protection Forum, which is a group comprised of the plant variety protection authorities of the ten ASEAN countries, in addition to China, Japan, and South Korea. The Forum was founded in 2007 following a regional workshop that 'recognised the importance of the existence of an effective and internationally harmonised plant variety protection system' based on the 'mutual recognition and the understanding of the importance of the UPOV Convention.'[74] Since 2008, the Forum has organised annual meetings in a different member country each year, in addition to seminars whose purpose is to present the presumed benefits of the UPOV 1991 paradigm.[75]

Furthermore, actors from within the UPOV Convention itself have actively promoted the UPOV 1991 plant breeders' rights model throughout Asia generally, and in ASEAN countries in particular.[76] For instance, UPOV Convention representatives have assisted ASEAN member countries with the development of their national plant variety protection laws through workshops and consultations. Since at least 1994, many of these events have been organised in Southeast Asian nations. They are often funded by Japan, which has

72 The Asia and Pacific Seed Association (ASPA). 2017. *APSA Position on Intellectual Property Rights for the Seed Industry*. Bangkok: ASPA. Accessed May 16 2019. https://apsaseed.org/wp-content/uploads/2017/02/FINAL-APSA-IPR-Position-Paper.pdf

73 Ibid.

74 East Asian Plant Variety Protection Forum (EAPVPF). 2007. *Joint Statement of the Workshop on the Cooperation and Harmonization in Plant Variety Protection in the Asian Region*. Akasaka Minato-Ku: EAPVPF. Accessed May 16 2019. www.eapvp.org/about/docs/jointstatement_en.pdf

75 East Asia Plant Variety Protection Forum (EAPVPF). *Forum History*. Akasaka Minato-Ku: EAPVPF. Accessed May 16 2019. www.eapvp.org/about/index.html

76 Kanniah, R. and C. Antons. 2012. 'Plant Variety Protection and Traditional Agricultural Knowledge in Southeast Asia.' *Australian Journal of Asian Law* 13 (1): 1–23, 8–9.

been a UPOV Convention member since 1982.[77] More recently, in 2016 and 2017, the UPOV Convention 'provided advice and assistance on the development of plant variety protection legislation according to the 1991 Act of the UPOV Convention' to numerous countries throughout Asia, including Brunei, Cambodia, Indonesia, Laos, Malaysia, Myanmar, Nepal, and Thailand.[78] During this same period, seminars and training courses were organised by or in conjunction with the UPOV Convention in Japan, Vietnam, Myanmar, and Thailand, and participants from multiple countries participated in UPOV-run distance learning courses.[79]

Political and educational initiatives that enhance the visibility of the UPOV 1991 plant breeders' rights model tend to create the illusion that implementing national legislation based on this paradigm is the only effective option that countries have in order to comply with the terms of the TRIPS Agreement. This perception results from the fact that UPOV Convention-driven training activities are not counterbalanced with similar events designed to educate local actors about how to establish non-UPOV Convention, *sui generis* systems of intellectual property for plant varieties. When coupled with the hard influences embodied in the bilateral, regional, and trans-regional trade agreements discussed earlier in this chapter, it is perhaps unsurprising that numerous countries throughout Asia are moving increasingly towards the adoption of UPOV 1991-based plant breeders' rights laws. As section 2.4 demonstrates, several Southeast Asian territories have recently enacted new plant breeders' rights regimes modelled on UPOV 1991, while others have proposed reforms to existing plant variety protection laws that are designed to bring these frameworks into greater alignment with the UPOV Convention standard.

2.4 Legal manifestations of the Asian turn towards UPOV 1991

Until recently, the treatment of plant varieties as intellectual property in the Southeast Asian subregion was patchy. As of May 2019, Vietnam was the only one of the six mainland Southeast Asian countries[80] to have acceded formally to the UPOV Convention. Meanwhile, Malaysia and Thailand protected plant varieties through *sui generis* intellectual property legislation, though it was likely that both countries would introduce future reforms to bring their respective national laws into greater alignment with UPOV 1991. For their part, Cambodia, Laos, and Myanmar recently designed UPOV 1991-based plant breeders' rights frameworks,

77 Ibid, page 9.
78 World Trade Organization, Council for Trade-Related Aspects of Intellectual Property Rights. 2018. *Technical Cooperation Activities: Information from Other Intergovernmental Organizations: International Union for the Protection of New Varieties of Plants (UPOV)*. Document No. IP/C/W/633/Add.8. Geneva: World Trade Organization.
79 Ibid, pages 2–3, 7.
80 These territories include Cambodia, Laos, Malaysia, Myanmar, Thailand, and Vietnam.

even though as of May 2019 these countries were not formal members of the UPOV Convention. Thus, in all of the mainland Southeast Asian territories, a clear shift towards the UPOV 1991-based plant breeders' rights paradigm is evidenced in both proposed and enacted legislative reforms.

A prominent example of this dynamic is found in Myanmar. The UPOV Council evaluated the Burmese *Draft Law on New Plant Variety Protection* in September 2017 and determined that the framework was compliant with UPOV 1991.[81] The result of this assessment is that once the bill is adopted, Myanmar can accede to UPOV 1991 without making any changes to its prospective national plant breeders' rights system.[82] The text of the Burmese *Draft Law on New Plant Variety Protection* recapitulates the provisions of UPOV 1991, providing protection for all plant genera and species based on the conditions of novelty, distinctness, uniformity, and stability.[83] The scope of the rights granted to plant breeders extends to the harvested material of protected varieties,[84] essentially derived varieties (EDVs), varieties that are not clearly distinguishable a protected variety, and varieties whose production requires the repeated use of a protected variety.[85] The periods of exclusivity specified in the Draft Law of Myanmar also track UPOV 1991, at 25 years for trees and vines and 20 years for all other species.[86]

The only exceptions to the intellectual property rights of plant breeders that the *Draft Law on New Plant Variety Protection* of Myanmar provides are those that UPOV 1991 explicitly enumerates, in addition to its Article 15(2) optional exception relating to the 'farmer's privilege.' According to these provisions, plant breeders' rights do not extend to acts done for non-commercial or experimental purposes, or to breed new varieties.[87] Additionally, the Draft Law of Myanmar stipulates that 'small farmers shall not infringe the breeder's right, in relation to varieties included in a list of agricultural plants in the manner prescribed by the Ministry,' if use is for propagating purposes only, on their own holdings, 'provided that this use is within reasonable limits and subject to the safeguarding of the legitimate interests of the breeder.'[88]

This formulation of the farmer's privilege is narrow, in that it only applies to 'small farmers,' a term that is not defined in the Draft Law of Myanmar. Furthermore, the farmers' privilege solely permits small farmers to save the propagating material of specific species of plants that the Ministry elects to designate. An

81 International Union for the Protection of New Varieties of Plants (UPOV). 2017. *Examination of the Conformity of the Draft Law on New Plant Variety Protection of Myanmar with the 1991 Act of the UPOV Convention.* UPOV Pub. No. C/51/21. Geneva: UPOV. www.upov.int/edocs/mdocs/upov/en/c_51/c_51_21.pdf

82 UPOV, note 34.

83 *The New Plant Variety Protection Draft Law of Myanmar.* 2017. Section 9.

84 Ibid, Section 25.

85 Ibid, Section 27.

86 Ibid, Section 32.

87 Ibid, Section 28(a).

88 Ibid, Section 28(b).

additional limitation is that small farmers are exempted from paying royalties on protected breeders' varieties only when these plants are used for propagating purposes, on these farmers' own holdings. This means that seed saving is not allowed where the use of the harvested material from a subsequent generation would be employed for other purposes, such as exchange with other farmers or sale in local markets. Lastly, seed saving by small farmers is qualified by the language, 'within reasonable limits' and 'subject to the safeguarding of the legitimate interests of the breeder,' phrases which remain ambiguous in the current version of the Burmese Draft Law.

Although the Draft Law of Myanmar has been favourably evaluated by the UPOV Council, as of May 2019 the national legislature had not yet approved the bill. In contrast, Cambodia and Laos recently enacted binding plant breeders' rights laws modelled on UPOV 1991, though the UPOV Council has not yet evaluated these frameworks for compliance with the Convention. First, the *Law on Seed Management and Plant Breeder's Rights* of Cambodia – which is a legislative framework that amalgamates systems of seed certification and intellectual property for plant varieties – was enacted in April 2008. The preface of this text expressly acknowledges that the primary factor that motivated the adoption of the law was that Cambodia joined the World Trade Organization in 2004. However, the language that the preface employs suggests that some confusion may have existed surrounding the country's actual obligations under the TRIPS Agreement.

According to the terms of a 2013 decision by the Council for TRIPS, least-developed members such as Cambodia do not need to comply with the TRIPS Agreement until July 2021.[89] Nevertheless, the Cambodian *Law on Seed Management and Plant Breeder's Rights* states that because the country has joined the World Trade Organization, 'Cambodia must introduce many laws to meet the requirements of [the Organization].'[90] The preface goes on to declare, 'we need to provide protection of plant breeder's rights consistent with [the UPOV Convention].'[91]

While this language may be intended simply to clarify the priorities of the Cambodian lawmakers, it could also reflect a misunderstanding about the obligations that Cambodia assumed by joining the World Trade Organization. Notably, the Working Party Report for the accession of Cambodia to the World Trade Organization stated that the Cambodian government was considering joining the UPOV Convention, 'and a new law was being drafted to this end with the assistance of UPOV.'[92] However, as discussed in earlier sections of this chapter, the

89 World Trade Organization. 2013. 'Extension of the Transition Period under Article 66.1 for Least Developed Country Members.' *Council for Trade-Related Aspects of Intellectual Property Rights*, June 12. Accessed May 16 2019. www.wto.org/english/tratop_e/trips_e/ldc_e.htm

90 *Kingdom of Cambodia, Law on Seed Management and Plant Breeder's Rights.* 2009. Preface, paragraph 2.

91 Ibid, paragraph 3.

92 World Trade Organization. 2003. *Report on the Working Party on the Accession of Cambodia.* World Trade Organization Document WT/ACC/KHM/21. Geneva: World Trade Organization, paragraph 172.

terms of the TRIPS Agreement do not obligate World Trade Organization members to adhere to the UPOV Convention as a means to provide intellectual property for plant varieties. Furthermore, the Working Party Report does not contain any language that would suggest that membership in the World Trade Organization was made contingent on Cambodia joining the UPOV Convention.

In any event, the provisions of the *Law on Seed Management and Plant Breeder's Rights* of Cambodia create a form of intellectual property that is consistent with the UPOV 1991 model. The law reinscribes the novelty, distinctness, uniformity, and stability criteria as the fundamental conditions for the grant of plant breeders' rights,[93] and the scope of the rights granted includes propagation, offering for sale, selling or other marketing, exporting, importing, and stocking protected varieties for commercial purposes.[94] The rights granted to breeders also extend to harvested material, EDVs, varieties that are not clearly distinguishable from a protected variety, and varieties that require repeated use of a protected variety.[95] The periods of protection for plant breeders' rights in Cambodia also mirror those that UPOV 1991 mandates, at 25 years for trees and vines and 20 years for all other species.[96]

The only exceptions to the intellectual property rights of plant breeders that are included in the Cambodian legislation are for acts done: for experimental purposes; privately and for non-commercial purposes; and for the purposes of breeding other varieties.[97] The law itself does not recognise a farmer's privilege exception to plant breeders' rights, but it does mandate that two government ministries must cooperate 'to issue regulations that limit the rights of owners of protected varieties in order to permit farmers to use [such] varieties for propagating purposes, on their own holdings.'[98] This language suggests that, consistent with UPOV 1991, farmers would not be permitted to exchange the planting material of protected varieties with other growers, or to sell such material in local seed markets.

Further reinforcing the marginalisation of customary agricultural practices is the fact that the Cambodian legislation stipulates that all seed trade in the country requires a licence from the Ministry of Agriculture, Forestry, and Fishery.[99] Additionally, the law creates a system of seed inspection that authorises its agents to monitor and supervise all seed-related businesses and activities in the country; to inspect farms that are suspected of violating the seed certification law; and to confiscate offending material, among other powers.[100] Lastly, the infringement of plant breeders' rights in Cambodia is punishable by civil actions, confiscation and

93 *Kingdom of Cambodia, Law on Seed Management and Plant Breeder's Rights.* 2009. Article 6.
94 Ibid, Article 15.
95 Ibid.
96 Ibid, Article 19.
97 Ibid, Article 16.
98 Ibid.
99 Ibid, Article 42.
100 Ibid, Article 65.

destruction of seeds, and monetary damages,[101] while offences related to the seed trade are conceptualised as criminal and the possible penalties for violations include imprisonment.[102] These provisions represent instances of ultracompliance with UPOV 1991, which does not specify the type of sanctions that should be imposed for the infringement of plant breeders' rights.

Given the legislation that Myanmar and Cambodia recently enacted, it is perhaps unsurprising that neighbouring Laos similarly revised its national intellectual property law in 2011 to create a new system of plant variety protection. Like the Burmese and Cambodian regimes, the Laos legislation is based on UPOV 1991. Thus, intellectual property for plant varieties is contingent on meeting the criteria of novelty, distinctness, uniformity, and stability;[103] and the scope of plant breeders' rights over seeds and other propagating materials of protected varieties includes production and reproduction; conditioning for the purpose of propagation; offering for sale; selling or other marketing; exporting and importing; and stocking for commercial purposes.[104] Protection also extends to EDVs, varieties that are not clearly distinguishable from a protected variety, and varieties that require the repeated use of a protected variety.[105] Lastly, plant breeders' rights in Laos have a duration of 25 years for trees and vines and 20 years for all other species.[106]

The revised intellectual property law of Laos recognises the UPOV 1991-based exceptions to plant breeders' rights, including: for acts done privately and for non-commercial purposes; for experimental purposes; and to breed other varieties.[107] A limited farmer's privilege is also incorporated into the legislation, such that a farmer 'may use for propagating purposes, on his or her own holdings, the product of the harvest obtained by planting [the protected variety] on his or her own holdings.'[108] However, this exception only applies if the protected variety was obtained with the authorisation of the rightsholder. This means that farmers who acquire the planting material of a protected variety through a transaction not sanctioned by the breeder would not be exempted from infringement.

While Myanmar, Cambodia, and Laos elected to follow the UPOV 1991 model from the outset, Malaysia and Thailand represent Southeast Asian countries that previously enacted independent, *sui generis* plant variety protection legislation. Nevertheless, these countries are also taking steps to align their laws with UPOV 1991. For its part, Malaysia submitted its *Protection of New Varieties Act* of 2004 to the UPOV Council in 2005 for an examination of conformity with UPOV

101 Ibid, Article 70.
102 Ibid, Article 74.
103 *Lao People's Democratic Republic, Law on Intellectual Property (Amended 20 December 2011)*. Article 68.
104 Ibid, Article 78.
105 Ibid.
106 Ibid, Article 79.
107 Ibid, Article 82(1).
108 Ibid, Article 82(2).

1991. Following this evaluation, the Council noted several areas of discrepancy between the Malaysian legislation and UPOV 1991, as described in section 2.1 of this chapter. Nevertheless, when it signed the CPTPP in 2018, Malaysia assumed the obligation to comply with UPOV 1991 upon ratification of the treaty. This means that Malaysia will likely soon be subject to a formal legal requirement to amend its national plant variety protection system in a way that could favour industrial agriculture, while detrimentally affecting customary farming practices in the country.

Similar to Malaysia, Thailand established a *sui generis* plant variety protection system in 1999, through legislation that amalgamates elements of the UPOV Convention with aspects of the 1992 *Convention on Biological Diversity*. The Thai *Plant Varieties Protection Act* thus endeavours to accomplish multiple policy goals, including granting intellectual property protection to plant breeders; establishing a system of protection for farmers' plant varieties; facilitating the sharing of benefits derived from the exploitation of varieties registered by local communities; and supporting biodiversity conservation, research, and development. Thus, the framework institutes mechanisms for the protection of different categories of plant varieties, which include local domestic varieties, general domestic varieties, and wild varieties. Furthermore, the Thai Act creates a Plant Varieties Protection Fund, which functions as a mechanism for benefit sharing.

Although some scholars have criticised the Thai system of intellectual property for plant varieties as vague and limited in certain respects,[109] other observers have cited the law as an example that other developing countries could follow as a means to balance TRIPS compliance with local priorities and interests.[110] In either case, it appears that the plant variety protection regime of Thailand may be reformed in the future. In October 2017, the Thai Ministry of Agriculture and Cooperatives released a draft amendment to the *Plant Varieties Protection Act* that contained provisions designed to reconcile the law with UPOV 1991.[111]

One of the key changes that the draft amendment proposed is that new plant varieties not based on native Thai varieties (i.e., wild, local domestic, and general domestic varieties) would be exempted from the revenue-sharing requirements that are currently mandated pursuant to the terms of the government-administered Plant Varieties Protection Fund.[112] Furthermore, the draft amendment proposed to

109 Lertdhamtewe, P. 2013. 'Plant Variety Protection in Thailand: The Need for a New Coherent Framework.' *Journal of Intellectual Property Law & Practice* 8 (1): 33–42, 40.

110 Correa, et al., note 16.

111 As reported in Prasertsri, P. 2017. 'Thai Plant Variety Protection Act Amendment Update.' *United States Department of Agriculture Foreign Agricultural Service GAIN Report No. TH7147*, November 2. Accessed May 16 2019. https://gain.fas.usda.gov/Recent%20GAIN%20Publications/Thai%20Plant%20Variety%20Protection%20Act%20Amendment%20Update_Bangkok_Thailand_11-2-2017.pdf

112 Ibid.

redefine the term 'general domestic plant variety'[113] to not include varieties that have undergone formal breeding.[114] This means that a plant variety that was developed by a professional breeder – such as a public research institution or a private firm – but was subsequently adapted to local growing conditions and cultivated widely by local farmers would no longer meet the definition of 'general domestic plant variety.'

If enacted, these changes could effectively limit the number of plant varieties that are subject to the obligation of obtaining prior informed consent and negotiating mutually agreed terms for benefit sharing. The Thai Seed Trade Association and other interests aligned with multinational firms support this proposed amendment, based on the contention that the Plant Varieties Protection Fund has discouraged investment in improved plant varieties and the development of Thailand as a 'seed hub.'[115] Meanwhile, opponents of the proposal argue that the proposed redefinitions of the terms 'native plant' and 'general domestic plant variety' in the draft amendment would disempower local communities, by reducing the number of plant varieties subject to prior informed consent and benefit sharing requirements.[116]

The draft amendment also proposes additional changes to the *Plant Varieties Protection Act* that would bring Thailand into greater alignment with the UPOV 1991 model. For instance, the term of plant breeders' rights protection would be reclassified and lengthened to the UPOV 1991 compliant periods of 25 years for perennials and vines, and 20 years for all other species.[117] Furthermore, the proposed reform would eliminate the requirement to undertake an environmental impact assessment prior to developing genetically modified varieties, and it would also extend plant breeders' rights to cover EDVs.[118]

Lastly, it is notable that the draft amendment to the Thai regime of intellectual property for plant varieties would limit the scope of the farmers' privilege that is recognised in the current law. Under the *Plant Varieties Protection Act*, farmers are permitted to save the seeds of protected plant varieties in an amount of up to three times the quantity originally received.[119] In contrast, the draft amendment would require authorisation from the breeder for all uses of protected plant

113 For a thorough analysis of the scope of the term 'general domestic plant variety' as currently defined in the Thai *Plant Varieties Protection Act*, see Chapter 8 of this volume.

114 Sujintaya, S. 2018. 'First Draft Amendment to the Plant Varieties Protection Act.' *Insight, Baker McKenzie*, January 23. Accessed May 16 2019. www.bakermckenzie.com/en/insight/publications/2018/01/first-draft-amendment-plant-varieties/

115 Prasertsri, note 111.

116 Bunyamanee, S. 2017. 'Agriculture Dept Sows Seeds of Discontent.' *Bangkok Post Opinion Page*, October 18. Accessed May 16 2019. www.bangkokpost.com/opinion/opinion/1344478/agriculture-dept-sows-seeds-of-discontent

117 Under the current Act, the protection terms are set at 12 years for plants capable of yielding fruits within two years; 17 years for plants capable of yielding fruits after a period of more than two years; and 27 years for trees. *Thailand Plant Varieties Protection Act, B.E. 2542 (1999)*. Article 31.

118 Sujintaya, note 114.

119 *Thailand Plant Varieties Protection Act, B.E. 2542 (1999)*. Article 33.

varieties, except for acts that are not intended for propagation or commercialisation; acts that only are intended for research and development in plant breeding; and cultivation and propagation activities that are conducted exclusively on the farmer's own land.[120] As of May 2019, it remained unclear whether the draft amendment to the Thai *Plant Varieties Protection Act* would be enacted. Public comment was accepted during October and November 2017, but since that time no formal governmental action has been taken to convert the proposal into law.

2.5 Conclusion

This chapter has surveyed the tendency of countries throughout Asia to shift increasingly towards implementing plant breeders' rights legislation modelled on UPOV 1991. The argument was substantiated by focussing on concrete changes that have been either proposed or enacted in five mainland Southeast Asian nations, namely Myanmar, Cambodia, Laos, Malaysia, and Thailand. As the chapter has shown, across Asia multiple 'hard' and 'soft,' external and internal factors have impelled the expansion of the UPOV 1991 model of plant breeders' rights. In some instances, this has resulted in ultracompliance with the TRIPS Agreement, where countries that are members of the World Trade Organization but not the UPOV Convention have elected to follow the UPOV 1991 model of intellectual property for plant varieties.

As the most prominent example of a hard, external influence, it is undeniable that TRIPS has left a lasting legacy, by creating the foundational impetus for many Asian governments to protect plant varieties as intellectual property. The appeal of participation in the World Trade Organization has influenced domestic policymaking, including in ways that render national seed and agricultural economies more legible and accessible to foreign actors. However, it is unfortunate that at least in some instances, confusion about the nature of the TRIPS obligation to protect plant varieties as intellectual property apparently has pushed lawmakers towards the UPOV 1991 plant breeders' rights model. Although TRIPS does not require compliance with the UPOV Convention, several Asian countries have drafted national plant breeders' rights legislation using UPOV 1991 as a template.

Other hard influences that have shaped national-level lawmaking include the numerous bilateral, regional, and trans-regional free trade agreements that many Asian countries have executed with relatively wealthier nations subsequent to the entry into force of the TRIPS Agreement. In many instances, these trade agreements do contain explicit language requiring signatories to ratify UPOV 1991, and to implement national laws based on this standard. Meanwhile, a number of

120 Siriwat, S. 2018. 'Draft Bill Provides Updates to Protection of New Plant Varieties in Thailand.' *Tilleke & Gibbons*, February 20. Accessed May 16 2019. www.tilleke.com/sites/default/files/2018_Feb_Draft_Bill_Updates_New_Plant_Varieties.pdf

'soft' dynamics have motivated the widespread adoption of intellectual property for plant varieties based on the UPOV 1991 model. These include direct political lobbying efforts undertaken by representatives of multinational and regional seed industries. Other soft external influences include the educational 'capacity building' initiatives sponsored by actors including the East Asia Plant Variety Protection Forum and UPOV itself. These events may have promoted the misconception that UPOV 1991 is the only 'effective' – to invoke the parlance of TRIPS – means through which plant varieties may be protected as intellectual property.

Although as of May 2019, China, Japan, South Korea, and Vietnam were the only Asian States to have joined the UPOV Convention officially, many other countries in the region will likely do so in the near future. For instance, all five of the mainland Southeast Asian nations – namely Myanmar, Cambodia, Laos, Malaysia, and Thailand – have already taken steps to bring their domestic plant variety protection laws into greater alignment with UPOV 1991. This phenomenon also can be observed in other Asian subregions, and it is possible that participation in free trade agreements will eventually require large, populous countries including China and India to adhere to UPOV 1991. If this were to occur in these two countries alone, customary agricultural practices such as seed exchange and local sale could be restricted for more than one-third of the global population.

The result of the various hard and soft, external and internal factors that this chapter has described is that an increasing number of countries throughout Asia are adopting a narrow conception of how to regulate relationships between human actors and plants. The predominance of the plant breeders' rights model that UPOV 1991 encapsulates marginalises other ways of imagining how these relationships might be governed. While this chapter does not intend to argue for or against UPOV 1991 as a means to protect plant varieties as intellectual property, it is important to emphasise that this model is solely concerned with enabling the commercial exploitation in capitalist markets of the new, distinct, uniform, and stable plant varieties that plant breeders develop.[121]

According to this logic, plants are conceived as innovative economic objects or goods, while the subjectivity of plant breeders is favoured over that of other actors. Thus, in recognition of their ingenuity, these individual 'inventors' should be entitled to commercial exclusivity, awarded in the form of intellectual property. Under this paradigm, other groups of people – such as farmers – are not the subjects of rights, let alone the plants themselves that circulate in agricultural economies.[122]

121 Button, P. 2016. *Proceedings of the Symposium on Possible Interrelations between the ITPGRFA and the UPOV Convention. Overview of the UPOV Convention.* Geneva: UPOV. Accessed 29 May 2019. www.upov.int/edocs/mdocs/upov/en/upov_itpgrfa_sym_ge_16/upov_itpgrfa_sym_ge_16_ppt_1.pdf

122 While it may seem like a radical idea to conceive of non-human actors as the subjects of legal rights, consider that some national laws have recognised the legal rights of non-

Notwithstanding the spread of this model for governing the way that people and plants interrelate, alternative ontologies remain important to the lifeworlds of many communities in Asia. For this reason, countries that choose to follow the UPOV 1991 paradigm for plant breeders' rights should consider a strategy of compliance with resistance. Doing so would allow for participation in the World Trade Organization and compliance with the TRIPS Agreement, while also attending to other important national policy priorities. These could include establishing systems that would protect and foment customary forms of agriculture, and the ancestral practices and knowledge that make farming possible. Although the UPOV 1991-based plant breeders' rights model continues to gain traction throughout Asia, it is important to observe that numerous countries in the region continue to rely on small-scale, customary agriculture to fulfil important national goals.

For this reason, governmental and civil society actors alike should consider approaches to elevate alternative solutions to order the relationships between human actors and plants. Potential strategies include resisting the hard and soft influences that could pressure lawmakers to draft legislation based on the UPOV 1991 standard. To oppose hard influences, representatives of countries that have not yet joined UPOV and who participate in negotiations towards the finalisation of the RCEP or other, future free trade agreements could take a strong stance against the inclusion of language that would require compliance with UPOV 1991.

In countries that have already assumed formal obligations to adhere to UPOV 1991 pursuant to international agreements, reforms could be considered to both legislative and regulatory regimes that would broaden the national conceptualisation of protections – including according to the logic of intellectual property – for plant varieties. Asian countries such as India, Malaysia, and Thailand have already shown that this can be done, by establishing systems that grant protections to a broader suite of plant varieties, beyond the new, distinct, uniform, and stable varieties that professional breeders obtain. Furthermore, separate legal frameworks could be envisaged and implemented to realise alternative policy goals, such as safeguarding customary agricultural practices, protecting traditional knowledge, conserving plant genetic resources, ensuring food security, or promoting food sovereignty.

Other strategies could be deployed to counter soft influences. One would involve support for alternatives to local and regional capacity building initiatives that exclusively promote the UPOV 1991-based plant breeders' rights model. Government agencies or civil society organisations could sponsor events that would educate lawmakers and other interested parties to think broadly about the regulation of plants and different peoples' knowledge about how to

humans. A notable example is the Constitution of Ecuador, which grants rights to nature or '*Pachamama.*' See *Constitución de la República del Ecuador*. 2008. Articles 71 and 72.

use them. Simultaneously, channels could be opened to ensure that diverse interest groups might participate in the formation of policy at national and local levels. Together, these actions would aim to complement intellectual property systems that grant plant breeders' rights with legal frameworks that recognise alternative strategies to govern the myriad ways that people and plants interrelate.

Chapter 3

Essentially derived varieties

A workable compromise against free-riding breeders?

Charles Lawson

3.1 Introduction

The *International Convention for the Protection of New Varieties of Plants* (UPOV Convention) was concluded in Paris in 1961 and followed with revisions in 1972, 1978 and 1991. These agreements establish a system of intellectual property for plant varieties in the form of plant breeders' rights. The 1961, 1978 and 1991 Acts of the UPOV Convention all provide protection for plant varieties that are new, distinct, uniform, and stable compared to other varieties.[1] Furthermore, all versions of the UPOV Convention limit the exclusive rights of plant breeders such that protected plant varieties can be used without authorisation of the rightsholder to breed other varieties.[2]

This allowance means that a protected plant variety could be used to develop a new variety that itself is eligible for protection, even though the differences the new variety displays in comparison to the initial variety are extremely minor. For instance, the new variety may be protectable even where it differs only cosmetically from the initial variety. The problem here was that breeders of new varieties could reap commercial benefits that mostly are attributable to the efforts of prior breeders. To address this situation, the 1991 Act of the UPOV Convention (UPOV 1991) introduced the concept of 'essentially derived varieties' (EDVs). This notion expanded the scope of plant breeders' rights to include any variety that was selected on the basis of a very minor difference from an existing protected variety. The relevant text of UPOV 1991 conceptualises an EDV as a variety that is:

i Predominantly derived from the initial variety, or from a variety that is itself predominantly derived from the initial variety, while retaining the expression of the essential characteristics that result from the genotype or combination of genotypes of the initial variety;
ii Clearly distinguishable from the initial variety; and

1 UPOV Convention. Article 6(1)(a); UPOV 1978. Article 6(1); and UPOV 1991. Article 5(1).
2 UPOV Convention. Article 5(3); UPOV 1978. Article 5(3); and UPOV 1991. Article 15(1)(iii).

iii Except for the differences which result from the act of derivation, the EDV conforms to the initial variety in the expression of the essential characteristics that result from the genotype or combination of genotypes of the initial variety.[3]

UPOV 1991 further clarifies that EDVs may be obtained through diverse breeding methods. These could include, for example, the selection of a natural or induced mutant, or of a somaclonal variant; the selection of a variant individual from plants of the initial variety; backcrossing; or transformation by genetic engineering.[4]

The effect of finding that a variety is an EDV is to extend the scope of the breeder's right to an initial protected variety to cover also the EDV,[5] provided that the initial protected variety is not itself an EDV.[6] Where the initial variety is protected by a breeder's right this means that any act of production, reproduction, conditioning for the purpose of propagation, offering for sale, selling or other marketing, exporting, importing, and stocking for any of these purposes of the EDV (and its harvested materials and certain products) requires the authorisation of the breeder of the initial protected variety.[7] Furthermore, where the EDV also is protected, these acts of production, reproduction, and so on, require the authorisation of both the breeder of the initial protected variety and the breeder of the EDV, until the term of protection ends.[8]

Although this chapter does not focus on Asia, all legal issues and concerns that it raises in relation to the conceptualisation of EDVs remain important for Asian countries for two main reasons. First, as discussed in several chapters of this volume, the plant variety protection laws of Asian countries do not diverge from how UPOV 1991 defines EDVs or aims to protect EDVs. Second, there has not been any significant development in relation to the registration and protection of EDVs in Asian countries. In other words, despite the creation of legal arrangements to extend protections for EDVs, both public and private sector breeders in Asian countries are finding it difficult to register EDVs for intellectual property protection. Of the Asian countries that this volume analyses, only India is a country where from the period of 2008 to 2018, the Protection of Plant Varieties and Farmers' Rights Authority received 180 applications for the registration of EDVs. Of these, so far only one application has been approved.[9]

3 UPOV 1991. Article 14(5)(b).
4 Ibid, Article 14(5)(c).
5 Ibid, Article 14(5)(a).
6 Ibid, Article 14(5)(a)(i).
7 Ibid, Article 14(1).
8 Ibid, Article 14(5)(a).
9 See Chapter 5 of this volume. See also Protection of Plant Varieties and Farmers' Rights Authority of India. 2018. *Compendium of Registered Varieties under PPV&FR Act, 2001*. New Delhi: Department of Agriculture and Co-operation, Ministry of

Realising that the legal regulation of EDVs is gaining increased recognition in Asian and other countries and that there exists a number of ambiguities to protect these new categories of plant varieties, this chapter undertakes a broader, critical approach to examine how the EDV provisions in UPOV 1991 likely should be interpreted. Section 3.2 of the chapter explores the UPOV 1991 delimitation of EDVs in detail. Section 3.3 highlights the scope of the terms 'predominantly derived,' 'essential characteristics,' 'clearly distinguishable' and 'conforms to the initial variety,' as explicated in official UPOV documents. Section 3.4 sheds light on an apparent conflict inherent to the UPOV definition of EDVs. Section 3.5 analyses some of the legal cases that have litigated the conceptualisation of EDVs in different countries whose domestic plant breeders' rights laws are based on UPOV 1991. Section 3.6 concludes the chapter by arguing that while many of the legal issues about EDVs remain unresolved, the practical effect of the EDV provisions in UPOV 1991 has been to limit free riding by minor advances in plant breeding on previous breeding efforts.

3.2 Delimitation of EDVs in UPOV 1991

A breeder's right is a right of exclusivity for certain acts related to the use of protected plant varieties. This right is limited territorially, in that it is granted following an assessment that is undertaken according to the domestic laws of UPOV members. The breeder's right balances short-term exclusivity (an exemption from certain kinds of competition in the market) against free and open access to new plant varieties. This term of exclusivity operates as an incentive to promote more breeding. Meanwhile, the framework promotes open access through various limits on exclusivity, including exemption, exclusions, and exhaustion.[10]

The EDV language in UPOV 1991 is included within the grouping of provisions that deal with the rights that the regime grants to plant breeders.[11] The subject matter covered in this chapter about UPOV 1991 includes the definition of the scope of the breeder's right[12] and exceptions to it,[13] and exhaustion.[14] Also covered are certain restrictions,[15] co-application of plant breeders' rights with other laws,[16] and the duration of the breeder's right.[17] A key feature of the UPOV 1991 framework of intellectual property for plant varieties, and a key difference from other similar schemes such as patenting, is that the breeder's right

Agriculture. Accessed May 29 2019. http://plantauthority.gov.in/pdf/Compendium Final27Oct2018.pdf

10 UPOV 1991. Article 16.
11 Ibid, Articles 14–19.
12 Ibid, Article 14.
13 Ibid, Article 15.
14 Ibid, Article 16.
15 Ibid, Article 17.
16 Ibid, Article 18.
17 Ibid, Article 19.

does not limit acts done for the purpose of breeding other varieties.[18] This breeder's exemption is intended to promote the development of new plant varieties using existing varieties, and it reflects a longstanding practice among plant breeders of improving existing varieties 'by standing on the shoulders of giants.'[19]

In addition to the plant variety for which protection is sought under UPOV 1991, the exclusive rights that breeders may obtain also cover three additional categories of varieties: EDVs,[20] varieties that are not clearly distinguishable on the basis of 'distinctness,'[21] and varieties whose production requires the repeated use of the protected variety.[22] While this listing uses the conjunctive 'and' rather than the disjunctive 'or' the preferable interpretation probably is that the exclusive rights that are conferred for the initial variety extend to varieties in each grouping. In other words, a variety satisfying only the EDV threshold[23] does not also need to satisfy the other thresholds[24] to gain the extended breeder's right to cover EDVs. The remaining parts of this chapter are premised on this notion that the EDV threshold alone is sufficient to extend the breeder's right to cover EDVs.

3.3 Scope of the UPOV 1991 conceptualisation of EDVs and certain other varieties

The following points follow from an interpretation of the provisions in UPOV 1991 that deal with EDVs and certain other varieties:

- *The protected variety is not itself an EDV.*[25] This is the threshold requirement; the variety that is alleged to be an EDV cannot itself be derived from an EDV and still obtain protection. In other words, the extended scope of the breeder's right only applies to an EDV that is derived from a non-EDV initial variety.
- *The EDV is derived predominantly from the initial variety.*[26] This means that an EDV must be predominantly derived from one variety, and be a direct descendant of the initial variety.
- *The EDV retains the expression of the essential characteristics.*[27] The essential characteristics that the EDV must express are the heritable (genotype)

18 Ibid, Article 15(1)(iii).
19 Turnbull, H., ed. 1959. *The Correspondence of Isaac Newton, Volume 1.* Cambridge: Cambridge University Press, page 416.
20 UPOV 1991. Article 14(5)(a)(i).
21 Ibid, Article 14(5)(a)(ii).
22 Ibid, Article 14(5)(a)(iii).
23 Ibid, Article 14(5)(a)(i).
24 Ibid, Articles 14(5)(a)(ii) and (iii).
25 Ibid, Article 14(5)(a)(i).
26 Ibid, Article 14(5)(b)(i).
27 Ibid, Article 14(5)(b)(i).

characteristics from the initial variety, even where these characteristics are assessed as expressed characteristics (phenotype).

- *The EDV must result from the genotype or combination of genotypes.*[28] The relevant characteristics are only heritable characteristics (i.e., genotype) that are expressed (i.e., phenotype). They cannot include characteristics that are only a response to the environment (i.e., phenotype).
- *The EDV itself is clearly distinguishable.*[29] The EDV needs to be clearly distinguishable by whatever means (genotypic or environmental) from the initial variety.
- *The only differences that distinguish the EDV from the initial variety result from the act of derivation.*[30] This reaffirms that the differences that result from the act of derivation should only be minor – perhaps 'one or very few.'[31]

The practical effect of this scheme is that the process of establishing an EDV requires the following factors to be met:

- The initial variety from which the putative EDV was derived independently must satisfy the requirements for a breeder's right. This means that the initial variety must be new, distinct, uniform, and stable as compared to other common varieties. Without a protected initial variety, there are no breeder's rights to protect by a finding of EDV.
- The putative EDV itself must satisfy the requirements for a breeder's right. This means that the EDV must be new, distinct, uniform, and stable as compared to other common varieties. Because essential derivation is concerned only with varieties that are clearly distinguishable by whatever means from an initial variety, the putative EDV almost certainly will be protectable with a breeder's right independently from the initial variety.
- The three cumulative criteria for determining EDV must be satisfied. These are: (1) be predominantly derived from the initial variety, or from a variety that was predominantly derived from the initial variety, while retaining the expression of the essential characteristics; (2) be clearly distinguishable; and, (3) conform to the expressed essential characteristics of the initial variety (note the apparent conflict between (1) and (3), which is discussed at length in section 3.4 of this chapter).

In assessing the putative EDV, the initial variety must be compared against the putative EDV, and a determination must be made of how these two varieties differ. This involves a quantitative comparison of differences (e.g., morphological,

28 Ibid, Articles 14(5)(b)(i) and (iii).
29 Ibid, Article 14(5)(b)(ii).
30 Ibid, Article 14(5)(b)(iii).
31 International Union for the Protection of New Varieties of Plants (UPOV). 1992. *Sixth Meeting with International Organizations: Essentially Derived Varieties.* UPOV Pub. No. IOM/6/2, Section 12. Geneva: UPOV.

genetic, biochemical, and so on, and including commercial, economic, and industrial differences), and a qualitative assessment of whether the differences are enough to confound a finding of EDV (or not enough, thus resulting in a finding of essential derivation). UPOV 1991 provides several examples of the means through which an EDV may be obtained.[32] Notably, however, the use of the word 'may' means that a variety obtained through the methods that UPOV 1991 specifically enumerates are not necessarily EDVs, and that EDVs also can be obtained in other ways.

There are several key terms in the UPOV 1991 conceptualisation of EDVs that the Convention itself does not define. Nevertheless, these terms are central to understanding how to determine whether a given variety is essentially derived from an initial variety. The relevant terms are 'predominantly derived;' 'essential characteristics;' 'clearly distinguishable;' and 'conforms to the initial variety.' These are considered respectively below.

3.3.1 'Predominantly derived'

The relevant provisions of UPOV 1991 stipulate that the threshold of essentially derivation is to be determined based on an assessment of whether the putative EDV is predominantly derived from the initial variety or from a variety that is itself predominantly derived from the initial variety.[33] What constitutes predominantly derived is uncertain, although there are indicators for how different actors have interpreted these terms. For instance, the document prepared for the Fourth Meeting with International Organizations in 1989, which contained an explanation of the proposed text on EDVs to be incorporated into the forthcoming revision to the UPOV Convention stated, 'the derived variety must retain almost the totality of the genotype of the mother variety and be distinguishable from that variety by a very limited number of characteristics (typically by one).'[34]

Subsequently, the Basic Proposal that was presented at the Diplomatic Conference for the Revision of the UPOV Convention in 1991 defined an EDV as a variety that:

> is predominantly derived from the initial variety, or from a variety that is itself predominantly derived from the initial variety, particularly through methods which have the effect of conserving the essential characteristics that are the expression of the genotype or of the combination of genotypes of the initial variety, such as the selection of a natural or induced mutant of the somaclonal variant, the selection of a variant, backcrossings or transformation by genetic engineering.[35]

32 UPOV 1991. Article 14(5)(c).
33 Ibid, Article 14(5)(b)(1).
34 International Union for the Protection of New Varieties of Plants (UPOV). 2013. *Explanatory Notes on Essentially Derived Varieties under the 1991 Act of the UPOV Convention (Revision)*. UPOV Pub. No. CAJ-AG/13/8/2. Annex, Section 3. Geneva: UPOV.
35 Ibid, Annex, Section 5.

One year later, the document prepared for the Sixth UPOV Meeting with International Organizations stated, 'a variety should only be essentially derived from another variety when it retained virtually the whole genotype of the other variety' and a 'derived variety could not in practice retain the expression of the essential characteristics of the variety from which it is derived unless it is almost entirely derived from that variety.'[36]

The document prepared for the Sixth Meeting further clarified that:

> Article 14(5)(b) lays down those conditions that must be satisfied in order that a later variety shall be deemed to be essentially derived from another variety ('the initial variety') … The first such condition (established in Article 14(5)(b)(i)) requires that the later variety be derived from the initial variety which in turn requires that genetic materials of the initial variety have been used in the creation of the later variety. The first condition is accordingly concerned with the genetic origin of the later variety. The third such condition (established in Article 14(5)(b)(iii)) requires that the later variety conforms to ('is made similar to') the initial variety in the expression of the inherited essential characteristics of the initial variety apart from the differences which result from the act of derivation. The third condition is accordingly concerned with the degree of similarity of the later variety to the initial variety. Whilst the first condition also makes reference to the degree of similarity, the primary function of the first condition is to establish a requirement relating to the genetic origin of the variety.[37]

Furthermore, this document revealed that the International Association of Plant Breeders (ASSINSEL):

> also went along with the interpretation that the words 'predominantly derived from the initial variety' meant that derivation could only exist from one variety. However, it had discussed a case … in which a variety A was crossed with a variety B and the progeny was selected in such a way that the new variety came very close to the genome of variety B. It was ASSINSEL's view that such a case was to be dealt with rather like the case of a backcross and could indeed be covered by the phrase in question. ASSINSEL felt, however, that such cases should be examined with great prudence and that the question of the threshold value had to play a decisive part.[38]

At the same meeting, another organisation, the Association of Plant Breeders of the European Economic Community, expressed the 'view that the interpretation

36 UPOV, note 31, Section 8.
37 Ibid, Section 13.
38 Ibid, Section 19, extracted in International Union for the Protection of New Varieties of Plants (UPOV). 2011. *Explanatory Notes on Essentially Derived Varieties under the 1991 Act of the UPOV Convention (Revision)*. UPOV Pub. No. CAJ-AG/11/6/3. Annex II. Geneva: UPOV.

of the [term "predominantly derived from the initial variety"] was correct and that indeed only one variety could be the initial variety.'[39] Lastly, the document prepared for the Sixth Meeting with International Organizations in 1992 concluded by stating, 'The decisive fact was whether the new variety essentially contained the genome of one of the parent varieties. The method of breeding was not laid down at any point.'[40]

More recently, UPOV meetings have continued to discuss the meaning of 'predominantly derived.' This ongoing negotiation is evidenced in documents prepared for the Administrative and Legal Committee Advisory Group meeting in 2014. The UPOV Council *Explanatory Notes*, published in 2017, reference this document, stating:

> The requirement of predominant derivation from an initial variety means that a variety can only be essentially derived from one variety. The intention is that a variety should only be essentially derived from another variety when it retains virtually the whole genotype of the other variety. A derived variety could not, in practice, retain the expression of the essential characteristics of the variety from which it is derived unless it is almost entirely derived from that initial variety.[41]

Together, these various records support the interpretation that the term 'predominantly derived' refers to the origin of the putative EDV, such that the putative EDV must be derived from an initial variety. In contrast, a variety that expresses the same essential characteristics and but is bred from a variety other than the initial variety cannot be an EDV. This interpretation also is preferable because it reconciles the apparent conflict between Article 14(5)(b)(i) and Article 14(5)(b)(iii) of UPOV 1991, which is addressed in greater detail in section 3.4 of this chapter.

3.3.2 'Essential characteristics'

The relevant sections of UPOV 1991 provide that as with the term 'predominantly derived,' the threshold of 'essential characteristics' is assessed against the characteristics that the initial variety displays. The precise scope of 'essential characteristics' is not defined in the text of the UPOV Convention, although other

39 Ibid.

40 Ibid.

41 International Union for the Protection of New Varieties of Plants (UPOV). 2014. *Explanatory Notes on Essentially Derived Varieties under the 1991 Act of the UPOV Convention (Revision)*. Pub. No. UPOV/EXN/EDV/2 Draft 5, Section 4. Geneva: UPOV; and International Union for the Protection of New Varieties of Plants (UPOV). 2017. *Explanatory Notes on Essentially Derived Varieties under the 1991 Act of the UPOV Convention (Revision)*. UPOV Pub. No. UPOV/EXN/EDV/2, Section 4. Geneva: UPOV.

UPOV sources provide indications for how this term might be interpreted. For instance, the document prepared for the 1992 Sixth Meeting with International Organizations stated:

> The essential characteristics are those which are indispensable or fundamental to the variety. 'Characteristic' would seem to embrace all features of a variety including, for example, morphological, physiological, agronomic, industrial and biochemical characteristics. It is suggested that the result of a biochemical test conducted on a variety, for instance, a screening test using a genetic probe, is a characteristic of the variety. [The term in Article 14(5)(b)(i)] 'while retaining' requires that the expression of the essential characteristics be derived from the initial variety.[42]

This document further clarified:

> A judgement on the question of the degree of similarity must be reached on the basis of the essential characteristics which result from the genotype. 'Essential' has the meanings 'fundamental' or 'indispensable.' The language finally adopted in Article 14(5)(iii) replaced Article 14(2)(b)(iii) of the Basic Proposal considered by the Diplomatic Conference. Article 14(2)(b)(iii) of the Basic Proposal provided that the essentially derived variety must 'conform to the genotype or combination of genotypes of the initial variety …' This language was initially replaced by the adoption by the Conference of the proposal of Japan … which proposed that Article 12(2)(iii) of the Basic Proposal be reworded to read, '(iii) the characteristics that are the expression of its genotype or its combination of genotypes conform to those of the initial variety apart from the differences which result from the method of derivation.'[43]

The suggestion is that Article 14(2)(b)(iii) of the Basic Proposal and the Japanese proposal that replaced it both called for the degree of similarity between varieties to be assessed on the basis of the characteristics of the initial variety taken as a whole and not on the basis of individual characteristics taken in isolation. The language of the Japanese proposal was subsequently amended by the Drafting Committee, but it is suggested that no change in substance was intended. A further implication is that it should not be possible to conclude that a derived variety does not attain the necessary degree of similarity simply because it does not express one single characteristic, taken in isolation, of the initial variety.

The document prepared for the 1992 Sixth UPOV Meeting with International Organizations elaborated on these proposals by providing an example:

42 UPOV, note 31, Section 9.
43 Ibid, Section 19.

> Theoretically, if variety A is crossed with variety B and variety X is selected from the resulting progeny, if variety X derives less than half of its essential heritable characteristics (i.e., of its genotype) from A and more than half from B, it will be essentially derived from B since apart from the characteristics derived from A, it conforms to the expression of the essential characteristics of B. This is clearly not the intended interpretation. A later variety cannot fulfil the conditions of Article 14(5)(b)(i) unless it is predominantly derived from the initial variety while retaining, without qualification in Article 14(5)(b)(i), the expression of the essential heritable characteristics of the initial variety.[44]

More recently, the document prepared for the Administrative and Legal Committee Advisory Group in 2014 provided examples to clarify the meaning of 'essential characteristics:'

> The following might be considered in relation to the notion of 'essential characteristics:' (i) characteristics that are indispensable or fundamental; (ii) ... heritable traits that are determined by the expression of one or more genes, or other heritable determinants, that contribute to the principal features, performance or value of the variety; (iii) characteristics that are important from the perspective of the producer, seller, supplier, buyer, recipient, or user; (iv) characteristics that are essential for the variety as a whole, including, for example, morphological, physiological, agronomic, industrial and biochemical characteristics, (v) essential characteristics may or may not be characteristics used for the examination of distinctness, uniformity and stability (DUS); (vi) essential characteristics are not restricted to those characteristics that relate only to high performance or value (for instance, disease resistance may be considered as an essential characteristic when the variety has susceptibility to disease); (vii) essential characteristics may be different in different crops/ species.[45]

This document further provided examples of characteristics that may not meet the threshold of 'essential.' 'The following might provide an illustration of non-essential characteristics: Colour of anthers in a wheat variety; Colour of flower in an apple variety.'[46]

The UPOV Council *Explanatory Notes*, which were published in 2017, closely follow the parameters outlined in the document prepared for the Administrative and Legal Committee Advisory Group in 2014. Thus:

44 Ibid, Section 21.
45 International Union for the Protection of New Varieties of Plants (UPOV). 2014. *Explanatory Notes on Essentially Derived Varieties under the 1991 Act of the UPOV Convention (Revision)*. UPOV Pub. No. UPOV/EXN/EDV/2 Draft 5, Section 6. Geneva: UPOV.
46 Ibid, Section 7.

> The following might be considered in relation to the notion of 'essential characteristics:' (i) … heritable traits that are determined by the expression of one or more genes, or other heritable determinants, that contribute to the principal features, performance or value of the variety; (ii) characteristics that are important from the perspective of the producer, seller, supplier, buyer, recipient, or user; (iii) characteristics that are essential for the variety as a whole, including, for example, morphological, physiological, agronomic, industrial and biochemical characteristics; (iv) essential characteristics may or may not be phenotypic characteristics used for the examination of [DUS]; (v) essential characteristics are not restricted to those characteristics that relate only to high performance or value (for instance, disease resistance may be considered as an essential characteristic when the variety has susceptibility to disease); (vi) essential characteristics may be different in different crops/ species.[47]

Taken together, these sources support an interpretation of 'essential characteristics' as any feature of a variety that is indispensable or fundamental to the initial variety. Notably, the essential characteristics to which the UPOV 1991 provisions refer include intrinsic factors including the morphological, physiological, biochemical, genetic, etc. features of a variety, and also extrinsic characteristics, including those which are commercial, economic, and industrial in nature.

3.3.3 'Clearly distinguishable'

As with the terms discussed in subsections 3.3.1 and 3.3.2, UPOV 1991 stipulates that the threshold of 'clearly distinguishable' should be assessed against the initial variety. Although the UPOV Convention does not explicitly define the term 'clearly distinguishable,' other UPOV documents provide guidance. The first of these is the document prepared for the Sixth UPOV Meeting with International Organizations in 1992, which clarified that the words 'clearly distinguishable from the initial variety' 'establish that essential derivation is concerned only with varieties that are clearly distinguishable from an initial variety and which are accordingly protectable independently from the initial variety.'[48] This document elaborated the following detailed explanation:

> Article 14(5)(b) lays down those conditions that must be satisfied in order that a later variety shall be deemed to be essentially derived from another variety ('the initial variety'). The second of those conditions … requires only

47 International Union for the Protection of New Varieties of Plants (UPOV). 2017. *Explanatory Notes on Essentially Derived Varieties under the 1991 Act of the UPOV Convention (Revision)*. UPOV Pub. No. UPOV/EXN/EDV/2, Section 6. Geneva: UPOV. See also UPOV, note 45, Section 4.

48 UPOV, note 31, Section 11.

> that the later variety be clearly distinguishable from the initial variety and requires no further comment.[49]

Likewise, the document prepared for the Administrative and Legal Committee Advisory Group in 2014 and the 2017 UPOV Council *Explanatory Notes* both note that:

> The phrase 'it is clearly distinguishable from the initial variety' establishes that essential derivation is concerned only with varieties that are clearly distinguishable, in accordance with Article 7, from the initial [protected] variety and which are accordingly protectable independently from the initial [protected] variety. Article 14(5)(a)(ii) would apply if the variety is 'not clearly distinguishable in accordance with Article 7 from the protected variety.'[50]

These explanations establish that the best interpretation is that 'clearly distinguishable' in the context of UPOV 1991 requires that the putative EDV be protectable independently of the initial variety.

3.3.4 'Conforms to the initial variety'

The final key term that remains vague in the UPOV 1991 conceptualisation of EDVs is 'conforms to the initial variety.' As with the three phrases analysed in subsections 3.3.1 to 3.3.3, UPOV 1991 requires the threshold of 'conforms to the initial variety' to be assessed against the initial variety. The meaning of this term is not precisely defined in the UPOV Convention, but it is discussed in detail in other official UPOV documents. The first of these, namely the document prepared for the Fourth Meeting with International Organizations in 1989, which contained an explanation of the proposed EDV text, stated, 'the derived variety must retain almost the totality of the genotype of the mother variety and be distinguishable from that variety by a very limited number of characteristics (typically by one).'[51]

Subsequently, the document prepared for the 1992 Sixth UPOV Meeting with International Organizations provided:

> The words [in Article 14(5)(b)(iii)] 'except for the differences which result from the act of derivation' do not set a limit to the amount of difference which may exist where a variety is considered to be essentially derived. A limit is, however, set by the words of [Article 14(5)(b)(i)]. The differences must not be such that the variety fails 'to retain the expression of the essential characteristics that result from the genotype or combination of genotypes of

49 Ibid, Section 13.
50 UPOV, note 47, Section 7; and UPOV, note 45, Section 8.
51 UPOV, note 34, Annex, Section 3.

the initial variety.' A comparison between subparagraphs (i) and (iii) of Article 14(5)(b) is somewhat problematic in that (i) would seem to require the whole of the expression of the essential characteristics that result from the genotype of the initial variety while (iii) requires only that the derived variety conforms to the initial variety except for differences resulting from the act of derivation ... The examples of essential derivation given in Article 14(5)(c) make clear that the differences which result from the act of derivation should be one or very few.[52]

This document further explained:

Article 14(5)(b) lays down those conditions that must be satisfied in order that a later variety shall be deemed to be essentially derived from another variety ('the initial variety') ... The third such condition (established in Article 14(5)(b)(iii)) requires that the later variety conforms to ('is made similar to') the initial variety in the expression of the inherited essential characteristics of the initial variety apart from the differences which result from the act of derivation. The third condition is accordingly concerned with the degree of similarity of the later variety to the initial variety.[53]

Two other documents that help to substantiate the meaning of the term 'conforms to the initial variety' are the guidance documents for the Administrative and Legal Committee Advisory Group (2014) and the UPOV Council *Explanatory Notes* (2017). These documents state, 'A judgment on the question on the degree of conformity must be reached on the basis of the essential characteristics which result from the genotype of the initial variety.'[54] Moreover:

The words 'except for the differences which result from the act of derivation' do not set a limit to the amount of difference which may exist where a variety is considered to be essentially derived. A limit is, however, set by [Articles 14 (5)(b)(i) and (iii)]. The differences must not be such that the variety fails 'to retain the expression of the essential characteristics that result from the genotype or combination of genotypes of the initial variety' ... The examples given in Article 14(5)(c) make clear that the differences which result from the act of derivation should be one or very few. However, if there are only one or few differences that does not necessary mean that a variety is essentially derived. The variety would also be required to fulfil the definition stated in Article 14(5)(b).[55]

52 UPOV, note 31, Section 12.
53 Ibid, Section 13.
54 UPOV, note 47, Section 8; and UPOV, note 45, Section 9.
55 UPOV, note 47, Sections 9–10; and UPOV, note 45, Section 10.

Lastly, the 2017 UPOV Council *Explanatory Notes* reinscribe the language of the document prepared for the Fourth Meeting with International Organizations in 1989, stating 'The derived variety must retain almost the totality of the genotype of the initial variety and be different from that variety by a very limited number of characteristics.'[56] Read together, these various documents suggest that 'conforms to the initial variety' refers to a comparison that must be made between the initial variety and the putative EDV. The result of this comparison should be a finding of a high degree of similarity, with the differences that result from the act of derivation being only 'one or very few.' Put differently, more than one or very few differences between the initial variety and the putative EDV suggest there is no essential derivation.

3.4 Resolving the apparent conflict inherent to the UPOV 1991 conceptualisation of EDVs

One component of the UPOV 1991 definition of EDVs provides that the putative EDV must be predominately derived from an initial variety while also 'retaining the expression of the essential characteristics that result from the genotype or combination of genotypes of the initial variety.'[57] Meanwhile, another component of this definition stipulates that 'except for the differences which result from the act of derivation, [the putative EDV] conforms to the initial variety in the expression of the essential characteristics.'[58] There appears to be conflict between these two provisions, because the former suggests that the 'essential characteristics' are those which are genotypic in nature, while the latter does not contain this limitation.

Some clarification is provided in the document prepared for the Sixth UPOV Meeting with International Organizations in 1992, which stated:

> Article 14(5)(b) lays down those conditions that must be satisfied in order that a later variety shall be deemed to be essentially derived from another variety ('the initial variety') ... The first such condition (established in Article 14(5)(b)(i)) requires that the later variety be derived from the initial variety which in turn requires that genetic materials of the initial variety have been used in the creation of the later variety. The first condition is accordingly concerned with the genetic origin of the later variety. The third such condition (established in Article 14(5)(b)(iii)) requires that the later variety conforms to ('is made similar to') the initial variety in the expression of the inherited essential characteristics of the initial variety apart from the differences which result from the act of derivation. The third condition is accordingly concerned with the degree of similarity of the later variety to the initial

56 UPOV, note 47, Section 11.
57 UPOV 1991. Article 14(5)(b)(1).
58 Ibid, Article 14(5)(b)(iii).

> variety. Whilst the first condition also makes reference to the degree of similarity, the primary function of the first condition is to establish a requirement relating to the genetic origin of the variety.[59]

One way to resolve this apparent conflict is to interpret Article 14(5)(b)(i) as requiring only that the putative EDV be genetically related to the initial variety, or in other words, that there is a genetic lineage between the putative EDV and the initial variety. Meanwhile, for its part, Article 14(5)(b)(iii) may be understood to impose a quantitative and qualitative comparison of phenotypic (being the expression results of the genotype) essential characteristics. Notably, this comparison should also involve the identification of any differences between the two varieties that result from the act of derivation.

To understand how this formulation might be applied in practice, it is useful to consider the example of selecting varieties from within existing variations and induced mutations. Where such selections are made, it is likely that three main issues will arise: (1) how to determine the differences between the initial variety and the putative EDV; (2) how to identify the essential characteristics of the initial variety and the putative EDV; and (3) how to identify the differences that result from the act of derivation. After these three issues are resolved, the inquiry will then shift to an assessment of: (4) whether the initial variety and the putative EDV are clearly distinguishable; and (5) whether the essential characteristics of the initial variety and the putative EDV are sufficiently similar to establish essential derivation, or different enough for there to be no essential derivation.

Notably, the document prepared for the Sixth UPOV Meeting stated that when conducting such evaluations:

> The question of the genetic origin of the later variety ... is primarily a question of fact to be established using all available evidence including the personal testimony of individual witnesses, laboratory and field record books, knowledge concerning the inheritance of particular characteristics, the results of biochemical tests and so on.[60]

Meanwhile:

> The question of degree of similarity of the later variety to the initial variety primarily calls for a value judgement whether the later variety does or does not conform to the initial variety in the expression of its essential, heritable characteristics.[61]

59 UPOV, note 31, Section 13.
60 Ibid.
61 Ibid.

The salient point here is that the question of the genetic origin of the putative EDV is a question of fact that requires the presentation of evidence that would detail the origins and biological or genetic similarities or differences between the initial variety and the putative EDV. Meanwhile, establishing the degree of similarity when assessing the essential characteristics of the initial variety and the putative EDV requires the presentation of evidence that would describe any similarities or differences between the initial variety and the putative EDV. In this latter determination, differences transcend the genetic and biological realm to include also evidence of commercial, economic, and industrial similarities between the two varieties.

3.5 What do the cases say?

Unfortunately, litigation about essential derivation has been infrequent internationally, and the resolutions of the relevant cases have not provided much clarity as to the meaning of EDVs. The basic provisions of UPOV 1991 have been implemented in domestic legislation in several countries, sometimes with variations that are designed to rectify certain drafting compromises and oversights that are apparent in the UPOV 1991 EDV provisions. Although the exact parameters of the EDV concept remain unclear, the cases that have been litigated in countries including the Netherlands, Germany, Italy, Israel, and Australia do provide interesting insights into the kinds of evidence required to establish essential derivation. Furthermore, these cases reveal the significant effect that the determination of which party bears the burden of proof has in establishing or rebutting a finding of essential derivation.

In an early Dutch case, *Van Zanten Plants B.V. v Hofland B.V.*[62] it was clear that the variety in dispute was an EDV. The case concerned a freesia variety denominated 'Ricastor,' which was protected with plant breeders' rights in the Netherlands. Another variety marketed as 'Mercurius' was alleged to be an EDV of Ricastor. The evidence showed that there were no genetic differences between the two varieties (there was 100 percent homology between Ricastor and Mercurius), and that the morphological differences were minor. Thus, the two varieties were almost identical. Ultimately, the court found that Mercurius was an EDV of Ricastor. No evidence was presented to counter the data that showed 100 percent genetic similarity between the two varieties.[63] Furthermore, the argument that Mercurius was cultivated from seedlings was not a credible explanation for its high degree of genetic homology with Ricastor. In short, both plants were 100 percent homologous, and it was a foregone conclusion – indeed, there was a presumption of infringement – that Mercurius was essentially derived from Ricastor.

62 *Van Zanten Plants B.V. v Hofland B.V.* (2008) 310918/KG ZA 08-594, District Court of The Hague (August 6 2008).

63 The assessment of genetic homology was conducted based on an amplified fragment length polymorphism (AFLP) data, using a Jaccard index.

In contrast, three cases that litigated the question of essential derivation for varieties of *Gypsophila*, namely *Astée Flowers B.V. v Danziger 'Dan' Flower Farm,*[64] *Danziger 'Dan' Flower Farm v Astée Flowers B.V.*,[65] and *Danzinger Flower Farm v Hanania Azulai and Astee Flowers B.V.*[66] provided less clarity, thus leaving a legacy of uncertainty about the meaning of EDVs. These cases turned on questions of essential derivation related to three *Gypsophila* cultivars, namely 'Blancanieves,' 'Summer Snow,' and 'Million Stars.' In the Dutch case *Astée Flowers B.V. v Danziger 'Dan' Flower Farm*, the lower court accepted that the evidence provided established that Blancanieves and Summer Snow both were created through the application of chemicals (colchicines) to achieve polyploidisation. The court determined that Blancanieves was not an EDV of Summer Snow because 17 of the 21 observable phenotypic characters were different. Significantly, the court bypassed the technical genetic evidence because it was considered to be biased and unreliable.

On appeal, in *Danziger 'Dan' Flower Farm v Astée Flowers B.V.*, the plaintiff provided evidence that the genetic homology between the two varieties was high, having a Jaccard index of ranging from 0.937 to 0.944. Meanwhile, the defendant's expert presented Jaccard index evidence of genetic similarity between 0.82 and 0.87. As in the initial decision, the Dutch Court of Appeal rejected this evidence, concluding that the amplified fragment length polymorphism (AFLP) technique was 'open to objection,' and that:

> although similarity, measured by the Jaccard index, and affinity are correlated, an individual index value will not provide the degree of certainty about an affinity, which is required in order to conclude (on a preliminary basis) that evidence of derivation has been produced.[67]

The court then considered the phenotypic similarity between the two varieties by examining the morphological data. As with the lower court, the Court of Appeal again considered that the finding by the Community Plant Variety Office of 17 morphological differences between the two varieties during the registration process exceeded the threshold of 'one or a few inheritable characteristics' required for a finding of essential derivation.[68] Based on the numerous morphological differences between the two varieties, the court concluded that 'proof that Blancanieves is an EDV … has therefore not been furnished,' and further attempts to furnish evidence were not permitted.[69]

64 *Astée Flowers B.V. v Danziger 'Dan' Flower Farm* (2005) 198763, Court of The Hague (July 13 2005).
65 *Danziger 'Dan' Flower Farm v Astée Flowers B.V.* (2009) 105.003.932/01, Court of Appeal, The Hague (29 December 2009).
66 *Danzinger Flower Farm v Hanania Azulai and Astee Flowers B.V.* (2009) 1228/03, District Court, Tel-Aviv-Jaffa.
67 *Danziger 'Dan' Flower Farm v Astée Flowers B.V.*, note 65, page 16.
68 Ibid, page 22.
69 Ibid.

In addition to the issues that the appeal in *Danziger 'Dan' Flower Farm v Astée Flowers B.V.* raises about the role of genetic homology data in establishing essential derivation, the case failed to resolve definitively the question of burden of proof. In the appeal, the court cited the relevant regulation of the European Council on European Community Plant Variety Rights,[70] stating that the burden of proof was with the plaintiff (Danziger) to establish essential derivation. This meant that the Danziger needed to prove that Blancanieves was an EDV, which the Court of Appeals justified by stating:

> The Court is of the opinion that according to Dutch procedural law, as the occasion arises, (virtually) the same result can be achieved as with reversal of the burden of proof, by taking the ground, based on evidence furnished by the breeder of the initial variety, that evidence of an EDV has been furnished for the time being and allowing the other party to prove the contrary. The difference with a reversal of the burden of proof is that the risk of evidence continues to lie with the breeder of the initial variety, which is only important in the event that any uncertainty about the derivation continues to exist.[71]

Applying this standard, any evidence that would reveal a genealogical link between the putative EDV and the initial variety will be relevant. Thus, if a plaintiff provides credible evidence of the genealogical link, then the other party will be obliged to refute that evidence, in effect shifting the burden of proof to the defendant.[72] The result is, in practice, the same as formally transferring the onus to the defendant once the plaintiff has established a reasonable allegation.

However, as discussed earlier, in the *Danziger 'Dan' Flower Farm v Astée Flowers B. V.* appellate case the court rejected evidence based on the AFLP technique that showed close genetic similarity between the two varieties in question. Instead, the court based its ruling on evidence of the existence of numerous phenotypic differences between the two varieties, in effect favouring phenotype over genotype. The result was that the plaintiff retained the burden of proof and was unable to rely on the evidence of Jaccard indexes showing genetic similarity of 0.944 and 0.937, which might have been expected to shift the burden to require a credible explanation from the defendant. Interestingly, this is exactly what happened in the Israeli litigation, during which evidence that was nearly identical to that invoked in the Dutch appellate case was presented.

In the Israeli case *Danzinger Flower Farm v Hanania Azulai and Astee Flowers B.V.*, [73] the litigation was pursued under the Israeli Plant Breeders' Rights legislation.[74] Under this law, the burden of proof rests on the defendant

70 *Regulation (EC) 2100/94 of the Council Concerning Community Plant Variety Rights of 27 July 1994*, L 277/1.
71 *Danziger 'Dan' Flower Farm v Astée Flowers B.V.*, note 65, page 12.
72 Ibid.
73 *Danzinger Flower Farm v Hanania Azulai and Astee Flowers B.V.*, note 66.
74 *Plant Breeders Right Law 5733–1973* of Israel (as amended in December 1983 and February 1996). 1999.

to establish that the variety in question was not an EDV if evidence to establish 'genetic conformity' is presented by the plaintiff. The relevant language of the Israeli plant breeders' rights regime is as follows:

> Where an action is brought by the holder of an original protected variety (hereafter: plaintiff) against the holder of a variety, in respect of which it is argued that it is an essentially derived variety (hereafter: defendant), the defendant shall bear the burden of proof that the variety is not essentially derived, if the plaintiff has proven one of the following:

1 genetic conformity between the original variety protected and the variety, in respect of which it is claimed to be essentially derived variety;
2 the variety, claimed to be essentially derived variety maintains, except for minor differences, the expression of the essential characteristics that arise out of the genotype or out of a combination of genotypes of the original protected variety.[75]

Based on these provisions, the Israeli District Court rejected the defendant's argument that only morphological characters might be considered – as had happened in the litigation in the Netherlands – and accepted the genetic AFLP evidence that the plaintiff had presented. This evidence showed that of 214 markers using six primers, the contested varieties differed by only five markers.[76] The court also rejected the assertion by the defendant's expert that AFLP was not an appropriate measure of EDV because the randomly selected primers targeted genetic differences that were not necessarily linked to markers of significant traits for EDV. Notably, this assertion had been accepted by the Dutch courts.[77]

The Israeli District Court reasoned that what the legislated standard required was genetic conformity, and that the AFLP analysis addressed that issue. Once the burden of proof was shifted, the defendant was unable to prove credibly how Blancanieves was created,[78] and was unable to provide any credible morphological evidence of the differences between the varieties. This latter issue was due to the fact that the defendant's expert witness died before the hearing, and the replacement expert did not conduct a thorough morphological examination, but rather only an 'initial examination.'[79]

Surprisingly, the court interpreted the EDV threshold of conforming to the initial variety as not being limited to 'one trait or a small number of morphological traits.'[80] This meant that evidence of multiple morphological differences – in

75 Ibid, Section 62A.
76 *Danzinger Flower Farm v Hanania Azulai and Astee Flowers B.V.*, note 66, page 14.
77 Ibid.
78 Ibid, page 21.
79 Ibid, pages 14 and 19.
80 Ibid, page 18.

addition to the fact that the Israeli government accepted that the varieties were distinct when it registered them separately – did not constitute proof against a finding of EDV. This conclusion directly contradicted the result of the analogous litigation in the Netherlands. Meanwhile, the plaintiff presented its own evidence of comprehensive morphological examinations, which tended to show only minor phenotypic differences between Blancanieves and the initial variety:

> [The plaintiff's expert witness] personally supervised the planting of the plants in a standard greenhouse, in two different areas, where in every plot the two varieties were planted in several repetitions. Approximately half a year after their planting, and after they firstly blossomed, the plants were trimmed and a new wave of florescence was observed. The comparison between the morphological characteristics of the varieties has been conducted by Prof Weiss continuously during the whole length of the growing period – while paying attention to a great number of parameters; and its findings were, that the essential characteristics of the Registered Variety are retained in Blancanieves. The only morphological differences which were found by [the plaintiff's expert witness] were as follows: the Registered Variety had longer stems than those of Blancanieves, flowering date of Blancanieves was approximately two weeks later than the flowering date of the Registered variety, and the flowers of Blancanieves contained more petals than the flowers of the Registered Variety. Based on these findings, [the plaintiff's expert witness] established that the morphological difference which was found, results from the act of derivation of the genotype.[81]

The outcome of the decision is significant because it demonstrates that based on almost identical evidence, courts in the Netherlands and Israel reached different conclusions, by interpreting the EDV thresholds very differently.

This lack of clarity has not been resolved in subsequent litigation, as can be seen in the German case *Probstdoder Saatzucht GmbH & Co. KG v Pflanzzucht Oberlimpurg*.[82] This litigation arose when the owner of one protected plant variety became aware of a similar variety that was also protected under the German plant breeders' rights law. The owner of the first variety conducted tests, the results of which revealed no genetic or other differences, which suggested a very close genetic relationship between the two varieties. After attempting unsuccessfully to negotiate with the owner of the second variety, the owner of the initial variety filed a claim for relief.

To resolve the question of genetic similarity, the court appointed an expert to conduct a marker analysis using microsatellite markers. The results of this evaluation showed a genetic homology of 99 percent between the two varieties. Based

81 Ibid, page 20.
82 *Probstdoder Saatzucht GmbH & Co. KG v Pflanzzucht Oberlimpurg* (101) 7 0 442t04, Court of First Instance of Mannheim, Civil Chamber (10 December 2010).

on this evidence, the court accepted that the later variety was an EDV. The defendant then filed an appeal to challenge the genetic analysis and the failure by the court of first instance to consider phenotypic analysis. However, this appeal was never litigated because the parties settled and the case was dropped.

A logical interpretation of the *Probstdoder Saatzucht GmbH & Co. KG v Pflanzzucht Oberlimpurg* case could be that where no or very few genetic differences exist between an initial variety and an alleged EDV, credible evidence must be provided to explain the high degree of similarity. In the absence of such an explanation, there is an incontestable EDV. This conclusion would also be supported by the findings of the court in the Dutch case *Van Zanten Plants B.V. v Hofland B.V.*

A similar interpretation could also be derived from the decision of a 2015 Italian case, *Almo s.p.a. v Sardo Piemontese Sementi Soc. Coop. Società Agricola.*[83] This case turned on a question of essential derivation concerning the GLADIO rice variety owned by Almo and the SIRIO CL rice variety owned by Sardo. Both of these varieties were protected with plant breeders' rights under the relevant Italian law. Almo asserted that SIRIO CL was derived simply by crossing the GLADIO plant with another plant that was resistant to imidazolinone herbicides, likely followed by a backcross with a GLADIO plant. Thus, Almo argued that SIRIO CL was nothing more than a variety essentially derived from GLADIO – or in other words, SIRIO CL was the GLADIO variety with the additional trait of resistance to imidazolinone herbicides.

The evidence that Almo presented showed that only three out of 38 characters differed between the two varieties, apart from the trait of resistance to imidazolinone herbicides. The evidence presented by Sardo was similar, demonstrating that four characters were different, in addition to imidazolinone herbicide resistance. Meanwhile, the genetic analysis conducted by the court appointed expert found that out of the 25 genetic markers identified, 21 were inherited from GLADIO, while only four were derived from the other parent.[84] The court analysed the findings of the court appointed expert as follows:

> after having indicated the essential characteristics of a rice variety and the specific characteristics of GLADIO that are reproduced in SIRIO CL, ruled out the possibility of the latter variety being derived from the former, owing to the fact that some of the characteristics were not 'unique and specific' to GLADIO but were instead already present, in combination, in other, earlier rice varieties, while other characteristics (productive capacity, rice quality obtained or yield after industrial processing, tillering capacity and plant vigour) could not be regarded as essential characteristics for the purposes of this case, since those were strongly influenced by the environment, and in the

83 *Almo s.p.a. v Sardo Piemontese Sementi Soc. Coop. Società Agricola* (2015) 3519/2015, Turin Trial Court (14 May 2015).

84 Ibid, page 12.

> case of some, were not specific to GLADIO but were instead present in earlier varieties, together with other characteristics relating to the grain type and the duration of the vegetative cycle. [The expert] then went on to note that SIRIO CL derived the characteristic of 'resistance to herbicides' not from GLADIO but rather from the other parent.[85]

In order to issue a ruling on the question of essential derivation under the relevant European Community regulation,[86] the Italian court first had to determine the meaning of 'essential characteristics' for rice. Thus, the court considered that the essential characteristics of a rice variety are: grain type, duration of the vegetative cycle, productive capacity, quality of the rice obtained or yield after industrial processing, plant vigour, tillering capacity, and resistance to herbicides.[87] Of these characteristics, plant vigour and tillering capacity were not determined to be relevant for the assessment of essential derivation, while grain type, duration of the vegetative cycle, productive capacity, and quality of the rice obtained or yield after industrial processing were relevant.

The court found that GLADIO and SIRIO CL shared all of these essential characteristics.[88] On this basis, the court concluded that SIRIO CL was essentially derived from GLADIO.[89] The evidence that the court considered to be most significant apparently was that SIRIO reproduced the same four genotype characteristics of grain type, the same vegetative cycle duration, the same productive capacity, and the same rice quality or yield as the GLADIO variety. Furthermore, it appears significant that of the 25 genetic markers considered, 21 were inherited by SIRIO CL from GLADIO.[90] Put simply, the court found that taking a commercially successful variety, introducing a single gene to confer herbicide resistance, and then backcrossing the progeny to the parent, satisfied the threshold for essential derivation.

The Australian approach to determining whether a variety is an EDV under the terms of that country's domestic plant breeders' rights law[91] provides an interesting contrast to the *Almo s.p.a. v Sardo Piemontese Sementi Soc. Coop. Società Agricola* decision. The Australian *Plant Breeder's Rights Act 1994* included two important elaborations on the UPOV 1991 conceptualisation of EDVs. First, the law defined 'essential characteristics' as 'heritable traits ... that contribute to the principal features, performance and value of the variety.'[92] Second, the Australian regime shifted the burden of proof, requiring the 'important (as distinct from

85 Ibid, page 9.

86 *Regulation (EC) 2100/94 of the Council Concerning Community Plant Variety Rights of 27 July 1994*, L 277/1. 1994.

87 *Almo s.p.a. v Sardo Piemontese Sementi Soc. Coop. Società Agricola*, note 83, page 11.

88 Ibid.

89 Ibid, page 12.

90 Ibid.

91 *Plant Breeder's Rights Act 1994* of Australia. 1994.

92 Ibid, Section 3.

cosmetic) features' to be demonstrated if the second variety is not to be declared an EDV.[93]

The effect of these elaborations was to introduce commercial imperatives into the EDV assessment. For example, the 2005 decision *Sir Walter v B12* considered a dispute between a protected lawn grass variety denominated 'Sir Walter' and a second variety called 'B12,' which was bred using Sir Walter as the initial variety.[94] The characteristics that differed between the two varieties were colour and internode (the stalk between leaves) length differences, which assumedly would not be considered important features as required by the Australian *Plant Breeder's Rights Act 1994*.[95]

However, the evidence presented in the case demonstrated that the shortened internode length was in fact important, because it increased the 'thatch' of the grass. This increased the wear tolerance of the B12 variety, a feature that was desirable for commercial use, such as on golf courses. The results of two separate growing trials demonstrated that there was a statistically significant node length difference to a high degree of confidence. Based on this evidence, the breeders' rights registration authority rejected the assertion of essential derivation. Other Australian cases that have adopted similar rulings include the 2007 decision *Sir Walter v Kings Pride*.[96]

These cases from several international jurisdictions reveal the complex interplay between genotypic and phenotypic evidence, and some of the nuances in how courts might deal with these kinds of evidence. However, perhaps the most important conclusion from the litigation discussed in this chapter is that the cases reveal that by carefully tracing the sources of germplasm and by maintaining detailed breeding records, parties substantially can resolve questions about essential derivation. The cases also show that where an alleged EDV and an initial variety are very closely related, and where the alleged EDV does little to improve on the initial variety, a finding of essential derivation is likely.

3.6 Conclusion

The extension of plant breeders' rights to cover EDVs was intended to limit the possibility that later plant breeders could unfairly free ride on the time and investments of another, earlier breeder. Thus, UPOV 1991 prohibits the grant of a full plant breeder's right for varieties that constitute only very minor improvements over initial varieties by recognising the concept of essential derivation. This legal development probably was inspired by the model of dependent patents. Accordingly, plant breeders could obtain adequate remuneration for their

93 Ibid, Section 4.

94 International Union for the Protection of New Varieties of Plants (UPOV). 2013. *Seminar on Essentially Derived Varieties*. UPOV Pub. No. UPOV/SEM/GE/13. Geneva: UPOV, pages 54–55.

95 *Plant Breeder's Rights Act 1994* of Australia, note 91, Section 4(c).

96 UPOV, note 94, pages 56–57.

breeding efforts when later breeders exploited their work by realising only minor breeding advances.

The major scientific development that made essential derivation a much more attainable possibility for many breeders was that genetic modification techniques became ubiquitous beginning in the 1980s and early 1990s. This allowed for the targeted modification of a commercially successful plant variety by introducing a single gene – the herbicide resistance gene considered in *Almo s.p.a. v Sardo Piemontese Sementi Soc. Coop. Società Agricola* exemplifies this concern. The UPOV 1991 EDV provisions attempt to respond to this scenario and to ensure balance, by capturing fair returns for the original breeder while still allowing and promoting new breeding initiatives. Importantly, the finding of an EDV does not nullify the breeder's right granted either for the initial variety or for the EDV. This means that where essential derivation is established, the owner of the EDV must negotiate with the owner of the initial variety to obtain authorisation to exploit the EDV.

That there remains uncertainty about EDVs is reflected in the ongoing work of UPOV to find a clear explanation of this concept. The most recent *Explanatory Notes on Essentially Derived Varieties under the 1991 Act of the UPOV Convention* provide for a workable scheme.[97] However, as the litigation in the Netherlands and Israel in *Danziger 'Dan' Flower Farm v Astée Flowers* and *Danzinger Flower Farm v Hanania Azulai and Astee Flowers B.V.* respectively illustrates, national laws implementing the UPOV 1991 standards vary substantially. These domestic regimes sometimes impose additional requirements or procedural hurdles that may have a decisive effect on resolving the question of essential derivation.

Jurisdictional differences may include the kinds of evidence considered important to establish essential derivation. For instance, in *Danziger 'Dan' Flower Farm v Astée Flowers B.V.* the Dutch court rejected the genetic evidence obtained from applying the AFLP technique. Likewise, the burden of proof to establish or negate a finding of essential derivation may vary. For instance, the Dutch court in *Danziger 'Dan' Flower Farm v Astée Flowers B.V.* found that the threshold had not been met to shift the burden of proof. Meanwhile, the Israeli court in *Danzinger Flower Farm v Hanania Azulai and Astee Flowers B.V.* analysed essentially the same evidence and made an opposite determination, thus shifting the burden of proof to the defendant.

As the decisions in *Van Zanten Plants B.V. v Hofland B.V.* and *Probstdoder Saatzucht GmbH & Co. KG v Pflanzzucht Oberlimpurg* illustrate, a credible explanation for the high degree of genetic similarities between varieties is necessary to counter a finding of essential derivation. Likewise, the Australian cases *Sir Walter v B12* and *Sir Walter v Kings Pride* demonstrate that even where there are small differences between two varieties, where these have an important commercial effect that (arguably) constitutes more than simply free riding on earlier breeding, then subsequent breeders can be accommodated. This contrasts with cases such as

97 UPOV, note 47.

the Italian decision in *Almo s.p.a. v Sardo Piemontese Sementi Soc. Coop. Società Agricola*, where the mere incorporation of a gene for herbicide resistance into an already commercially valuable variety led the court to conclude that there was essential derivation.

While these findings may be interesting to some, the issue remains of whether this all actually matters. Perhaps the introduction of the EDV standard into legal frameworks based on UPOV 1991 has effectively achieved its purpose of preventing unfair free riding. This interpretation is based on the observation that, by establishing a process, albeit flawed, to determine essential derivation, lawmakers have signalled to would-be breeders of new varieties to document their source materials carefully, and to maintain scrupulous records of their breeding activity. The lack of recent cases in any international jurisdiction suggests that breeders may have heeded the decisions analysed in this chapter. Thus, in effect, the threat that the conceptualisation of EDVs was intended to address may have been resolved, even if underlying technical legal questions remain unsettled.

Chapter 4

Implementation of the plant variety protection laws of Indonesia, Malaysia, and the Philippines

Trends and future prospects

Rajeswari Kanniah

4.1 Introduction

The agricultural sectors of Indonesia, Malaysia, and the Philippines share many commonalities. A diverse array of actors, including subsistence farmers, industrial producers, national and international agri-business firms, government research institutions, and universities comprise the agricultural sectors of these countries. Their staple crops, geographies, and climates are similar, as are the environmental, social, and economic issues that affect farming in these territories. Furthermore, Indonesia, Malaysia, and the Philippines have in some ways taken analogous approaches to establishing national intellectual property laws for plant varieties. All three countries have enacted and implemented *sui generis* plant variety protection (PVP) legislation that responds to the needs of both industrial and subsistence-based farming systems.

The PVP laws of Indonesia, Malaysia, and the Philippines were influenced partially by the plant breeders' rights model that has been popularised by the *International Convention for the Protection of New Varieties of Plants* (UPOV Convention). However, as of May 2019, none of these countries was a member of the UPOV Convention, and therefore all three governments remained free to experiment with systems of intellectual property for plant varieties that would accommodate the interests of diverse stakeholders. Despite this *sui generis* approach to lawmaking, Indonesia, Malaysia, and the Philippines all have been influenced increasingly by the plant breeders' rights paradigm in recent years. For instance, all three countries are members of the East Asia Plant Variety Protection Forum (EAPVPF), a group that advocates for regional harmonisation to render domestic PVP laws consistent with the 1991 Act of the UPOV Convention (UPOV 1991).[1] Thus, there is increasing pressure on lawmakers in Indonesia, Malaysia, and the Philippines to abandon their respective local approaches to the governance of plant varieties in favour of a standardised form of plant breeders' rights.

This chapter explores the experiences that actors in Indonesia, Malaysia, and the Philippines have had with the development and implementation of

1 East Asian Plant Variety Protection Forum (EAPVPF). 2019. 'What We Aim For.' EAPVPF. Accessed May 13 2019. http://eapvp.org

sui generis systems of intellectual property for plant varieties. The chapter also considers recent trends that have affected the way that plant varieties are governed as intellectual property in these three countries, while discussing prospects for future impacts on Indonesian, Malaysian, and Filipino farming systems.

Following this introductory section, the chapter is divided into six sections. Section 4.2 provides an overview of the nature of the agricultural sector in Indonesia, Malaysia, and the Philippines, thereby contextualising the structure of the countries' national seed systems and the enactment of their respective PVP laws. Section 4.3 highlights the innovative elements of these countries' PVP laws that render each regime as distinct from, and in some instances non-compliant with, the plant breeders' rights model that the UPOV Convention embodies. Section 4.4 outlines the relationship between UPOV and the *sui generis* laws of Indonesia, Malaysia, and the Philippines. Section 4.5 describes the ongoing engagement between these countries and the UPOV Council, both directly, and indirectly through the EAPVPF. Section 4.5 also speculates on the likelihood that Indonesia, Malaysia, and the Philippines might revise their existing national PVP laws based on interactions with the UPOV Council, the EAPVPF, and other actors. Section 4.6 analyses how the PVP laws of these countries have been utilised by different actors in the Indonesian, Malaysian, and Filipino seed sectors. Section 4.7 provides concluding observations.

Overall, the chapter demonstrates that in Indonesia, Malaysia, and the Philippines, it is likely that both farmers' seed systems and the systems operated by public and private seed entities will continue to coexist. However, it is uncertain how possible future reforms to these countries' plant breeders' rights frameworks could affect farmers' seed systems. Areas of concern centre especially on whether the Indonesian, Malaysian, and Filipino governments would elect to follow the model of UPOV 1991 to protect plant varieties as intellectual property.

4.2 Background of agriculture and seed systems in Indonesia, Malaysia, and the Philippines

Farming trends in Indonesia, Malaysia, and the Philippines have unfolded in parallel in recent years. For instance, although the contribution of agriculture to the national gross domestic product of each country has declined steadily over the past several decades, farming remains vital to Indonesian, Malaysian, and Filipino societies as a means to provide employment and food security for persons living in rural areas. In 2017, agriculture accounted for 8.8 percent of Malaysian gross domestic product,[2] while providing 11 percent of employment

2 The World Bank. 2019. 'World Development Indicators: Malaysia.' The World Bank DataBank. Accessed May 13 2019. https://databank.worldbank.org/data/reports.aspx?source=2&country=MYS

in that country.[3] In Indonesia, the share of agriculture to gross domestic product was 13.2 percent[4] while 31 percent of the population was employed in agriculture.[5] Lastly, agricultural activities comprised 9.7 percent of Filipino gross domestic product[6] and provided employment for 25 percent of the population.[7]

While in all three countries commercial cash crop cultivation is carried out on large-scale plantations, a higher percentage of agricultural land is devoted to food crop cultivation on small-sized holdings. These smallholdings are tended by families and individual farmers, who mostly live below the national poverty line and rely predominantly on customary practices of seed saving, exchange, and sale. In Indonesia, Malaysia, and the Philippines alike, smallholder farmers remain the dominant actors in the respective national agricultural sectors. In Malaysia, small farms, the majority of which contain fewer than 2 hectares, account for 75 percent of the total agricultural acreage.[8] Similarly, in Indonesia, 85 percent of agricultural land is divided into farms of fewer than 2 hectares, which are managed by smallholders.[9] Lastly, in the Philippines, about 80 percent of the rural population lives on small-scale farms.[10]

Another common aspect that characterises the agricultural sectors of Indonesia, Malaysia, and the Philippines is the fact that none of these countries is self-sufficient in food production. Instead, all three are dependent on food imports, including for rice, which is the staple crop of Indonesian, Malaysian, and Filipino societies. Therefore, in theory, these countries' national PVP laws have been designed to boost agricultural productivity. For instance, one of the essential aims of the Indonesian, Malaysian, and Filipino PVP regimes is to bolster domestic seed

3 International Labour Organization. 2019. 'Employment in Agriculture (% of total employment) (modeled ILO estimate).' The World Bank. Accessed May 13 2019. https://data.worldbank.org/indicator/sl.agr.empl.zs
4 The World Bank. 2019. 'World Development Indicators: Indonesia.' The World Bank DataBank. Accessed May 13 2019. https://databank.worldbank.org/data/reports.aspx?source=2&country=IDN
5 International Labour Organization, note 3.
6 The World Bank. 2019. 'World Development Indicators: Philippines.' The World Bank DataBank. Accessed May 13 2019. https://databank.worldbank.org/data/reports.aspx?source=2&country=PHL
7 International Labour Organization, note 3.
8 Zaeim, Muhammad. 2016. 'Overview of the Agriculture Sector in Malaysia.' Ministry of Agriculture and Agro-Based Industry of Malaysia. Accessed May 13 2019. www.scribd.com/presentation/73250479/Overview-of-Agriculture-Sector-in-Malaysia-1230823436347415-1
9 Sudaryanto, T. 2015. 'Strategies for Facilitating Structural Transformation of Smallholder Farms in Indonesia.' Food and Fertilizer Technology Center for the Asian and Pacific Region. Accessed May 13 2019. http://ap.fftc.agnet.org/ap_db.php?id=564
10 Aquino, A., A. B. Ani, and M. Festejo. 2013. 'An Overview of Policies and Public Sector Investments in Philippine Agriculture.' Food and Fertilizer Technology Center for the Asian and Pacific Region. Accessed May 13 2019. http://ap.fftc.agnet.org/ap_db.php?id=65

industries so that they are able to develop and/or market high-yielding plant varieties to increase crop productivity. However, although systems for PVP have been in place in Indonesia, Malaysia, and the Philippines for several years, the extent to which these laws have contributed concretely to the development of the national seed industries remains unclear.

As of May 2019, in all three countries the public sector was still the primary supplier of seeds for improved plant varieties. This was especially the case for staple food crops. For instance, in 2014 the Indonesian government provided the majority of seeds that farmers grew that year, in the proportions of 75 percent for open-pollinated rice, 90 percent for hybrid rice, 75 percent for open-pollinated corn, 50 percent for hybrid corn, and 75 percent for soybeans.[11] Likewise, the Malaysian government historically has subsidised rice cultivation to enable farmers to meet food security needs, generate income, and thereby reduce poverty. Public support for farming in Malaysia includes strategies such as a guaranteed minimum price for rice, in addition to input subsidies such as the seeds of improved plant varieties, fertilisers, pesticides, and other new technologies.[12] In the Philippines, rice farmers also receive government assistance and subsidies, which take the forms of credit, market infrastructure, postharvest equipment and facilities, seeds, fertilisers, and farm machinery.[13] However, it is important to recognise that notwithstanding the importance of public sector institutions as the primary providers of seeds to farmers in these three countries, numerous other phenomena – including the sale of seeds by private companies and customary practices of seed saving, use, and farmer-to-farmer seed exchange and sale – also operate to fulfil local seed requirements.

4.3 Innovative aspects of the plant variety protection laws of Indonesia, Malaysia, and the Philippines

As with many other countries in Asia,[14] participation in the World Trade Organization and adherence to its 1995 *Agreement on Trade-Related Aspects of Intellectual Property* (TRIPS) formed the initial basis for the establishment of laws that grant intellectual property for plant varieties in Indonesia, Malaysia, and the Philippines. Although these countries incorporated certain aspects of the UPOV plant

11 Rafani, I. 2015. 'Seed Development Policy in Indonesia.' Food and Fertilizer Technology Center for the Asian and Pacific Region. Accessed May 13 2019. http://ap.fftc.agnet.org/ap_db.php?id=382

12 Harun, R. 2015. 'Policies and Economic Development of Rice Production in Malaysia.' Food and Fertilizer Technology Center for the Asian and Pacific Region. Accessed May 13 2019. http://ap.fftc.agnet.org/ap_db.php?id=393; Harun, R. and E. E. Engku Ariff. 2017. 'The Role of Institutional Support in Malaysia's Paddy and Rice Industry.' Food and Fertilizer Technology Center for the Asian and Pacific Region. Accessed May 13 2019. http://ap.fftc.agnet.org/ap_db.php?id=737

13 Aquino, et al., note 10.

14 See, for example, other chapters of this volume.

breeders' rights model into their domestic PVP laws, they also exploited the formal policy space available in TRIPS to create *sui generis* regimes. Thus, Indonesia, Malaysia, and the Philippines developed intellectual property laws for plant varieties that responded to the needs of their respective local agricultural sectors, in some ways deviating from the UPOV model.

The national PVP laws that Indonesia, Malaysia, and the Philippines adopted were drafted amidst significant debate and controversy. Diverse domestic actors shaped these policies, including private seed entities, farmers' groups, and other civil society organisations. External legal constraints such as membership in trade agreements or other treaties beyond TRIPS also affected the form that the national PVP legislation assumed. Lastly, a host of 'soft' influences also played a role in the development of the Indonesian, Malaysian, and Filipino laws. These included the technical assistance that the UPOV Secretariat or UPOV member countries provided for national policy development, the desire to avoid trade sanctions or to be placed on the 'watch list' of the Special 301 Report on Intellectual Property Rights that the United States Trade Representative compiles, and aspirations to foster the development of local biotechnology industries and to modernise the national agriculture sector.[15]

Many experts have recognised that UPOV is best suited for industrialised countries whose agricultural sectors are characterised principally by large-scale farms, and industrial and commercial seed systems, and where farming and plant breeding operate as distinct and specialised professions.[16] The nature of agriculture in countries such as Indonesia, Malaysia, and the Philippines is fundamentally distinct from the industrialised agricultural model, characterised instead by a mixture of large-scale cash crop plantations and smallholder farms growing produce for subsistence and to some extent for local markets. In these three countries, farmers regularly perform a variety of functions at the community level, including plant breeding, conservation, and cultivation. Meanwhile, these countries' commercial seed systems, which are characterised by the participation of public and private seed entities, are in the early stages of development. Furthermore, it is notable that unlike the situation in many wealthy countries, in

15 Kanniah, R. and C. Antons. 2017. 'The Regulation of Innovation in Agriculture and Sustainable Development in India and Southeast Asia.' In *Routledge Handbook of Asian Law*, edited by C. Antons. Abingdon: Routledge, pages 287–309; Kanniah, R. and C. Antons. 2012. 'Plant Variety Protection and Traditional Agricultural Knowledge in Southeast Asia.' *Australian Journal of Asian Law* 13 (1): 1–23; Kanniah, R. 2011. *Breeders vs Farmers: The Contest for Rights over Plant Varieties in Selected Asian Countries.* Saarbrucken: VDM Verlag Dr Müller; and Kanniah, R. 2005. 'Plant Variety Protection in Indonesia, Malaysia, the Philippines and Thailand.' *Journal of World Intellectual Property* 8: 283–310.

16 Correa, C. M., with contributions from S. Shashikant and F. Meienberg. 2015. *Plant Variety Protection in Developing Countries. A Tool for Designing a Sui Generis Plant Variety Protection System: An Alternative to UPOV 1991.* Bonn: Association for Plant Breeding for the Benefit of Society. Accessed May 28 2019. www.apbrebes.org/files/seeds/ToolEnglishcompleteDez15.pdf

Indonesia, Malaysia, and the Philippines, national poverty eradication programmes require the public sector to support small-scale farmers by providing credit, improved seeds, fertilisers, and subsidised technology.

Given these considerations, the PVP systems that each of these countries has established contain elements that in some ways deviate from UPOV, thus responding to the needs of a variety of local actors. Furthermore, in addition to domestic concerns, Indonesia, Malaysia, and the Philippines have also committed to international obligations beyond TRIPS that relate to the governance of plant genetic resources. These include the 1992 *Convention on Biological Diversity* (CBD)[17] and the 2001 *International Treaty on Plant Genetic Resources for Food and Agriculture* (the Plant Treaty). As with TRIPS, these multilateral agreements contain provisions that affected the form that the national PVP laws assumed in Indonesia, Malaysia, and the Philippines.

These three countries all joined the CBD in 1994, several years before the enactment of their respective national PVP laws. Meanwhile, Indonesia and the Philippines both acceded to the Plant Treaty in 2006, after their national intellectual property systems for plant varieties were already established. Nevertheless, the influence of concepts that were cemented in both treaties on the PVP legislation in all three countries is evident. From the CBD, the Indonesian, Malaysian, and Filipino PVP laws adopted provisions related to obtaining prior informed consent and benefit sharing. Specifically, the CBD provides that access to genetic resources, including plants that are used in agriculture, is contingent on obtaining prior informed consent from the party that provides these resources.[18] In addition, benefits arising from the commercial or other utilisation of genetic resources, including agricultural plants, are required to be shared in a fair and equitable manner between the resource users and the providers.[19] The PVP laws of Indonesia, Malaysia, and the Philippines all contain, to a greater or lesser extent, similar language.

Meanwhile, these countries also recognised the concept of farmers' rights, as recognised by the Plant Treaty, in their respective national PVP laws. The Plant Treaty provides that farmers have certain rights related to the utilisation of agricultural plants, including the right to save, use, exchange, and sell farm-saved seeds or other propagating material, subject to relevant national laws.[20] According to the Plant Treaty, national legislation to guarantee farmers' rights could also provide protection for farmers' traditional knowledge, ensure equitable benefit sharing, and recognise farmers' participation in national-level decision making on matters related to the conservation and sustainable use of plant genetic resources

17 This includes two other supplementary agreements to the *Convention on Biological Diversity* (CBD), namely the 2000 *Cartagena Protocol on Biosafety*, and the 2010 *Nagoya Protocol on Access to Genetic Resources and the Fair and Equitable Sharing of Benefits Arising from their Utilization* (Nagoya Protocol).

18 CBD. Article 15.5.

19 Ibid, Article 15.7.

20 *International Treaty on Plant Genetic Resources for Food and Agriculture*. 2001. Article 9.

and associated traditional knowledge for food and agriculture. These issues are further explored through an examination of the Indonesian, Malaysian, and Filipino legislation in subsections 4.3.1 to 4.3.3.

4.3.1 Indonesia

The *Plant Variety Protection Act No. 29 of 2000* of Indonesia (Indonesian PVP Act) was enacted in December 2000. Two years later, the national Plant Variety Protection Office was established, though it only began to operate in May 2003. The Indonesian PVP Act was implemented primarily through *Government Regulation No. 13 of 2004 regarding the Naming, Registration, and Use of Original Variety for the Making of Essentially Derived Variety*. Subsequent regulatory instruments also were published to elaborate procedures for administrative and technical matters relating to the implementation of the national PVP system. Lastly, Indonesia drafted and enacted a separate law to deal specifically with the registration of horticultural plants. The relevant legislation is *Law No. 13 of 2010 Governing Horticulture in Indonesia*, which was implemented through the Minister of Agriculture *Regulation No. 38 of 2011 Implementing Rule of Law on Agriculture*. This rule established a framework for the registration of horticultural plant varieties.

One of the ways in which the Indonesian PVP Act deviates from the UPOV model and provides protections for actors in the national agricultural sector other than plant breeders relates to the ownership, registration, and use of local plant varieties. Specifically, the Indonesian law recognises that local varieties owned by communities can be registered and thus obtain legal protection. Although this is an innovative provision, the legal protection of local varieties is limited by two factors. The first is that the law stipulates that local varieties owned by communities will be controlled by the State, as represented by the national government.[21] The second is that the Indonesian PVP Act does not define the term 'community' or specify the criteria that local plant varieties should meet in order to merit protection.

Meanwhile, for new plant varieties, the Indonesian PVP Act mirrors the criteria originally established in the UPOV Convention: novelty, distinctness, uniformity, and stability. However, the Indonesian framework imposes an additional requirement. Specifically, applications for the registration of transgenic varieties must include 'details of the variety's molecular description and genetic stability of the proposed traits, the reproductive system of the original parent, existence of its wild relatives, compound content that can affect the environment and human health and the destruction methods in the event of any deviations; together with a declaration on the safety for human health and the environment.'[22]

21 *Plant Variety Protection Act No. 29 of 2000* of Indonesia (Indonesian PVP Act). Sections 7.1, 7.2, and 7.3.

22 Ibid, Section 11.4.

Another area in which the Indonesian PVP Act transcends the standard plant breeders' rights model developed by UPOV relates to the requirement of benefit sharing between plant breeders and the relevant local government authority. Specifically, Indonesian *Government Regulation No. 13 of 2004 regarding the Naming, Registration, and Use of Original Variety for the Making of Essentially Derived Variety* stipulates that where a local variety has been used to develop an essentially derived variety, the breeder must enter into a benefit sharing agreement with the authority responsible for the area in which the local variety is found. This entity could be the governor of a certain province or district, the mayor of a city, or the Plant Variety Protection Office within the Ministry of Agriculture.[23]

Government Regulation No. 13 of 2004 provides that the benefit sharing agreement 'may' include compensation for the relevant local community, but this is not a mandatory requirement.[24] If compensation is provided, the relevant local authority is required to use it for a range of purposes such as raising the prosperity of the community, conserving the local variety itself, and fostering conservation efforts related to all genetic resources in the area from which the variety originates.[25] While this is an innovative provision that could, potentially, provide benefits for actors other than plant breeders, the benefit sharing language of the Indonesian PVP framework is relatively weak, in that it applies only to essentially derived varieties and requires only that compensation optionally be provided to the resource-supplying community.

The Indonesian PVP Act contains other protections for local communities and farmers, but they are similarly limited. For instance, the law recognises a farmers' privilege provision[26] that allows the use of part of the produce harvested from protected breeders' varieties for non-commercial purposes. However, an explanatory note to the relevant section clarifies that the farmers' privilege is only intended to apply to individual small farmers who use material from protected varieties for personal consumption.[27] This interpretation of the farmers' privilege is consistent with the optional exception to plant breeders' rights provided in Article 15.2 of UPOV 1991, indicating that the Indonesian PVP Act would likely be deemed compliant with UPOV if the country were to adhere to the Convention.

The Indonesian PVP Act also balances exclusive proprietary rights with other important national interests, as evidenced in its broad prohibition on the grant of intellectual property for plants 'whose use contradicts the prevailing laws, public order, decency, religious norms, health and environmental sustainability.'[28] The

23 *Government Regulation No. 13 of 2004 regarding the Naming, Registration, and Use of Original Variety for the Making of Essentially Derived Variety*. Sections 5, 7, and 9.

24 Ibid, Sections 9.4 and 9.10.

25 Ibid, Section 10.

26 Indonesian PVP Act. Section 10.1.

27 The note clearly states that this provision is meant to protect the market for the protected variety and the interests of the PVP owner. Indonesian PVP Act. Explanatory Note to Section 10.1(a).

28 Ibid, Section 3.

explanatory note to this provision provides examples of plant varieties that would likely be prohibited, including those which are psychotropic, or which use genes from animal sources that countervene the norms of particular religions. This provision is broader than the prohibition on the grant of plant breeders' rights that the UPOV Convention contains. Given that the UPOV Council has never evaluated the Indonesian PVP Act for compliance with the Convention, it is unclear whether the law would be deemed consistent with the UPOV conceptualisation of public interest as a rationale for restricting the breeder's right.

Lastly, it is notable that the Indonesian PVP Act establishes a system of compulsory licences to render protected plant varieties broadly available. This may occur where, after a period of 36 months from the issuance of PVP rights, the owner has failed to exercise his/her rights, or where the rights have been exercised in a manner that is not beneficial to the public interest.[29] The issuance of compulsory licenses for protected plant varieties in Indonesia requires the payment of a royalty to the PVP owner, to be determined based on comparable licensing agreements. These provisions would likely be consistent with UPOV, although it is arguable that failure to exploit a protected variety would not meet the threshold of 'public interest' under UPOV 1991.

4.3.2 Malaysia

The *Protection of New Plant Varieties Act 2004 (Act 634)* of Malaysia (Malaysian PVP Act) was passed in 2004 but only entered into force three years later, in January 2007. The Regulations that implemented the Act are the *Protection of New Plant Varieties Regulations 2008*, the *Protection of New Plant Varieties (Size of Holdings) Regulations 2008*, and the *Administrative Guidelines on Application and Registration of New Varieties of Plants 2008*. The Act appointed the Department of Agriculture as the entity responsible for administering the PVP system in Malaysia, and the law also established a new Plant Variety Protection Office for this purpose.

One of the most noteworthy features of the Malaysian PVP Act – and one of the areas in which the law most substantially departs from the UPOV model – is its creation of forms of intellectual property for breeders' plant varieties on the one hand, and farmers' and community varieties on the other hand. These two categories of plant varieties must meet separate requirements for protection. While breeders' plant varieties are evaluated based on the same novelty, distinctness, uniformity, and stability criteria as delimited in the UPOV Convention, farmers' and community plant varieties are assessed based on whether they are new, distinct, and identifiable.[30]

29 Ibid, Sections 44.1 and 44.2. The explanatory note to Section 44.2 of the Act states that failure of a PVP owner to exercise his or her rights does not apply to situations that are not technical in nature, or to *force majeur* (natural catastrophe, fire, uncontainable diseases, and policies of the government).

30 *Protection of New Plant Varieties Act 2004 (Act 634)* of Malaysia (Malaysian PVP Act). Section 14.2.

Identifiability is a concept that is *sui generis* and unique to the Malaysian PVP Act. Rather than require that farmers' and community varieties comply with the standards of uniformity and stability – criteria which may be difficult for actors who are not professional breeders to meet[31] – the condition of identifiability provides a more flexible standard for claiming the specific characteristics that make a particular variety special. Identifiability is achieved when a person skilled in the art is able to identify a claimed plant variety by the specific characteristics that it exhibits. A unique combination of a few distinguishing traits would be sufficient to qualify that variety for protection. The identifiability criterion is open to considerable interpretation, underscoring the notion that uniformity may not always be a desirable feature for all types of plant varieties.

According to the UPOV Council, the section of the Malaysian PVP Act that deals with farmers' and community plant varieties essentially creates an intellectual property right that is distinct from plant breeders' rights. The Council has reasoned that this is the case because the protection of farmers' and community varieties is restricted to a particular group of applicants, it relates to different subject matter and conditions for protection, and the period of protection granted is distinct. Because of these deviations from the form of plant breeders' rights imagined in the UPOV Convention, the Council has advised Malaysian lawmakers that the protection of farmers' and community plant varieties should be given a different name and should be codified in a separate system of protection.[32] However, the opinion of the UPOV Council does not currently have any formal effect on policy development in Malaysia, given that as of May 2019 the country was not a member of the UPOV Convention.

Another example of how the Malaysian PVP Act represents an innovative, locally adaptive approach to intellectual property for plant varieties is that it contains a disclosure of origin requirement for new variety registration. The relevant provision mandates disclosure of the source of the genetic material or of the immediate parental lines of the plant variety that is claimed in a PVP application.[33] Furthermore, it is also necessary to demonstrate that written consent from an authority representing the local community or indigenous group has been obtained in cases where the claimed plant variety has been developed based on 'traditional varieties.'[34] A further requirement is to provide evidence of compliance

31 Louwaars, N. and F. Burgaud. 2016. 'Variety Registration: The Evolution of Registration Systems with a Special Emphasis on Agrobiodiversity Conservation.' In *Farmers' Crop Varieties and Farmers' Rights: Challenges in Taxonomy and Law*, edited by M. Halewood. Abingdon: Routledge, pages 184–211.

32 International Union for the Protection of New Varieties of Plants (UPOV). 2005. *Examination of the Conformity of the Protection of New Plant Varieties Act 2004 of Malaysia with the 1991 Act of the UPOV Convention.* UPOV Document C(Extr.)/22/2. Geneva: UPOV, page 3. Accessed May 13 2019. www.upov.int/edocs/mdocs/upov/en/c_extr/22/c_extr_22_2.pdf

33 Malaysian PVP Act. Section 12(e).

34 Ibid, Section 12.1(f).

with the national law that regulates access to genetic or biological resources,[35] and evidence of adherence to relevant Malaysian biosafety laws.[36]

Furthermore, unlike the UPOV Convention and other conventional systems for plant breeders' rights, the Malaysian PVP Act requires that right holders comply with applicable national laws regulating access to genetic resources.[37] As a signatory of the CBD, Malaysia is obliged to enact access and benefit sharing legislation. The Malaysian *Access to Biological Resources and Benefit Sharing Act 2017 (Act 795)* was passed in October 2017.

According to this Act, access to biological resources and associated traditional knowledge can be obtained only after the successful grant of an access permit by the competent authority. An access permit is necessary regardless of whether the intended exploitation of a particular biological resource or associated traditional knowledge is for commercial[38] or non-commercial[39] purposes. There are several conditions attached to the approval of these permits, the most important of which are benefit sharing and prior informed consent. The Malaysian PVP Act is expressly designed to operate in conjunction with this national framework for access and benefit sharing, thus protecting the rights and interests of a variety of actors in the national agricultural sector.

Similar to the Indonesian PVP Act, the Malaysian legislation also contains certain safeguards for farmers surrounding the use of protected breeders' plant varieties. Specifically, the Malaysian PVP Act recognises a farmers' privilege that allows for the exchange of reasonable amounts of seeds and other propagating materials derived from protected breeders' varieties among small farmers. Unlike the way that the farmer's privilege is imagined in UPOV, the Malaysian system allows for the sale of farm-saved seeds. However, the ability of farmers to sell farm-saved seeds is limited to situations in which a small farmer cannot make use of the saved seeds on his/her own holding due to natural disaster, emergency, or any other factor beyond his/her control. Furthermore, the amount sold may not exceed what is required on the farmer's own holding.[40]

A further means through which the Malaysian PVP Act is designed to balance the interests of plant breeders with those of other actors in the national agricultural sector involves a limitation on the grant of breeders' rights. Specifically, under the Malaysian legislation, rights may not be granted for new plant varieties where doing so would negatively affect public order or morality, or where there is a reasonable basis to believe that the cultivation, reproduction, or other use of the plant variety in question would negatively impact the environment.[41] When the

35 Ibid, Section 12(g).
36 Ibid, Section 12(h).
37 Ibid, Section 12.1(g).
38 *Access to Biological Resources and Benefit Sharing Act 2017 (Act 795)* of Malaysia. Section 12.
39 Ibid, Section 15.
40 Malaysian PVP Act. Section 31.1.
41 Ibid, Sections 15(a) and 15(b).

UPOV Council examined the Malaysian PVP Act for conformity with the UPOV Convention, it proposed that this section be deleted. According to the Council, the limitation on the grant of breeders' rights in the Malaysian law does not conform to UPOV 1991.[42] As a remedy, the UPOV Council recommended that Malaysian lawmakers develop a separate legal mechanism that could be applied uniformly to all activities concerning the commercialisation of plant varieties, independent of whether they are protected as intellectual property.[43]

A final way in which the Malaysian PVP Act represents a unique *sui generis* approach to intellectual property for plant varieties concerns compulsory licensing. Under the Malaysian regime, the government may grant compulsory licenses for protected varieties beginning three years after the grant of a PVP certificate. This may occur only in situations where the protected plant variety is not available in reasonable quality, quantity, and price, and where the farming community's needs for the propagating material are not being met, or where an excessive proportion of the plant variety is being imported.[44] As with other provisions described earlier, the UPOV Council challenged the Malaysian system of compulsory licenses when it examined the country's law for conformity with UPOV. The Council specifically recommended that the compulsory licensing provisions be modified to cover only cases of public interest. Furthermore, the Council stated that in order to comply with UPOV, the breeder should not be obligated to produce the protected plant variety locally; rather, he/she should be able to elect to import the variety.[45]

4.3.3 The Philippines

The *Plant Variety Protection Act of 2002 (Republic Act No. 9168)* of the Philippines (Philippines PVP Act) entered into force in June 2002. The *Implementing Rules and Regulations of the Plant Variety Protection Act of 2002* were published soon thereafter in February 2003.[46] These policies appointed the Plant Variety Protection Office in the Bureau of Plant Industry of the Department of Agriculture as the agency responsible for the implementation of the national PVP system.

As with the Indonesian and Malaysian regimes, the Filipino PVP system contains many innovative features that are designed to address domestic concerns while still complying with TRIPS and other international commitments. These include the requirement that applications for PVP include a detailed declaration of

42 *International Convention for the Protection of New Varieties of Plants, Act of 1991* (UPOV 1991). Article 17.1.
43 International Union for the Protection of New Varieties of Plants (UPOV), note 32, page 4.
44 Malaysian PVP Act. Sections 34, 36.1 and 36.2.
45 International Union for the Protection of New Varieties of Plants (UPOV), note 32, page 6.
46 Department of Agriculture, Office of the Secretary. 2003. 'Administrative Order No. 7, Series of 2003.' February 20.

origin and breeding history for the claimed variety, which should include information about the source of the germplasm.[47] Furthermore, the Philippines PVP Act contains a farmers' privilege provision that is arguably broader than the exception to plant breeders' rights granted under the Indonesian and Malaysian laws. The Filipino formulation of the farmers' privilege permits small farmers to save, use, exchange, share, or sell farm produce obtained from the cultivation of protected breeders' plant varieties. The only significant limitation to this provision is that farmers are not permitted to sell seed or harvested material from protected varieties for the purpose of reproduction under a commercial marketing agreement.[48]

In its examination of the Philippines PVP Act, the UPOV Council advised the Filipino government to amend the farmers' privilege language. According to the Council, if any exchange or sale of the seeds of protected plant varieties is undertaken for the purpose of reproduction, it will be in contravention of the breeders' right under UPOV 1991, whether it is done pursuant to or outside a commercial agreement.[49] Similarly, the UPOV Council also disagreed with the wording of the Philippines PVP Act in relation to the farmer-to-farmer exchange or sale of the seeds of protected breeders' varieties. The rationale for the objection was that this language does not strictly follow the limits expressed in UPOV 1991. Specifically, UPOV 1991 permits farmers to use only the propagating material of protected breeders' varieties, and the harvested products that they have obtained by planting these varieties, for non-commercial purposes and on their own holdings.[50]

Another similarity between the PVP frameworks of the Philippines and those of Indonesia and Malaysia is the inclusion of compulsory licensing provisions. The Philippines PVP Act provides for compulsory licensing at any time beginning two years after the grant of a PVP certificate, when the rationale is to protect the public interest. Applicable situations could include where the reasonable

47 *Implementing Rules and Regulations of the Plant Variety Protection Act of 2002* of the Philippines. Article 27(a).

48 The specific language of the *Implementing Rules and Regulations of the Plant Variety Protection Act of 2002* of the Philippines is as follows:

The Board shall determine the conditions and issue the guidelines under which this exception shall apply, taking into consideration the nature of the plant cultivated, grown or sown. This exception shall also extend to the exchange and sale of seeds among and between said small farmers: Provided [that] the small farmers may exchange or [sell] seeds for reproduction and replanting in their own land. The right granted to small farmers under this provision does not include the right to sell the protected variety under the trademark or trade name of the holder which is associated with the registered denomination.

Article 67(d).

49 International Union for the Protection of New Varieties of Plants (UPOV). 2007. *Examination of the Conformity of the Philippine Plant Variety Protection Act of 2002 with the 1991 Act of the UPOV Convention.* UPOV Document C(Extr.)/24/2. Geneva: UPOV, page 5. Accessed May 29 2019. www.upov.int/edocs/mdocs/upov/en/c_extr/24/c_extr_24_02.pdf

50 Ibid.

requirements of the public for any part of the protected variety are not being met, where the needs of the overseas market in relation to the supply of any part of the protected variety are not being met, or where the protected variety is required for the production of medicine and/or any food preparation.[51] Interestingly – and in contrast to the experience of Malaysia – the insertion of the wording 'public interest' in the Philippines PVP Act convinced the UPOV Council that the compulsory licensing provisions of the Act are consistent with UPOV 1991.[52]

One final noteworthy *sui generis* feature of the Philippines PVP Act is that the law establishes a fund to support the conservation and development of indigenous plant varieties, and the stewardship of *in situ* genetic diversity. These aims are to be realised through the establishment of a Gene Trust Fund, administered by the Plant Variety Protection Board. The purpose of this Fund is to support organisations or institutions that manage or operate an accredited gene bank. An amount not exceeding 20 percent of the fees and charges levied under the Philippines PVP Act is designated to finance the Gene Trust Fund.[53] In relation to this section, the UPOV Council advised the Filipino government that measures relating to conservation of genetic resources pursue different objectives from those associated with plant breeders' rights. The Council reasoned that such legal mechanisms require different administrative structures, and therefore it would be more appropriate to include these measures in separate legislation.[54]

4.4 Relationship between the *sui generis* regimes and the UPOV Convention

As discussed earlier in this chapter, as of May 2019, Indonesia, Malaysia, and the Philippines were not members of UPOV. Therefore, they were not under any legal obligation to recognise any particular form of intellectual property for plant varieties, apart from the need to establish a TRIPS-compliant *sui generis* system. Notwithstanding the formal policy space that TRIPS provides, these three countries have all incorporated certain aspects of the UPOV model into their national PVP laws. However, this is not to say that the Indonesian, Malaysian, and Filipino laws, as currently written, would comply with UPOV 1991.

If these countries were to adhere to UPOV, they would need to remove any provisions from their PVP laws that are designed to reconcile the protection of

51 *Plant Variety Protection Act of 2002 (Republic Act No. 9168)* of the Philippines (Philippines PVP Act). Section 57; and *Implementing Rules and Regulations of the Plant Variety Protection Act of 2002* of the Philippines. Sections 69 and 70.

52 International Union for the Protection of New Varieties of Plants (UPOV). 2009. *Explanatory Notes on Exceptions to the Breeder's Right Under the 1991 Act of the UPOV Convention.* UPOV Document UPOV/EXN/EXC/1, page 5. Accessed May 29 2019. www.upov.int/edocs/expndocs/en/upov_exn_exc.pdf

53 Philippines PVP Act. Section 71.

54 International Union for the Protection of New Varieties of Plants (UPOV), note 52, page 7.

plant varieties as intellectual property with provisions related to the governance of biological and genetic resources, including those which are intended to implement the CBD and the Nagoya Protocol at the national level. Doing so would mean the elimination of language requiring PVP applicants to obtain prior informed consent from plant genetic resource providers, and to negotiate agreements for access and benefit sharing.

Furthermore, for these countries to comply with UPOV, it would be necessary to amend other provisions of their national PVP laws related to the recognition of farmers' rights, as conceptualised in the Plant Treaty. Specifically, the UPOV Convention allows for only a limited farmers' privilege, such that the propagating material of protected breeders' plant varieties may be saved for personal and non-commercial use by farmers on their own holdings. In other words, farmers would not be permitted to freely exchange the seeds of protected varieties with other farmers or to sell this seed under certain circumstances, as the *sui generis* laws of Indonesia, Malaysia, and the Philippines currently allow. Adopting the UPOV restrictions on the use of intellectual property-protected seeds by farmers could undermine important policy priorities in these three countries, including the objective to support farmers' seed systems, which are characterised by customary farming practices such as seed saving, use, exchange, and sale.

In its examination of the Malaysian PVP Act, the UPOV Council proposed that national PVP laws could incorporate a separate chapter that would be distinct from the system of protection for new, distinct, uniform, and stable plant varieties. This separate chapter could establish procedures for the registration of traditional and local plant varieties, according to criteria for protection that could deviate from the standards that breeders' varieties are required to meet under the UPOV model.[55] However, the establishment of two parallel PVP systems for breeders' varieties on the one hand and farmers' varieties on the other hand would not in itself resolve the question of the extent to which farmers should be allowed to use protected breeders' varieties. The tension between actors who believe that smallholder farmers should be allowed to freely use, save, sow, share, exchange, and sell the seeds of all varieties, and those who advocate for limited exceptions to the intellectual property rights of plant breeders, would likely not be easily resolved if Indonesia, Malaysia, or the Philippines were to accede to the UPOV Convention.[56]

4.5 Influence of the East Asia Plant Variety Protection Forum

As discussed in section 4.2 of this chapter, the governments of Indonesia, Malaysia, and the Philippines have all engaged directly with the UPOV Council. In the case of Malaysia and the Philippines, the Council conducted a formal evaluation of

55 International Union for the Protection of New Varieties of Plants (UPOV), note 32, page 3.
56 For a detailed exploration of such tensions, see Chapter 10 of this volume.

the compliance of these countries' laws with UPOV 1991. Furthermore, although as of May 2019 none of these three countries was a member of UPOV,[57] they have all benefitted from technical assistance provided by UPOV member countries and the UPOV Secretariat, both during the drafting stages of their national PVP laws and after these regimes were enacted. The forms that this assistance and support have assumed included study tours to UPOV member countries, participation in UPOV distance learning courses, technical training for staff at the Indonesian, Malaysian, and Filipino Plant Variety Protection Offices, development of testing criteria for the registration of plant varieties, and invitations to attend international seminars on PVP.[58]

In addition to the direct and indirect influence that the UPOV system itself has had on lawmaking in Indonesia, Malaysia, and the Philippines, the UPOV Convention model has been promoted in these countries through the participation of their representatives in the EAPVPF. Indonesia, Malaysia and Philippines, along with other members of the Association of Southeast Asian Nations (ASEAN), participated in the first EAPVPF meeting in 2007. This initial event was hosted by Japan,[59] but other UPOV members in Asia – including China and Korea – also acted as influential proponents of the EAPVPF. Japan, China, and Korea continue to provide support for the Forum and drive the initiatives and activities that it undertakes. For instance, Japan still plays a catalytic role by financing many of the PVP-related national workshops, study tours, and technical training workshops that are held in ASEAN countries.

The long-term goal of the EAPVPF is to 'establish effective PVP systems consistent with the 1991 version of the UPOV Convention among Forum members, towards achieving all Forum members' membership [in] UPOV.'[60] The

57 Indonesia, Malaysia, and the Philippines are the member states of the Association of South East Asian Nations (ASEAN). All ten ASEAN member countries have enacted PVP laws. Of these, only two, namely Singapore and Vietnam, were members of UPOV as of May 2019, having acceded to UPOV 1991. As of May 2019, the UPOV Council had approved the PVP laws of Brunei and Myanmar, but these two countries had not yet joined the UPOV Convention at that time. International Union for the Protection of New Varieties of Plants (UPOV). 2018. *Annual Report of the Secretary-General for 2017.* UPOV Document C/52/2, page 4. Accessed May 29 2019. www.upov.int/edocs/mdocs/upov/en/c_52/c_52_2.pdf

58 See Annual Reports of UPOV Secretariat from 2002 to 2018. These reports provide information on all of the meetings, consultations, seminars, training courses, and other events organised by UPOV in which representatives of these three countries have participated. In these reports, UPOV refers to these three countries as 'potential members.' See UPOV Secretariat. 2019. 'Annual Reports.' UPOV Secretariat. Accessed May 31 2019. www.upov.int/meetings/en/topic.jsp?group_id=251

59 For detailed information about the activities of the EAPVPF, see East Asia Plant Variety Protection Forum (EAPVPF). 2019. 'Introduction to the East Asia Plant Variety Protection Forum.' EAPVPF. Accessed 29 May 2019. www.eapvp.org/about/index.html

60 East Asian Plant Variety Protection Forum (EAPVPF). 2019. 'What We Aim For.' EAPVPF. Accessed May 13 2019. http://eapvp.org

organisation aspires to achieve this aim through two specific objectives. The first of these is to strengthen members' national PVP systems so that they are consistent with UPOV 1991, while the second is to institute a regionally harmonised mechanism for the examination of PVP applications for new plant varieties. Predictably, UPOV itself has supported the EAPVPF in achieving these goals and objectives, maintaining a regular presence in Forum meetings and technical workshops.

Given these dynamics, is it unsurprising that Indonesia, Malaysia, and the Philippines are all currently pursuing accession to the UPOV Convention. This is the case even though the initial consultations that the Indonesian, Malaysian, and Filipino governments had with the UPOV Council resulted in the Council advising all three countries that certain provisions of their current PVP laws do not conform with the UPOV Convention. As discussed earlier, Malaysia and the Philippines formally submitted their PVP laws for examination by UPOV, and the UPOV Council published responses in 2005 and 2007, respectively. For its part, Indonesia has been consulting with UPOV about the conformity of its national PVP law with the Convention, even though it has not yet initiated the formal process of accession.

It should be noted that at the time when Indonesia, Malaysia, and the Philippines began to draft their respective *sui generis* PVP laws, the 1978 Act of the UPOV Convention (UPOV 1978)[61] was still accepting accessions. This older Act of the UPOV Convention has been widely evaluated as more favourable to the customary agricultural practices of smallholder farmers than UPOV 1991.[62] However, Indonesia, Malaysia, and the Philippines were not able to elect to join UPOV 1978, due to delays in the drafting and enactment of their respective national PVP laws. UPOV 1978 ceased to accept new accessions in April 1999, and therefore the only option that remains available to Indonesia, Malaysia, and the Philippines is to adhere to UPOV 1991.[63]

Overall, the relationship between the Indonesian, Malaysian, and Filipino governments and the UPOV system is fraught. As demonstrated in the annual reports published by UPOV, all three countries have continuously engaged with the UPOV Secretariat since their national PVP laws were enacted. This is

61 Article 5.3 of the 1978 Act of the UPOV Convention (UPOV 1978) was considered favourable to the forms of agriculture typically practiced in developing countries. This is because the Article 5.3 'farmers' privilege' provision permitted seed saving and exchange on a private, non-commercial basis.

62 Tripp, R., N. Louwaars, and D. Eaton. 2007. 'Plant Variety Protection in Developing Countries: A Report From the Field.' *Food Policy* 32 (3): 354–371.

63 Article 37.3 of UPOV 1991 stipulated that UPOV 1978 would cease to accept new accessions for developing countries on December 31 1995 and for other countries on December 31 1993. However, the UPOV Council decided in 1999 to allow certain states to accede to UPOV 1978 at any time prior to the first anniversary of the entry into force of UPOV 1991. UPOV 1991 entered into force on April 24 1998, and therefore accession to UPOV 1978 closed on April 24 1999. International Union for the Protection of New Varieties of Plants (UPOV). 2000. *Report of the Council Thirty-Third Ordinary Session*. UPOV Document C/33/18, page 4. Accessed May 29 2019. www.upov.int/edocs/mdocs/upov/en/c/33/c_33_18.pdf

understandable given the fact that Indonesia, Malaysia, and the Philippines are dependent on UPOV and its members for technical assistance to implement their domestic PVP frameworks. Thus, although resistance to the UPOV Convention model of intellectual property for plant varieties continues to exist in these three countries, in some ways they rely on the Convention in order to render their *sui generis* laws effective.

4.6 Utilisation of the Indonesian, Malaysian, and Filipino PVP regimes by different actors

Given that the Indonesian, Malaysian, and Filipino *sui generis* PVP laws were all enacted and implemented over a decade ago, it is an opportune moment to evaluate how different actors in these three countries have utilised these regimes. As the statistics presented in subsections 4.6.1 to 4.6.3 demonstrate, the Indonesian, Malaysian, and Filipino laws have followed different trajectories.[64]

4.6.1 Indonesia

The Indonesian Plant Variety Protection Office began to accept PVP applications in 2004. Between that year and October 2017, 653 applications were received for new plant varieties, and to date a total of 407 PVP certificates have been granted.[65] Of the total number of PVP certificates granted, 48.9 percent were for vegetables and 31 percent were for staple food crops, including especially rice, corn, and soybean.[66] Of these, 68.3 percent of the certificates granted were obtained by actors from the domestic private sector, and 15.2 percent were awarded to government agricultural agencies. Foreign actors made up only 4.4 percent of the total number of owners of granted PVP certificates. One explanation for why the proportion of foreign PVP holders is so low could be that in Indonesia, many international companies have domestic subsidiaries or local joint venture partners.

In addition to the statistics that the Indonesian Centre for Plant Variety Protection and Agriculture Licensing compiles for PVP applications and grants, the government maintains a separate registry of local plant varieties and propagating materials. From the time when this registry was established in 2015 to October 2017, a total of 1,986 local varieties and propagating materials were registered in

64 It should be noted that the observations that this chapter makes are based solely on the data available to estimate the number of PVP certificates granted by the Indonesian, Malaysian, and Filipino Plant Variety Protection Offices. Further research designed to elucidate the experiences of different actors in interacting with these systems should be conducted before any conclusive characterisations can be drawn.

65 Indonesia Plant Variety Protection Office. 2017. 'Monthly Report October 2017.' page 7. Indonesia Plant Variety Protection Office. Accessed May 20 2019. http://pvtpp.setjen.pertanian.go.id/informasi-publik

66 Ibid, page 9.

the local plant variety database.[67] In addition, Indonesia manages a third registry for horticultural plants. The horticultural plant database was established in 2011, and from then until October 2017, 804 species of horticultural plants were included in this registry.[68] Of these, 67 percent were vegetables, 21 percent were fruits, 11 percent were ornamentals, and 1 percent were herbs and medicinal plants.[69]

A few conclusions may be drawn from the Indonesian PVP statistics. Foremost, it is notable that in Indonesia, the PVP system has been used predominantly to obtain rights over staple food crops and vegetables. This stands in contrast to the experience of certain other countries, where the national intellectual property regime has been mainly used to protect ornamental crops.[70] Another important finding is that the domestic private industry and public research institutions are both important developers of new plant varieties in Indonesia, but the private sector is well ahead of the public sector in registering new varieties.

Furthermore, and as mentioned earlier, many of the private sector entities that are officially classified as domestic are in fact linked to foreign companies. The recent upswing in PVP applications filed by these actors indicates that international firms are participating increasingly in the vegetable and food crop markets in Indonesia. National media reports have speculated that up to 90 percent of the domestic horticulture seed market in Indonesia is controlled by foreign companies, although the Director General of the Agriculture Ministry has stated that foreign and domestic seed companies own an approximately equal market share.[71]

In any event, the Indonesian government is apparently concerned about the increasing influence of external actors on the domestic agricultural sector. In 2010, the national legislature introduced *Law No. 13 of 2010 Governing Horticulture in Indonesia*, which capped the proportion of shares in domestic horticultural firms that may be held by overseas entities at 30 percent. After the *Law No. 13 of 2010* was enacted, the Indonesian Horticulture Seed Producers Association sought judicial review of the regime in the Constitutional Court. The Court ultimately rejected the Horticulture Seed Producers Association's arguments, holding the law to be valid.[72] Because Indonesia may join the UPOV Convention in the future, it remains to be seen how the Indonesian government

67 Ibid, page 10.
68 Ibid, page 13.
69 Ibid, page 15.
70 For instance, in Ecuador, 92 percent of the plant varieties registered through the national system of plant breeders' rights were flowers. Jefferson, D. J. 2019. 'Experimenting with the Governance of Plants as Intellectual Property: Limitations, Possibilities, and the Ecuadorian Experience.' PhD diss., University of Queensland.
71 Sandi, A. P. and A. Hidayat. 'Foreign Companies Dominate Local Crop Seed Market.' *Tempo*, April 10. Accessed May 13 2019. https://en.tempo.co/read/569599/foreign-companies-dominate-local-crop-seed-market
72 Iqbal, R. 2014. 'Law No. 13/2010 Governing Horticulture in Indonesia.' Food and Fertilizer Technology Center for the Asian and Pacific Region. Accessed May 13 2019. http://ap.fftc.agnet.org/ap_db.php?id=278

might prospectively regulate the participation of foreign investors in the domestic seed sector.

4.6.2 Malaysia

The Malaysian Plant Variety Protection Office began to accept PVP applications in 2008. As of 2017, 111 PVP certificates were granted for new plant varieties.[73] The majority of successful registrations were held by four Dutch companies, three Malaysian public research institutions (the Malaysian Agriculture and Research Development Institute, the Malaysian Cocoa Board, and the Sabah Forestry Development Authority), and one public university (Universiti Kebangsaan Malaysia). Of the applications received, ornamentals represented the largest number at 119 applications, followed by cereals and forest plants (20 applications each), fruits (19 applications), vegetables (12 applications), and herbs and mushrooms (three applications each).

As of 2017, 61 PVP certificates were issued for ornamental plants, and 55 of these certificates were owned by four Dutch companies. This number indicates that foreign breeders have successfully utilised the Malaysian PVP system to obtain rights over their plant varieties. The next highest proportion of PVP certificates that were granted pertained to forest plants (19 certificates). All of these were held by the Sabah Forestry Development Authority, a Malaysian public research institution. Similarly, of the applications filed for cereals, a total of 13 PVP certificates were granted, all for rice. These were owned by two institutions: the Malaysian Agriculture and Research Development Institute (seven certificates), and the Universiti Kebangsaan Malaysia (six certificates). The other categories of successful PVP awards were fruits (eight certificates granted to four Malaysian companies and three individuals), industrial crops (four certificates, of which three were granted to the Malaysian Cocoa Board, with the remaining one granted to the Universiti Kebangsaan Malaysia), vegetables (five certificates, of which one was granted to the Malaysian Agriculture and Research Development Institute and four were granted to a Dutch Company), and herbs (one certificate granted to a Malaysian company).

One of the innovative features of the Malaysian PVP Act is its creation of a separate system of registration for farmers' and local community plant varieties based on the criteria of distinctness and identifiability. The aspiration that smallholder farmers would register their varieties under the law is explicitly stated in the Preamble to the Malaysian PVP Act. Nevertheless, to date only one local plant variety successfully gained registration as a new plant variety and this was in 2008. Since then, there have not been any other local plant varieties registered as new plant varieties.

73 Jabatan Pertanian. 2019. 'Plant Variety Protection Malaysia.' Jabatan Pertanian. Accessed May 13 2019. http://pvpbkkt.doa.gov.my

One explanation for this could be that the Malaysian Department of Agriculture was charged with launching a parallel system for the registration of local plant varieties under the Malaysian PVP Act. Furthermore, the Act mandated that the Department of Agriculture use the information compiled in this registry to recommend local cultivars/varieties for cultivation. This 'National Crop List' was created pursuant to Section 4(g) of the Malaysian PVP Act, which empowered the Department of Agriculture to 'keep and maintain a record of other plant varieties which are not registered under the Register of New Plant Varieties.'

The objectives of the Malaysian system of registration for local plant varieties are to build an inventory of *in situ* genetic resources, to award recognition to the breeder of the variety, to enable official identification of the sources of the country's genetic resources, and to bolster the country's genetic resource pool. As of May 2019, a total of 706 local plant varieties, comprising vegetables, fruits, industrial crops (such as rubber, palm oil, and cocoa), cereals, ornamentals, and forest plants have been registered on the National Crop List.[74] The registered owners of these local plant varieties include individual farmers, local companies, universities, and government research institutions.

A final trend that may be identified in relation to PVP registrations in Malaysia concerns the principal actors that are involved in plant breeding in that country. At present, the majority of breeding activity in Malaysia – especially for non-ornamental plants – is undertaken by public research institutions and publicly funded universities. Indeed, the public sector, including government research institutes, public universities, and statutory bodies, has played a leading role in submitting applications for PVP. Among the public institutions that conduct plant breeding in Malaysia, the only obvious actors missing from the list of PVP registrations are the Malaysian oil palm and rubber research institutes, which have developed numerous high-yielding cultivars. Meanwhile, the enactment of the Malaysian PVP Act has not spurred an increase in plant breeding by the domestic private sector. The only significant industry holders of PVP certificates in Malaysia were foreign companies that owned rights related to ornamental plant varieties.

4.6.3 The Philippines

The Philippine Plant Variety Protection Office began to receive PVP applications in 2003. However, several years were required to develop the necessary protocols to test the distinctness, uniformity, and stability of plant varieties, and as such the first PVP certificates were granted only in 2006. As of 2018, a total of 240 certificates had been awarded. The majority of these were for food crops, including corn (106 certificates), vegetables (58 certificates) and rice (51 certificates). A smaller number of PVP certificates were issued for fruits (19 certificates) and field legumes (six certificates).[75]

74 For detailed data on the registration of local plant varieties, see Jabatan Pertanian. 2019. 'Varieties Registered for National Crop List.' Jabatan Pertanian. Accessed May 13 2019. http://pvpbkkt.doa.gov.my

75 Philippine Plant Variety Protection Office. 2019. 'Plant Variety Registry.' Philippine Plant Variety Protection Office. Accessed May 13 2019. https://pvpo.bpinsicpvpo.com.ph/search.php

In contrast to the situation in Malaysia, the Filipino PVP system has been used prolifically by private domestic and foreign companies, including Pioneer Hi-Bred, Monsanto, Bayer Crop Science, Syngenta, East-West Seed Co., Del Monte, and Dole. Of these, Pioneer Hi-Bred has been especially successful in obtaining intellectual property for its plant varieties. This company currently controls the largest number of PVP certificates for corn varieties in the Philippines (52 certificates), accounting for 49 percent of the total number of PVP registrations for corn in the country. Meanwhile, the East-West Seed Co., Inc. has dominated ownership of PVP certificates for vegetables, controlling 69 percent of total registrations.[76]

These findings indicate that it is likely that foreign companies will continue to represent an important source of seeds in the Philippines, especially for corn, rice, and vegetable crops. It is also interesting to note that since 2000, the Philippines has become one of the major producers of genetically modified corn in the world. By 2014, genetically modified varieties accounted for 62 percent of the total land area planted with corn.[77] Two of the most common of these varieties are claimed in PVP certificates owned by Pioneer Hi-Bred. In other words, this single company already controls a significant portion of the national seed supply for corn in the Philippines.

Of the three countries studied in this chapter, it is evident that foreign firms are already operating as important actors in the national seed markets of Indonesia and the Philippines. It is also notable that in these countries, domestic seed industries are likewise gaining traction. In contrast, in Malaysia the public sector plays a more important role than private firms in the breeding of new varieties of food crops, and by extension, the supply of seed. Lastly, it should be emphasised that in Indonesia and Malaysia, a significantly greater number of local plant varieties have been inscribed in national crop registries than have been protected as intellectual property through the PVP system. These registries serve an important purpose, because they potentially provide a form of protection for traditional and local plant varieties that are not eligible for PVP. Protecting these varieties can help to ensure that concerns related to food security and plant diversity are addressed, especially where a smaller number of actors increasingly supply seed from a more limited genetic pool.

4.7 Conclusion

The national PVP laws of Indonesia, Malaysia, and the Philippines were designed based on several overarching objectives. These included to comply with each country's respective obligations under the TRIPS Agreement, the CBD, and the Plant Treaty; to recognise and protect customary farming systems for the management of seeds; and to bolster public and private seed producing entities,

76 Ibid.
77 Gupta, K., J. Karihaloo, and R. K. Ketarpal. 2008. *Biosafety Regulations of Asia Pacific Countries.* Rome: Food and Agriculture Organization of the United Nations (FAO).

towards the ends of breeding and disseminating new plant varieties. While many scholars and other experts have lauded the *sui generis* approach that these three countries took to lawmaking, it is likely that Indonesia, Malaysia, and the Philippines will take actions in the future to align their national PVP laws with UPOV. This prospect is evidenced in the participation of all three countries in the EAPVPF, and in how their governments have engaged directly with the UPOV Secretariat. If Indonesia, Malaysia, and the Philippines were to adhere to UPOV 1991 and reform their national PVP frameworks accordingly, farmers' seed systems could be affected in several ways. Potential impacts include the curtailment of customary practices of seed saving, use, exchange, and sale.

As described earlier in this chapter, the UPOV Council has recommended that legal protections for farmers' and local plant varieties be separated formally from the national plant breeders' rights law. It is uncertain whether lawmakers in Indonesia, Malaysia, and the Philippines would heed this advice. Thus, it is similarly unclear whether these countries would continue to provide protection for farmers' and local communities' plant varieties if they elected to join the UPOV Convention.

Overall, it is likely that in all three countries, the public sector will cease to be the primary supplier of improved seeds, with this function shifting to the private sector. This is especially probable for cereals and vegetable crops in Indonesia and the Philippines. In Indonesia, the private domestic and foreign seed industries already predominate in the ownership of protected varieties of rice and other food crops. In the Philippines, foreign multinational firms own the majority of protected varieties of rice, corn, and vegetables. At some point in the near future, ownership of exclusive rights may lead to market dominance in the supply of these seeds, and perhaps even increased prices for farmers and consumers. The accelerating participation of private firms in the national seed sectors of Indonesia and the Philippines could also lead to a loss of genetic diversity for food crops, which could present concerns for sustainable agriculture and food security.

In contrast to the experience of Indonesia and the Philippines, it is notable that private actors do not own the majority of PVP certificates in Malaysia. Instead, public institutions have utilised the PVP system to a greater extent than have private companies, and farmers are still dependent on the public sector for seed breeding, development, and supply of improved seeds for food crops. While this trend would seem to indicate that small-scale farming remains more important than industrial agriculture in Malaysia, it should be reiterated that since the enactment of the country's PVP law, only one farmers' or local community plant variety has been registered. This fact suggests that a disconnect exists between the national government and smallholder farmers, such that this latter group does not have the necessary awareness of or interest in the PVP system to register local varieties for protection.

The trends observed surrounding the implementation of the national PVP systems in Indonesia, Malaysia, and the Philippines provide insights into the probable future structure of the seed industries in these three countries. The Indonesian,

Malaysian, and Filipino PVP laws were all enacted and implemented over a decade ago, and therefore these systems have matured sufficiently to have been tested by a variety of actors in the respective national agricultural sectors. Although there are differences in how actors in each country utilise the respective PVP systems and in the types of crops most commonly protected, certain general trends may be observed. As discussed throughout this chapter, all three countries appear to be likely to join the UPOV Convention and to adopt its model of intellectual property for plant varieties. However, at present no one set of actors or seed provision system is dominant in any of the three countries. Thus, it is likely that at least for the time being, the national seed systems of Indonesia, Malaysia, and the Philippines will continue to be characterised by both farmers' customary practices, and professional plant breeding spearheaded by public and private institutions alike.

Chapter 5

Opportunities and challenges created by the *Plant Variety Protection and Farmers' Rights Act* in India

R. C. Agrawal

5.1 Introduction

In the wake of the negotiations at the World Trade Organization that culminated in the *Agreement on Trade-Related Aspects of Intellectual Property Rights* (TRIPS), in 2001, the Government of India introduced the *Protection of Plant Varieties and Farmers' Rights Act.*[1] This law quickly gained notoriety among intellectual property law scholars, who scrutinised the regime with great interest. The Indian regime is widely regarded as significant, because it is one of the first *sui generis* systems of intellectual property for plants that protects the rights of plant breeders and farmers alike.[2] The rationale behind the implementation of a plant variety protection law designed to accommodate the interests of both breeders and farmers was based on at least two important factors.

First, identifying how intellectual property might support the interests of traditional farming communities was – and always has been – a policy priority for the Government of India. This is because a substantial proportion of the overall population of the country relies on traditional agricultural systems to meet important goals, including food security, economic opportunity, and social well-being. Specifically, 70 percent of rural households in India depend primarily on agriculture for their livelihoods, and 82 percent of Indian farmers are classified as small and marginal.[3] While these farmers may be poor in monetary terms, their

1 By virtue of being a member of the 1947 *General Agreement on Tariffs and Trade*, India became a founding member of the World Trade Organization in 1995. Following this, by January 2000 India was required to implement the TRIPS Agreement through different intellectual property laws. Because Article 27.3(b) of TRIPS required India to protect plant varieties by patents, a *sui generis* system, or both, India opted to develop a *sui generis* system. This decision manifested in the introduction of the *Protection of Plant Varieties and Farmers' Rights Act* in 2001.

2 Although Thailand had already introduced a TRIPS-compliant plant variety protection law to protect the rights of breeders and farmers, the Indian plant variety protection law is unique in the sense that it explicitly recognises the concept of farmers' rights.

3 Food and Agriculture Organization of the United Nations (FAO). 2019. 'India at a Glance.' FAO. Accessed May 20 2019. www.fao.org/india/fao-in-india/india-at-a-glance/en/

experience with agriculture is rich. Indian smallholders have been recognised for the numerous contributions that they make to conserve, use, develop, and circulate plant genetic diversity. These farmers possess substantive traditional knowledge in relation to local agricultural production, and they continue to innovate with customary practices, including the saving, use, exchange, and sale of seeds.

Second, the Indian government took seriously its international obligations beyond the TRIPS Agreement. Thus, officials determined that the national plant variety protection regime would be consistent with international agreements related to biodiversity conservation, such as the 1992 *Convention on Biological Diversity* (CBD) and the 2001 *International Treaty on Plant Genetic Resources for Food and Agriculture* (the Plant Treaty). India is not only a member of these international treaties, but the country also played a major role in the multilateral negotiations that resulted in the formal recognition of the rights of local, indigenous, and farming communities in the CBD and the Plant Treaty. Due to the requirement that India implement these two agreements through domestic legislation, the *Biological Diversity Act* – which complies with the CBD – and the *Protection of Plant Varieties and Farmers' Rights Act* – which complies with the TRIPS Agreement and the Plant Treaty – include multiple provisions that are designed to safeguard the interests and rights of local farming communities.[4]

Although the Indian plant variety protection law was enacted in 2001, several years were required for the government to create the necessary protocols to register plant varieties as intellectual property. In an attempt to expedite this process and to implement other provisions of the *Protection of Plant Varieties and Farmers' Rights Act*, the Government of India developed the *Protection of Plant Varieties and Farmers' Rights Rules* in 2003 and the *Protection of Plant Varieties and Farmers' Rights Regulations* in 2006. Once this regulatory infrastructure was in place, the Protection of Plant Varieties and Farmers' Rights Authority of India (PPV&FRA) began to register plant varieties and to issue plant variety rights certificates at a rapid pace. This is evidenced by the fact that from the period of 2007 to 2018, the PPV&FRA received 16,486 applications for the registration of different categories of plant varieties. Meanwhile, as of October 2018, the Authority had granted 3,504 plant variety rights certificates. Of these, 1,143 certificates were issued to public research organisations, 774 were granted to private seed companies, and 1,587 – the majority – were obtained by individual farmers or farming communities.[5]

4 For instance, *The Biological Diversity Act, 2002* of India stipulates that all local governments within the country must create a 'Biodiversitiy Management Committee,' whose purpose is to promote the conservation, sustainable use, and documentation of biological diversity, including the conservation of landrace plant varieties and folk varieties. *The Biological Diversity Act, 2002* of India. Article 41(1).

5 Protection of Plant Varieties and Farmers' Rights Authority of India (PPV&FRA). 2018. *Compendium of Registered Varieties under PPV&FR Act, 2001.* New Delhi: Department of Agriculture and Co-operation, Ministry of Agriculture. Accessed May 29 2019. http://plantauthority.gov.in/pdf/CompendiumFinal27Oct2018.pdf

The volume of plant varieties that public research organisations, private seed companies, and farmers have separately registered suggests that professional plant breeders and farmers alike are taking advantage of the Indian plant variety protection regime. Presumably, this is based on these actors' perceptions that there are benefits to obtaining intellectual property for their varieties. However, notwithstanding the success of the Indian plant variety protection system, there are several challenges that could complicate the realisation of the goals of the *Protection of Plant Varieties and Farmers' Rights Act*. For example, an ongoing area of debate surrounds how to ensure that Indian farmers derive tangible gains from the registration of their plant varieties under the Act. Likewise, it remains difficult for government officials to establish and promote institutional partnerships between the PPV&FRA and other actors, such as universities, research and breeding institutes, technology development and management centres, and *Krishi Vigyan Kendras* (farm science centres). In the past, the inability to establish such partnerships has limited the capacity of the Authority to support the breeding, development, and registration of plant varieties. This in turn complicates the realisation of the goals of agricultural development and food security, and the effectiveness of breeders' and farmers' rights.

The present chapter aims both to discuss the various opportunities and challenges that the *Protection of Plant Varieties and Farmers' Rights Act* creates, and to identify the means through which relevant stakeholders, including Indian farmers, could further benefit from this law. Following this introductory section, the chapter is divided into four sections. Section 5.2 outlines the key features of the Act, focussing especially on the types of intellectual property that the law makes available for different categories of plant varieties, including those developed by private sector breeders, public sector researchers, and farmers, respectively. This section also provides a brief summary of the procedures to which applicants must adhere to register their plant varieties and to obtain plant variety rights certificates in India.

Section 5.3 highlights opportunities that already exist for relevant stakeholders to benefit from the Act. These include the ability to obtain different kinds of rights related to the use of different categories of plant varieties; to benefit from resources generated by the National Gene Fund; and for farmers to receive a series of specific awards and rewards. Section 5.4 discusses some of the challenges that the Act should address to protect the interests of farmers, while section 5.5 concludes the chapter with a summary of the arguments presented.

5.2 Key features of the *Protection of Plant Varieties and Farmers' Rights Act*

The *Protection of Plant Varieties and Farmers' Rights Act* of India aims to 'provide for the establishment of an effective system [to protect] the rights of farmers and plant breeders and to encourage the development of new varieties of plants.'[6]

6 *The Protection of Plant Varieties and Farmers' Rights Act, 2001* of India. Preamble.

Subsections 5.2.1 to 5.2.4 present a brief analysis of some of the unique provisions that the Act implements.

5.2.1 Protections for different categories of plant varieties

The Indian framework of intellectual property for plant varieties provides different forms of protection for different categories of plant varieties. This typology includes new varieties, essentially derived varieties (EDVs), and several types of extant varieties, including farmers' varieties. Of these, the category of new varieties is most closely aligned with standard conceptions of intellectual property for plants, encompassing varieties that breeders develop and register. To receive protection, new varieties must meet the criteria of novelty, distinctiveness, uniformity, and stability (DUS).[7] According to the *Protection of Plant Varieties and Farmers' Rights Act*, 'novelty' means that the variety has not been sold or otherwise disposed of in India,[8] or outside India.[9] The criterion of 'distinctiveness' is met where the variety is distinguishable from all varieties of common knowledge by at least one essential characteristic. 'Uniformity' means that the variety must be sufficiently homogenous in its essential characteristics.[10] Lastly, to meet the requirement of 'stability,' the essential characteristics of the variety must remain unchanged after repeated propagation.[11] The Act requires new varieties to be tested for DUS in a replicated trial over two similar growing seasons, at two locations.

Another category of plant varieties for which the Indian framework offers protection includes the EDV. This concept is defined as a variety that is derived predominantly from an initial variety, or from a variety that itself is derived predominantly from an initial variety.[12] To be recognised as 'essentially derived,' the variety must retain the expression of the essential characteristics that result from the genotype or combination of genotypes of the initial variety, but also be clearly distinguishable from the initial variety.[13] Lastly, an essentially derived variety may only differ from the initial variety in characteristics that result from the act of derivation.[14]

7 Ibid, Article 15(1).
8 Specifically, to be considered novel a variety cannot have been sold or otherwise disposed of in India for earlier than one year prior to the filing date of the application for protection. Ibid, Article 15(3)(a)(i).
9 Specifically, to be considered novel a variety cannot have been sold or otherwise disposed of in India for earlier than six years in the case of trees or vines, and earlier than four years in the case of other crops, prior to the filing date of the application for protection. Ibid, Article 15(3)(a)(ii).
10 Ibid, Article 15(3)(c).
11 Ibid, Article 15(3)(d).
12 Ibid, Article 2(i)(ii).
13 Ibid, Article 2(i)(i).
14 Ibid, Article 2(i)(iii).

While many standard systems of intellectual property for plants recognise protections for new and EDVs, the Indian law is unique in its provision of protection for extant varieties. The *Protection of Plant Varieties and Farmers' Rights Act* defines these varieties as those which are available in India (i.e., they are not new), and which have been notified under the *Seeds Act, 1966 (Act No. 54 of 1966)* of the country. Furthermore, the Act clarifies that the category of extant varieties could also include varieties of common knowledge, or varieties that are in the public domain.[15] Although the Act conceptualises farmers' varieties as a subset of extant varieties, the law enumerates a series of special protections for these varieties, consistent with the aim to balance the rights of plant breeders with those of farmers.

The Indian legislation defines farmers' varieties as those that have been traditionally cultivated and developed by farmers in their fields, or those that are wild relatives or landraces about which farmers possess common knowledge.[16] As with other types of extant varieties, farmers' varieties are not required to meet the criterion of novelty to receive intellectual property protection in India. These varieties can be protected under the *Protection of Plant Varieties and Farmers' Rights Act*, if they meet the DUS criteria.[17] However, in an attempt to encourage farmers to register their varieties and to reduce the technical and financial burdens that farmers often face, the *2009 Protection of Plant Varieties and Farmers' Rights (Criteria for DUS for Registration) Regulations* relax the uniformity and stability requirements that farmers' varieties must meet.[18] For instance, where new varieties must undergo field-testing for two growing seasons, farmers' varieties need only be evaluated for one growing season.[19]

Another unique feature of the Act is that farmers can register their varieties under any of the above categories.[20] In other words, although the law creates a specific category of protection for farmers' varieties, farmers may still apply for protection in the same manner as professional breeders, if they believe that their varieties can meet the criteria that are enumerated for new varieties.

5.2.2 Recognition of the rights of breeders and farmers

Unlike models of intellectual property for plants that have become standard in many countries, the *Protection of Plant Varieties and Farmers' Rights Act* of India does not focus merely on granting rights to plant breeders. Instead, the law also creates a variegated system which recognises different kinds of rights that breeders and farmers separately may claim. The Act defines 'breeder' as 'a person or group

15 Ibid, Article 2(j).
16 Ibid, Article 2(l).
17 Ibid, Article 15(2).
18 See Chapter 10 of this volume.
19 *The Protection of Plant Varieties and Farmers' Rights Act, 2001* of India. Article 5(5).
20 Ibid, Article 39(1)(i).

of persons or a farmer or group of farmers or any institution which has bred, evolved or developed any variety.'[21] This definition is unusual in the context of standard intellectual property models because it expressly acknowledges that farmers may act as breeders when they improve particular plant varieties. The *Protection of Plant Varieties and Farmers' Rights Act* enables breeders to claim exclusive rights to produce, sell, market, distribute, import, or export the varieties that they protect,[22] which may include new varieties and EDVs.[23]

In addition to the definition of farmers qua breeders that the *Protection of Plant Varieties and Farmers' Rights Act* contains, the Act also provides a separate definition of 'farmer.' The purpose of this use of language is to address farmers' specific needs in relation to the conservation, use, and development of their traditionally cultivated varieties, including wild species. Thus, the Act states that a farmer is any person (1) 'who cultivates crops by cultivating the land [himself/herself]'; (2) 'who cultivates crops by directly supervising the cultivation of land [by] any other person'; and (3) 'who conserves and preserves, severally or jointly, with any person[,] any wild species or traditional varieties, or adds value to such wild species of traditional varieties through selection and identification of their useful properties.'[24]

As mentioned earlier, one of the key features of the *Protection of Plant Varieties and Farmers' Rights Act* is that it grants a set of rights and privileges to farmers that approximate the form of intellectual property that standard models allot only to breeders. For example, the Act recognises that farmers have the same right that plant breeders enjoy to register the varieties they have bred or developed.[25] Furthermore, the Act also grants a set of rights to farmers in relation to the use of plant varieties that third parties have protected. Thus, farmers are entitled to save, use, sow, re-sow, exchange, share or sell farm produce, including seeds, generated from the use of new varieties that third party breeders have protected.[26] The only limitation to this right is that farmers are not permitted to sell the seeds of protected breeders' varieties using a brand name.[27] The Indian framework additionally recognises other types of rights and protections for farmers, as elaborated below.

21 Ibid, Article 2(c).
22 Ibid, Article 28(1).
23 Ibid, Article 23(6) (stating that the breeders' rights enumerated in the section of the Act concerned with new varieties also apply to EDVs).
24 Ibid, Article 2(k).
25 Ibid, Article 14 (stating that any person may make an application to the Registrar for the registration of any variety).
26 Ibid, Article 39(1)(iv).
27 Ibid. An explanation to this provision states that in the context of the Act, 'branded seed' 'means any seed put in a package or any other container and labelled in a manner that such seed is of a variety protected under this Act.'

A Compensation for farmers

Farmers are entitled to compensation if a protected breeder's variety fails to perform as expected under the conditions that the breeder has specified.[28] Furthermore, any person or group of persons, or any governmental or non-governmental organisation can claim compensation on behalf of local or village communities (including individual farmers or farming groups), if it is found that these communities contributed significantly to the development of any variety that a third party has protected.[29]

B Claims for benefit sharing

In addition to providing a formal mechanism through which local or village communities may claim compensation, the Act also introduces a system of benefit sharing, thus aligning with the objectives of the CBD and the Plant Treaty. In doing so, the Act enables any person, group of persons, firm, or governmental or non-governmental organisation to file a claim for benefit sharing following the grant of a plant variety rights certificate to a third party.[30] When evaluating claims for benefit sharing, the PPV&FRA is required to consider: (1) 'the extent and nature of the use of genetic material of the claimant in the development of the [protected] variety'; and (2) 'the commercial utility and demand in the market of the [protected] variety relating to which the benefit sharing has been claimed.'[31]

C Compulsory licences

In an attempt to ensure that farmers benefit from the ability to access and use the plant varieties that third parties protect with intellectual property, the Act establishes a system of compulsory licensing. This framework allows any person to apply for the right to produce, distribute, and sell the seed or other propagating material of a protected variety.[32] However, compulsory licenses are limited such that they may only be issued three years after the date on which the relevant plant variety protection certificate was granted.[33] Furthermore, a compulsory license may be issued only if 'the reasonable requirements of the public for seed or other propagating material of the variety have

28 Ibid, Article 39(2).
29 Ibid, Article 41.
30 Ibid, Article 26(2).
31 Ibid, Article 26(5).
32 Ibid, Article 47(1).
33 Ibid.

not been satisfied,'[34] or if 'the seed or other propagating material of the variety is not available to the public at a reasonable price.'[35]

D Exemption from the payment of registration and other fees

The *Protection of Plant Varieties and Farmers' Rights Act* recognises that most farmers in India are poor and engaged in agriculture for the fulfilment of their basic needs. Thus, the Act accommodates farmers by exempting them from the payment of all administrative costs that are normally associated with activities including plant variety registration. Farmers also do not need to pay any fees incurred through the participation in legal proceedings before the PPV&FRA, the National Register of Plant Varieties, the Plant Varieties Protection Appellate Tribunal, or the High Court of India.[36]

E Protection for innocent infringement

In standard models of intellectual property for plants, where the infringement of plant breeders' rights is established, infringers are typically subject to the payment of a fine or another form of punishment. However, the Indian government aims to protect farmers from this kind of liability, and as a result the *Protection of Plant Varieties and Farmers' Rights Act* creates certain safeguards for farmers. For example, the Act provides that plant breeders' rights are not infringed by farmers who are not aware of the existence of these rights at the time of infringement.[37] The Act also clarifies that courts may not grant remedies to plant breeders where the accused farmer provides evidence to establish that at the time of infringement he/she was not aware that the variety in question was protected with plant breeders' rights.[38]

5.2.3 Recognition of the rights of researchers

Many standard models of intellectual property for plants recognise exceptions to plant breeders' rights for the use of protected varieties in scientific research, or in future breeding activities. The *Protection of Plant Varieties and Farmers' Rights Act* of India contains similar provisions, but it formulates protections for researchers as positive rights rather than as exceptions to the rights of plant breeders. Thus, the Act guarantees that researchers may use protected plant varieties for the purposes of conducting experiments or otherwise engaging in research.[39] The Act also grants researchers the right to use protected varieties as source breeding material for the development

34 Ibid.
35 Ibid.
36 Ibid, Article 44.
37 Ibid, Article 42(i).
38 Ibid, Article 42(ii).
39 Ibid, Article 30(a).

of a new variety.[40] However, this right is limited such that researchers who intend to use repeatedly a protected variety as a parental line for the commercial production of a new variety must obtain authorisation from the breeder of the source variety.[41]

5.2.4 Procedures to register plant varieties and to obtain plant variety protection certificates

The *Protection of Plant Varieties and Farmers' Rights Act* enumerates a series of procedures that an application for plant variety protection must undergo in order for a certificate to be awarded. These include: (1) the filing of an application to register the plant variety; (2) the examination of the application by the PPV&FRA; (3) field tests to evaluate the DUS of the claimed plant variety; (4) the publication of passport data in the *Plant Variety Journal of India*, so that any party who believes that he/she has a claim to benefit sharing may be notified of the application for plant variety protection; and, if the previous actions result in a positive assessment, (5) the grant of a plant variety protection certificate to the applicant/breeder.

A substantial volume of information must be included in the application for plant variety protection. For instance, the applicant must specify the denomination that will be assigned to the variety,[42] and also sign an affidavit to verify that the variety does not contain any gene or genetic sequence that constitutes a terminator technology.[43] Additionally, the application form is required to include complete passport data about the parental lines from which the claimed variety has been derived. In doing so, the applicant must both indicate the geographical location in India from which the genetic material was taken, and provide any relevant information about the contribution(s) that any farmers or other stakeholders have made to develop the variety.[44]

Furthermore, the application for plant variety protection must be accompanied by a declaration by the applicant that the genetic material used for the development of the variety was lawfully acquired.[45] A further requirement is to submit a statement containing a brief description about the DUS of the claimed variety.[46] For the purpose of the evaluation of these three characteristics, as of October 2018, the PPV&FRA had developed a series of crop-specific *Guidelines for the Conduct of Test for Distinctiveness, Uniformity and Stability*, for 156 different crop species. These guidelines cover parameters to evaluate many different species of cereals, legumes, fibre crops, oilseeds, sugar crops, vegetables, flowers and ornamentals, spices, fruits, medicinal and

40 Ibid, Article 30(b).
41 Ibid.
42 Ibid, Article 18(1)(b).
43 Ibid, Article 18(1)(b) and Article 18(1)(c).
44 Ibid, Article 18(1)(e).
45 Ibid, Article 18(1)(h).
46 Ibid, Article 18(1)(f).

aromatic plants, and plantation crops such as coconut and tea. A major feature of the crop-specific guidelines is that they provide practical details to inform the examination of the DUS of the variety.

The procedure through which applicants may obtain plant variety rights certificates in India is shown in Figure 5.1.

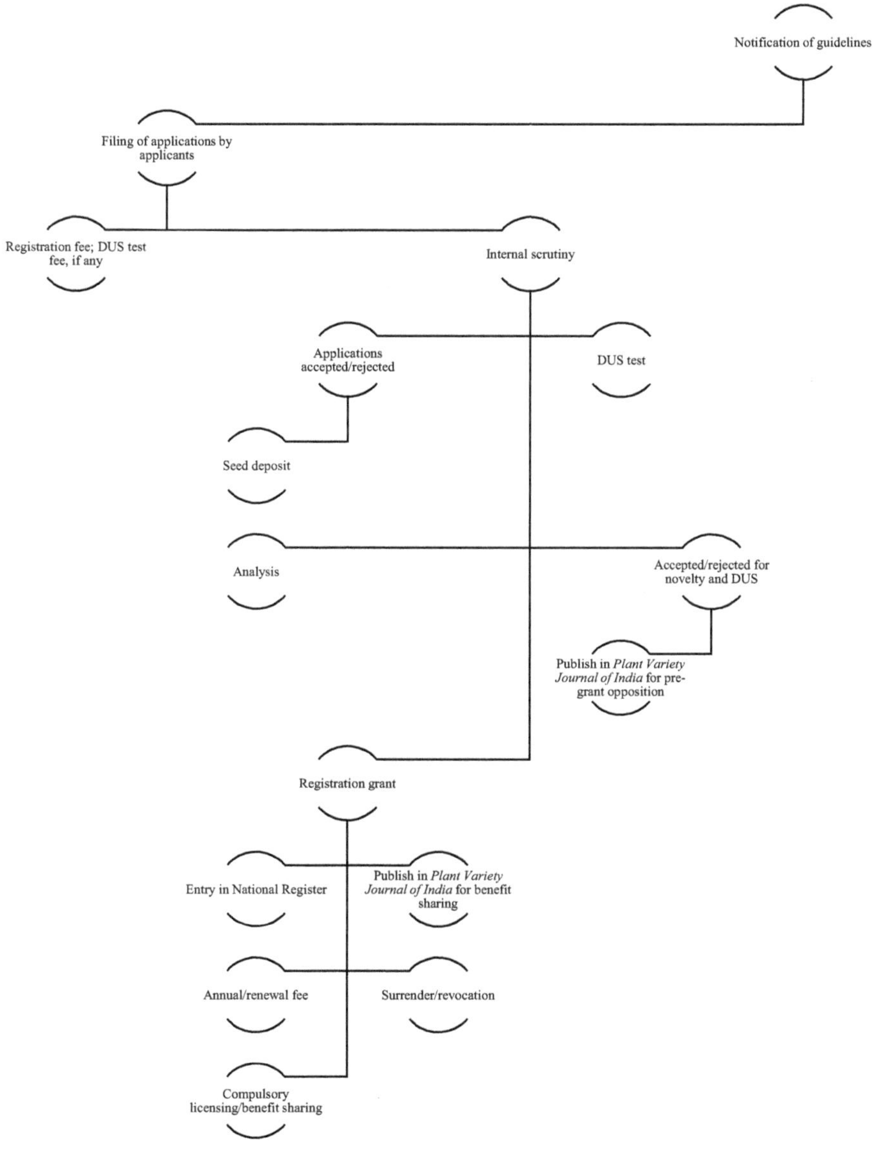

Figure 5.1 Registration process for plant variety protection in India

5.3 Opportunities created by the *Protection of Plant Varieties and Farmers' Rights Act*

The objectives of the *Protection of Plant Varieties and Farmers' Rights Act* clarify that the legislation is imbued with multiple aims. These include to create an 'effective' system of intellectual property for plant varieties – thereby complying with the obligations of the TRIPS Agreement – and to realise other important national policy goals. Some of these are contained in other international agreements, such as the CBD and the Plant Treaty. Thus, the Act articulates a series of specific aspirations, which are to: (1) protect the rights of farmers in respect of their important contributions to the conservation, improvement, and the availability of plant genetic diversity; (2) recognise plant breeders' rights to stimulate investment for research and development in public and private sectors; and (3) facilitate the growth of the seed industry to ensure that high quality seeds and planting material are available to local farmers.[47]

Evidence from the first decade since the *Protection of Plant Varieties and Farmers' Rights Act* was implemented suggests that at least some of these goals are being met. This is particularly clear in relation to the aims of the law to protect the rights of farmers and plant breeders surrounding the varieties that these groups develop. For instance, during the period of 2007 to 2018, a total of 16,486 applications were filed to protect plant varieties across the different categories that the law enumerates. Of these, 2,466 applications were lodged to claim protection for new varieties, 180 for EDVs, 2,932 for extant varieties, and 10,908 for farmers' varieties. These data are interesting, because they demonstrate that more than four times the number of applications were filed for farmers' varieties than for new varieties. This finding suggests that farmers believe that they will benefit from the registration of their varieties, although the numbers alone do not indicate why this might be the case.

Of the total number of applications that the PPV&FRA received since the Act was implemented in 2007, as of October 2018, 3,504 plant variety rights certificates were granted across all categories of plant varieties. In other words, approximately 22 percent of the total applications filed resulted in granted plant variety rights certificates. Of the applications granted, 480 certificates were issued for new varieties, one for an essentially derived variety, 1,437 for extant varieties, and 1,586 for farmers' varieties. Put another way, of the total number of applications filed to protect new varieties, 19 percent were granted. Meanwhile, 0.5 percent of the applications filed for EDVs were granted, 49 percent of the applications for extant varieties were granted, and approximately 15 percent of the applications for farmers' varieties were granted.

These statistics indicate that applications claiming extant varieties were far more likely to result in plant variety rights certificates, which likely can be explained by the fact that these varieties had previously met the conditions for notification

47 Ibid, Preamble.

under the *Seeds Act, 1966 (Act No. 54 of 1966)*.[48] Interestingly, even though the greatest volume of applications by far was filed to protect farmers' varieties, these were granted at a rate lower than that of all other categories, except EDVs. In other words, although farmers appear motivated to protect their varieties under the *Protection of Plant Varieties and Farmers' Rights Act*, they are experiencing difficulty in meeting the specified requirements for protection. Table 5.1 provides a visualisation of the number of plant varieties registered by year based on applications filed by farmers, the private sector, the public sector, and Indian agricultural universities, respectively.[49]

In addition to the opportunities that the *Protection of Plant Varieties and Farmers' Rights Act* created for diverse actors in India to obtain intellectual property protection for their plant varieties, the law also established other mechanisms to provide benefits to Indian communities. For instance, the Act mandated the creation of a National Gene Fund, which was designed specifically to support farmers on an individual and collective basis, and rural communities in general.[50] The Gene Fund pools resources gathered from diverse sources. These include the monetary benefits that the breeders are obligated to share when they use plant varieties over which third parties claim rights to develop new and EDVs.

Furthermore, the fees that applicants – except farmers, who are exempted from the payment of fees – incur to register and commercialise their varieties also are used to support the Gene Fund. Additional sources of income for the Fund include costs that breeders are mandated to pay as compensation to farmers, and occasional contributions from national or international organisations.[51] Whatever the original source of the resources that comprise the National Gene Fund, the *Protection of Plant Varieties and Farmers' Rights Act* stipulates that these funds be used for three specific purposes. These are: (1) for the purpose of equitable benefit sharing and compensation for losses associated with the use of protected breeders' varieties, which are made to village and local communities; (2) to foster conservation and sustainable use of *in situ* and *ex situ* genetic resources; and (3) to strengthen the capacities of *panchayats*, which are local government units whose purpose is to facilitate the conservation and sustainable use of plant genetic diversity.[52]

Based on these statutory parameters, from the period of 2009 to 2018, the PPV&FRA utilised the resources of the National Gene Fund for various purposes. For instance, the Fund was tapped to help to subsidise costs associated with the

48 In India, seed may only be sold if it: (a) is identifiable as to its kind or variety; (b) conforms to the minimum limits of germination and purity; and (c) it is packaged in a container that correctly identifies the seed. *The Seeds Act, 1966 (Act No. 54 of 1966)*. Article 7.

49 Protection of Plant Varieties and Farmers' Rights Authority of India (PPV&FRA), note 5.

50 *The Protection of Plant Varieties and Farmers' Rights Act, 2001* of India. Article 45.

51 Ibid, Article 45(1).

52 Ibid, Article 45(2).

Table 5.1 Status of the registration of plant varieties in India

Registrants	*Type of varieties*	*2009*	*2010*	*2011*	*2012*	*2013*	*2014*	*2015*	*2016*	*2017*	*2018*	*Grand total*
Farmers	Farmer	3	0	0	3	46	459	200	344	221	310	1,586
	New	0	0	0	0	0	0	0	1	0	0	1
	Sub-total	3	0	0	3	46	459	200	345	221	310	1,587
Private sector	Essentially derived	0	0	0	1	0	0	0	0	0	0	1
	Extant	14	0	9	29	62	45	64	78	56	58	415
	New	2	0	12	25	42	80	57	70	39	32	359
	Sub-total	16	0	21	55	104	125	121	148	95	90	775
Public sector	Extant	144	44	53	121	113	146	42	37	33	14	747
	New	0	0	3	1	11	25	7	51	7	1	106
	Sub-total	144	44	56	122	124	171	49	88	40	15	853
State agriculture universities	Extant	5	5	39	32	30	75	15	18	10	46	275
	New	0	0	0	0	0	3	0	6	5	0	14
	Sub-total	5	5	39	32	30	78	15	24	15	46	289
Grand total		168	49	116	212	304	833	385	605	371	461	3,504

Source: Protection of Plant Varieties and Farmers' Rights Authority of India (PPV&FRA). 2018. *Compendium of Registered Varieties under PPV&FR Act, 2001*. New Delhi: Department of Agriculture and Co-operation, Ministry of Agriculture. Accessed May 29 2019. http://plantauthority.gov.in/pdf/CompendiumFinal27Oct2018.pdf

scientific evaluation and registration of farmers' varieties. Resources were also directed to reward farmers for the contributions that they had made to the conservation, development, and availability of plant genetic diversity.

Specifically, the National Gene Fund was used to provide incentives to numerous farmers through three different programmes. These are: (1) the Plant Genome Saviour Community Award; (2) the Plant Genome Saviour Farmer Reward; and (3) the Plant Genome Saviour Farmer Recognition initiative (Table 5.2). The first programme, namely the Plant Genome Saviour Community Awards, recognises the contributions that Indian farming communities, especially tribal and rural communities, make towards the enhancement of quality in agricultural research and crop varietal development. The selection of awardees is conducted by a high-level national committee and is based on criteria designed to evaluate the engagement of farming communities in the conservation and improvement of domestic plant genetic resources and their wild relatives, particularly in areas that have been identified as agrobiodiversity hotspots.[53]

Meanwhile, and in contrast to the system of Plant Genome Saviour Community Awards, the Plant Genome Saviour Farmer Reward and the Plant Genome Saviour Farmer Recognition initiative are designed to recognise the contributions that individual farmers, rather than communities, have made towards the realisation of goals related to the conservation and genetic development of crops and wild relatives. All individual farmers who apply under these schemes must demonstrate their active involvement in the conservation and development of plant genetic resources, including landraces and crop wild relatives. This system of rewards to promote the con-

Table 5.2 Innovative schemes of awards and rewards for Indian farmers

	Number of farmers benefitted
Plant Genome Saviour Community Award *(consisting of cash of ₹1,000,000, as well as a citation and a memento)*	25
Plant Genome Saviour Farmer Reward *(consisting of cash of ₹150,000, as well as a citation and a memento)*	33
Plant Genome Saviour Farmer Recognition *(consisting of cash of ₹100,000, as well as a citation and a memento)*	66
Total	124

Source: Official records of the New Delhi-based PPV&FRA of India.

53 Protection of Plant Varieties and Farmers' Rights Authority of India (PPV&FRA). 2019. 'Plant Genome Saviour Community Award.' PPV&FRA. Accessed May 20 2019. http://plantauthority.gov.in/PGSFA.htm

servation and sustainable use of plant genetic resources for food and agriculture represents a unique component of the *Protection of Plant Varieties and Farmers' Rights Act*. Thus, the law transcends standard notions of intellectual property to provide benefits to a plurality of actors that operate in the national agricultural sector.

In addition to this system of rewards for individual farmers and rural communities, the PPV&FRA also has utilised the National Gene Fund to extend non-monetary benefits to farmers. For instance, the Authority has organised numerous farmer-centric capacity building and training programmes, including exhibitions and *Kisan Melas* (farmers' fairs).[54] These initiatives have been designed specifically to raise farmers' awareness of their rights – including to register their varieties for protection under the *Protection of Plant Varieties and Farmers' Rights Act* – and to help them understand the importance of conserving, developing, and registering their varieties.[55] The training programmes and exhibitions that the Authority has coordinated have reached thousands of farmers across India, and they likely constitute a primary reason for why farmers filed nearly 11,000 applications to register their varieties between the years of 2009 and 2018.

The organisation of capacity building and training programmes by the PPV&FRA also has helped to solidify relationships between local farmers and the governmental agencies and academic institutions that engage in crop variety development work in India. Some of the primary institutional actors involved in this space include the Indian Council of Agriculture Research, the Council for Scientific and Industrial Research, the Indian Council of Forestry Research and Education, *Krishi Vigyan Kendras*, public agricultural universities, and several non-governmental organisations. Thus, on the one hand the *Protection of Plant Varieties and Farmers' Rights Act* is a law that reinscribes certain aspects of standard models of intellectual property for plants. However, in practice, the Act has also been mobilised to restructure relations between various social actors in India, outside of the logic of property.

5.4 Enduring challenges surrounding the implementation of the *Protection of Plant Varieties and Farmers' Rights Act*

Although the *Protection of Plant Varieties and Farmers' Rights Act* has yielded numerous benefits for diverse stakeholders in the Indian agricultural sector since the law took effect in 2007, several challenges continue to complicate the realisation of the aims of the Act. Of these, there are four issues that should receive immediate attention. First, there is an enduring need to ensure that Indian farmers are able to derive tangible benefits from the registration of their plant varieties.

54 Protection of Plant Varieties and Farmers' Rights Authority of India (PPV&FRA). 2018. *Annual Report 2017–18*. New Delhi: Department of Agriculture, Co-operation and Farmers Welfare, Ministry of Agriculture and Farmers Welfare. Accessed May 20 2019. http://plantauthority.gov.in/pdf/E_Annual%20report%2017-18.pdf

55 Ibid.

During the period of 2007 to 2018, 1,586 plant varieties were registered under the Act as farmers' varieties. However, as of 2019, there has not been a single example of the use of farmers' varieties for the purposes of bioprospecting or the breeding of new varieties This means that there have been no instances to date in which farmers have received monetary or non-monetary benefit sharing from other actors who would access and utilise farmers' varieties. In other words, genetic material from farmers' varieties is not being used to develop new plant varieties. This means that the favourable characteristics of farmers' varieties have not yet had an impact on plant breeding in India, representing a missed opportunity for farmers and breeders alike.

Second, it is notable that as mentioned earlier, only a small proportion – approximately 15 percent – of the applications claiming farmers' varieties has been granted. One of the reasons for this is probably attributable to the fact that the seeds of farmers' varieties often contain impurities. Thus, when the PPV&FRA receives an application for the protection of a farmer's variety, it undertakes seed purification and also characterises these varieties. These processes require more time than is needed to evaluate breeders' varieties. Furthermore, the majority of the applications for protection that have been received for farmers' varieties were lodged beginning in 2015, so most of these were still undergoing characterisation or testing stage as of May 2019.

Although it is notable that the PPV&FRA already follows special procedures for the registration of farmers' varieties, the criteria on which these varieties are evaluated should still be adjusted to better accommodate their fundamental nature as heterogeneous and adaptable organisms. Furthermore, it is notable that even for the relatively small proportion of farmers' varieties that has received protection, no systematic analysis has been conducted to assess the performance of these varieties. It would be interesting to know, for example, how protected farmers' varieties compare to breeders' varieties, both in terms of seed production and sale in local markets. Lastly, it is important to recognise that to date, no concrete institutional support has been provided by the government or other actors to help farmers to develop commercialisation strategies for their varieties, or to become self-reliant in the production and supply of quality seeds.

Third, the *Protection of Plant Varieties and Farmers' Rights Act* did not provide clarity surrounding how certain components of the law should relate to the *Seeds Act, 1966 (Act No. 54 of 1966)*. For instance, it is ambiguous what kind of procedure should be used to notify protected farmers' varieties under the terms of the *Seeds Act, 1966 (Act No. 54 of 1966)*. It is recommended that the PPV&FRA and the Central Seed Committee (which administers the *Seeds Act*) work together to develop a system based on which farmers' varieties registered under the *Protection of Plant Varieties and Farmers' Rights Act* could efficiently obtain notification under the *Seeds Act, 1966 (Act No. 54 of 1966)*. Doing so would not only encourage more farmers to register their varieties, but also create legal certainty surrounding the commercialisation of these varieties.

Fourth, there is a continued need to create new partnerships and to strengthen existing relationships between the PPV&FRA and other actors in the Indian agricultural sector. Relevant institutions include universities, research and plant breeding institutes, technology development and management centres, and *Krishi Vigyan Kendras* (farm science centres). It would be especially important for these actors to collaborate towards the end of facilitating the breeding, development, and registration of new plant varieties. Furthermore, these institutions should devise better means through which they could collectively share responsibility for the evaluation of DUS for farmers' varieties.

5.5 Conclusion

As discussed throughout this chapter, the *Protection of Plant Varieties and Farmers' Rights Act* of India aims to create a system in which farmers and professional plant breeders alike are encouraged to develop and register their plant varieties. Thus, the Act makes different types of rights available to the various actors who participate in the Indian agricultural sector. These include commercial plant breeders, scientific researchers, and local farmers.

While some of these protections resemble those that are embodied in standard models of intellectual property for plants, the Act also creates alternative, *sui generis* mechanisms for the realisation of its goals. In so doing, the Indian regime grants intellectual property for diverse categories of plant varieties, including new varieties, EDVs, and different types of extant varieties, including farmers' varieties. While the kind of commercial exclusivity that the law offers might incentivise breeders – of all types, including farmers – to develop new plant varieties for the market, the Act also contains provisions that are designed to safeguard customary agricultural practices. As such, farmers are guaranteed the right to save, use, sow, re-sow, exchange, share or sell their farm produce, including the seeds of breeders' new varieties.

Evidence suggests that since the implementation of the *Protection of Plant Varieties and Farmers' Rights Act* in 2007, the Indian system of intellectual property for plant varieties has yielded some benefits for different actors in the national agricultural sector. For instance, to date the PPV&FRA has granted thousands of plant variety rights certificates, which have been awarded to all of the major stakeholders groups in India, including especially public research organisations, private seed companies, and individual farmers and farming groups. Likewise, the PPV&FRA has utilised the National Gene Fund to reward hundreds of farmers who have contributed to the conservation, development, and availability of plant genetic diversity in India.

While these achievements are laudable, several challenges continue to impede the full realisation of the aims of the *Protection of Plant Varieties and Farmers' Rights Act*. For instance, there is an enduring need to ensure that Indian farmers are able to derive tangible benefits from the registration of their plant varieties. This challenge could be overcome by establishing programmes through which professional plant breeders and farmers could collaborate in participatory plant breeding projects. When these initiatives result in new varieties that are commercialised, farmers should be entitled to share in any monetary and/or non-monetary benefits that the projects generate.

Likewise, some form of institutional support should be envisaged and offered by the government or other actors to help farmers to develop commercialisation strategies for their varieties, and to become self-reliant in the production and supply of quality seeds. To be effective, these systems of support should also incorporate systematic assessments of both the agronomic performance of registered and commercial viability of farmers' varieties, in addition to the needs of farming communities in general. Lastly, it is essential that a more effective partnership between the PPV&FRA and the Central Seed Committee be established. The purpose of this collaboration would be to develop streamlined procedures through which farmers' varieties could be both protected as intellectual property and notified under the *Seeds Act, 1966 (Act No. 54 of 1966)*. It is hoped that doing so would enable farmers' varieties to be commercialised more widely in India.

In its 2016 *National Intellectual Property Rights Policy*, the Government of India indicated that the large volume of filings and registrations of new and extant varieties (including farmers' varieties) should be interpreted as a positive signal. Furthermore, this Policy stipulated that the PPV&FRA should endeavour to facilitate the development of seeds and the commercialisation of farmers' plant varieties. Another recommendation was that the Authority should establish collaborations with universities, research and breeding institutes, technology development and management centres, and *Krishi Vigyan Kendras.*

This recent articulation of the national strategy for the use of intellectual property for plant varieties highlights that a framework that supports the protection of different categories of plant varieties already exists in India. However, the Policy also demonstrates that in certain ways, the country's extant plant variety protection regime is limited. It is therefore hoped that the PPV&FRA will work to address the challenges described in the present chapter, towards the end of more effectively protecting the rights of diverse actors in the national agricultural sector.

Chapter 6

Policy, politics, and implications of Pakistan's *Plant Breeders' Rights Act*

Muhammad Ahsan Rana and Kamalesh Adhikari

6.1 Introduction

Pakistan joined the World Trade Organization in January 1995, and pursuant to the *Agreement on Trade-Related Aspects of Intellectual Property Rights* (TRIPS), the country was required to establish a system to protect plant varieties as intellectual property by January 2000. According to the terms of Article 27.3(b) of the TRIPS Agreement, this protection could take the form of patents, a *sui generis* system, or both. Because local stakeholders rejected patents as a form of intellectual property for plant varieties,[1] in 1999 the Pakistani government prepared a draft *sui generis* plant variety protection law, known as the *Plant Breeders' Rights Ordinance*. This draft Ordinance was based essentially on the model embodied in the 1991 Act (UPOV 1991) of the *International Convention for the Protection of New Varieties of Plants* (UPOV Convention).[2] Although Pakistan was not a member of UPOV – a fact that remains true today – lawmakers used UPOV 1991 as a template following lobbying by domestic and international seed industries. These interests promoted the UPOV Convention model as a vehicle for the expansion of the national market for improved seeds in Pakistan.

In contrast to the private seed industry, some civil society groups, including the Islamabad-based Sustainable Development Policy Institute,[3] argued against the enactment of the 1999 *Plant Breeders' Rights Ordinance*. These groups criticised the draft Ordinance for its failure to address the needs of Pakistani farmers who

1 This decision is evidenced in the Pakistani *Patents Ordinance, 2000*, which expressly excludes plants from the scope of patentability. *Patents Ordinance, 2000* of Pakistan. Article 7(4)(b). Accessed May 24 2019. www.wipo.int/edocs/lexdocs/laws/en/pk/pk001en.pdf

2 For a detailed discussion on the UPOV Convention model, see Chapter 2 in this volume.

3 The Sustainable Development Policy Institute is ranked among the top global think tanks by the 'The Think Tanks and Civil Societies Program (TTCSP)' of the Lauder Institute at the University of Pennsylvania. See McGann, J. G. 2019. '2018 Global Go To Think Tank Index Report.' *TTCSP Global Go To Think Tank Index Reports*. Philadelphia: The Lauder Institute, The University of Pennsylvania. Accessed May 27 2019. https://repository.upenn.edu/cgi/viewcontent.cgi?article=1017&context=think_tanks

mostly rely on traditional agricultural systems. Specifically, civil society actors were concerned that the framework did not enable farmers to protect their locally cultivated varieties, and that it did not permit farmers to save, use, exchange, share, and sell the seeds of protected breeders' plant varieties.[4] Due at least in part to the tension between the private seed industry and civil society groups, the Pakistani Parliament did not pass the draft Ordinance.

It took nearly 17 years of public and parliamentary debates for a *sui generis* intellectual property law for plant varieties to be passed in Pakistan. The regime, entitled the *Plant Breeders' Rights Act*, was finally approved by the Parliament in September 2016. As of May 2019, the Pakistani government was still developing a set of rules and regulations to implement the Act, which will ultimately fulfil the country's obligations under the TRIPS Agreement. To facilitate the process of implementing the Act, in April 2019, the Pakistani government appointed the Director General of the Federal Seed Certification and Registration Department (FSC&RD) to hold the position of Registrar of the Plant Breeders' Rights Registry for a transition period of three months. It is expected that following the conclusion of this interim period, a full-time Registrar will be appointed. The prospective full-time Registrar will likely oversee the development of rules and regulations to give effect to the *Plant Breeders' Rights Act* in the near future.

As is common in the plant variety protection or plant variety rights laws of other countries, the 2016 *Plant Breeders' Rights Act* of Pakistan grants a set of exclusive rights that plant breeders can exercise to produce, reproduce, and commercialise newly bred or developed and discovered plant varieties. This means that the free circulation of novel plant varieties that are protected under the law will be restricted, a fact that will undoubtedly transform the nature of Pakistani agriculture. Historically, farming in Pakistan has been characterised by the unrestricted sharing of the germplasm of all kinds of plant varieties, including varieties bred by public sector institutions, varieties that have traditionally been cultivated by farmers, and varieties that were developed or imported by private seed firms.[5] Thus, it is likely that the implementation of the Act will have wide-ranging implications for diverse actors in the Pakistani agricultural sector, including private companies, public institutions, and local farming communities.

4 Suleri, A. Q. and Q. Shah. 2003. 'Trade-Related Aspects of Intellectual Property Rights (TRIPs) Agreement: Impact on Food Security of the People Living in HKH.' *Policy Brief Series Number 17.* Islamabad: The Sustainable Development Policy Institute. Accessed May 24 2019. www.sdpi.org/publications/files/PB17-Trade-Related%20Aspects%20of%20Intellectual%20Property%20Rights.pdf

5 Rana, M. A., D. J. Spielman, and Z. Fatima. 2016. 'The Architecture of the Pakistani Seed Industry: A Case of Market-Regulation Dissonance.' In *Agriculture and the Rural Economy in Pakistan: Issues, Outlooks, and Policy Priorities*, edited by D. J. Spielman, S. J. Malik, P. Dorosh, and N. Ahmad. Philadelphia: University of Pennsylvania Press on behalf of the International Food Policy Research Institute (IFPRI), pages 171–218.

The objective of the chapter is to analyse both the legal provisions and the political dimensions of the Pakistani *Plant Breeders' Rights Act*. Furthermore, the chapter explores the potential implications that the implementation of the law could have for diverse actors in the Pakistani agricultural sector, including private companies, public institutions, and local farming communities. In so doing, the chapter also aims to identify and discuss areas of convergence and divergence between the *Plant Breeders' Rights Act* and the national system of seed regulation in Pakistan, namely the 2015 *Seed (Amendment) Act* (2015 Seed Act). First introduced in 1976, the Pakistani Seed Act (1976 Seed Act) sets comprehensive standards for the release and registration of plant varieties, including the certification, production, and marketing of the seeds of registered plant varieties. Hence, the intersections and tensions between the *Plant Breeders' Rights Act* and the 2015 Seed Act may affect the interests of both breeders and farmers, while also having implications for national food security in Pakistan.

Following this introductory section, the chapter is divided into six sections. Section 6.2 traces the history of the Pakistani seed sector, describing the role that public and private institutions have played in the development and commercialisation of improved plant varieties in the country. This discussion also examines the nature of customary seed management practices, and the role that these and other seed transaction practices that have not been officially sanctioned play in the national seed economy. Section 6.3 analyses the politics of the implementation and oversight of the *Plant Breeders' Rights Act* in Pakistan. Section 6.4 explores the salient features of the Act, evaluating the ways in which the Pakistani framework is similar to or distinct from UPOV 1991. Section 6.5 discusses the possible implications that the *Plant Breeders' Rights Act* could have for different actors in the national seed economy, including public institutions, private industry, and local farming communities. Section 6.6 discusses areas of intersections and tensions between the 2016 *Plant Breeders' Rights Act* and the 2015 Seed Act. Section 6.7 concludes the chapter.

6.2 The history of the Pakistani seed sector

After Pakistan became independent following the end of the British Raj in 1947, the Lyallpur-based Punjab Agricultural College and Research Institute assumed control of research and development activities whose purpose was to breed new plant varieties for food production in Pakistan. Established by British colonists in 1906 as the first major institute of higher agricultural education in the then-undivided Punjab, the Institute was already endowed with a substantial research and development infrastructure, including crop-specific experimental stations. However, the young country lacked the adequate policies and governmental systems to register, approve, and disseminate new plant varieties. Thus, plant breeders working at the Punjab Agricultural College and Research Institute initially played a minor role in national seed provision.

Instead, farmers relied on customary practices of seed production and circulation to meet their food security needs.[6]

Later, in the 1960s, Pakistan began to promote agricultural research towards the end of crop varietal development and seed production through the establishment of a number of public institutions. For example, the Ayub Agricultural Research Institute was founded to pursue plant breeding, while the West Pakistan Agricultural Development Corporation was created to spearhead seed production. These institutions, in collaboration with the Mexico-based International Maize and Wheat Improvement Centre and the Philippines-based International Rice Research Institute, developed and disseminated numerous new varieties of wheat and rice in Pakistan throughout the decade.[7] In 1965, the Pakistani Parliament introduced the country's first seed law, namely *The West Pakistan Seeds and Fruit Plants Ordinance*. This Ordinance was enacted for the purpose of providing a system of registration for growers who would produce certified seeds, and to establish nurseries for plant propagation.[8] However, the limited scope of the Ordinance failed to address the burgeoning needs of the public seed sector, for example, in relation to new variety registration, seed certification, and the marketing and sale of new seeds.

In recognition of these policy limitations, in the 1970s, Pakistan launched a comprehensive seed industry project, with assistance from the World Bank. This initiative was designed to undertake a detailed review of the country's national seed system, including seed certification, and the development, breeding, and registration of new plant varieties.[9] One of the major outcomes of the Pakistani seed industry project was the drafting and enactment of the 1976 Seed Act. As the first comprehensive modern seed law of Pakistan, the 1976 Seed Act enumerated procedures for plant breeding, variety registration, seed production, seed certification, and seed sales and marketing. The Act also led to the formation of Seed Councils at federal and provincial levels, and to the creation of the FSC&RD, which henceforth became responsible for variety registration and seed certification in Pakistan.[10]

The 1976 Seed Act was passed at a time when public institutions were the primary actors engaging in agricultural research, plant breeding, and the development and circulation of new crop varieties in Pakistan.[11] Meanwhile, the role of

6 Ali, I. and S. M. Ali. 2004. 'A Note on the Seed Business in Pakistan.' Class Note prepared for the Lahore University of Management Sciences. Accessed May 24 2019. www.policy.hu/ali/LUMS%20paper%20on%20the%20seed%20industry.pdf

7 Nabi, I., N. Hamid, and Z. Shahid. 1986. *The Agrarian Economy of Pakistan: Issues and Politics*. Karachi: Oxford University Press.

8 *The West Pakistan Seeds and Fruit Plants Ordinance, 1965*. Preamble and Section 4.

9 Rana, M. A. 2014. 'The Seed Industry in Pakistan: Regulation, Politics, and Entrepreneurship.' *ReSAKSS Policy Note 16*. Washington, D.C.: International Food Policy Research Institute (IFPRI). Accessed May 24 2019. http://ebrary.ifpri.org/cdm/ref/collection/p15738coll2/id/128882

10 *Seed Act 1976* of Pakistan (1976 Seed Act). Sections 3, 5, and 9.

11 Spielman, D. J., H. Nazli, X. Ma, P. Zambrano, and F. Zaidi. 2014. 'Technological Opportunity, Regulatory Uncertainty, and the Economics of Bt Cotton in Pakistan.' *PSSP Working*

the private sector in the 1970s was limited to seed multiplication on private land, and the sale of improved seeds to local farmers. However, following the market liberalisation measures that Pakistan adopted in the 1980s, the role of the private sector extended from multiplication and sale of improved seeds, to include also plant breeding and crop varietal development. The first Pakistani seed company was registered formally in 1981,[12] while other domestic firms were established in the next few years. Four multinational seed companies also commenced operations in Pakistan in the 1980s. These multinational firms established local affiliates to participate in the national market, which were Monsanto Pakistan Agritech Private Limited, ICI Pakistan Limited, Pioneer Pakistan Seeds Limited, and Syngenta Pakistan Limited. By 1994, the seed trade was recognised formally as an industry in Pakistan.[13] As of May 2019, 878 seed companies, of which five were multinational corporations, had been registered with the FSC&RD.[14]

One of the primary impacts that the enhanced participation of private seed entities has had in the Pakistani seed economy is that the public sector – which used to operate as the main provider of certified seeds in the country – has been relegated to a marginal role. As shown in Table 6.1, most certified seeds today are produced locally. The public sector provides only 16 percent of certified seeds and 5 percent of the total national seed requirement. Importation is an important source of certified seeds, but only for maize (hybrid varieties), vegetable crops, and feed crops. The certified seeds of these imported varieties are expensive, but adoption by farmers has been strong notwithstanding the high costs. The availability of certified seeds varies substantially from one crop species to another, ranging from a low of 1.8 percent of the official estimated seed requirement for potato, to 105 percent for rice and 141 percent for vegetable crops. Overall, certified seeds provide a mere 33 percent of the national seed requirement, which means that the remainder is sourced through customary, as well as unofficial seed transaction practices.

In Pakistan, customary seed management practices include farmer-to-farmer seed exchange on a non-commercial basis; small-scale sale among farmers; and seed saving and replanting in subsequent growing seasons.[15] The practices of

Paper 25. Washington, D.C.: International Food Policy Research Institute (IFPRI). Accessed May 24 2019. http://ebrary.ifpri.org/cdm/ref/collection/p15738coll2/id/128681

12 Sarwar, M. B. 2007. *Formal and Informal Seed Supply System in Pakistan: A Perspective for Farmers' Seed Rights*. Islamabad: Federal Seed Certification and Registration Department (FSC&RD), Ministry of Food Security and Research, Government of Pakistan.

13 Ali and Ali, note 6.

14 Data collected from the office of the FSC&RD. See also *The Nation*. 2018. 'Seed Certification, Registration to be Enhanced.' *The Nation*. Accessed May 27 2019. https://nation.com.pk/07-Sep-2018/seed-certification-registration-to-be-enhanced (stating that as of September 2018, about 800 private seed companies were already operating in Pakistan).

15 Rana, note 9; See also Sarwar, note 12.

Table 6.1 Availability of certified seeds in Pakistan (2016–2017) (metric tonnes)

Crop	*Total seed requirement*	*Certified seed availability*				*Certified seed as % of total seed requirement*
		Local		*Imported*	*Total*	
		Public	*Private*			
Wheat	1,085,400	86,200	335,415	-	421,615	38.8
Cotton	40,000	687	28,677	-	29,364	73.4
Rice	44,800	3,322	43,097	619	47,038	105.0*
Maize	33,270	656	17,078	9,302	27,036	81.3
Pulses	47,496	704	2,436	-	3,140	6.6
Oilseed	10,582	3	529	99	631	6.0
Vegetables	5,570	96	874	6,872	7,842	140.8*
Fodders	40,138	5	7	16,054	16,066	40.0
Potatoes	372,725	-	-	6,839	6,839	1.8
Total	1,679,981	91,673	428,112	39,785	559,569	33.3

Source: Ministry of Finance. 2018. *Pakistan Economic Survey 2016–17*. Islamabad: Ministry of Finance, Government of Pakistan.

* These numbers indicate an underestimation of the requirement of the seeds of rice and vegetables in official data.

farmer-to-farmer seed exchange on a non-commercial basis and small-scale seed sale among farmers are common in Pakistan. However, these practices account for a small fraction of the total national seed requirement. This means that seed saving is the customary practice that most significantly contributes to ensure that farmers in Pakistan have the seeds that they require from one growing season to another.

The practice of seed saving is ancestral and well established among Pakistani farmers. The proportion of seeds that a given farmer will save from a given harvest depends on several factors, including the type of seed (open pollinated or hybrid), farm size, the availability and capacity of storage facilities, the presence of crop diseases, pest or other abiotic stressors, and farmers' knowledge and preferences. The proportion of farm-saved seeds also varies from one crop species to another. For example, wheat seeds may only be replaced every three to four years, while rice seeds may be replaced every year. Furthermore, it is common for farmers to purchase new seeds from seed markets to replace varieties that have fallen out of favour or that have become unproductive, and to replenish seed stocks that have deteriorated due to contamination or other factors.

In addition to these customary seed management practices, the unofficial, medium-to-large-scale sale of uncertified seeds also plays an important role in supplying seeds to Pakistani farmers. Uncertified seeds are those which are provided by seed companies, breeders, agricultural input dealers, and other members of the value chain (e.g., cotton ginners and sugar mills), whether in branded or unbranded form. These providers operate without official sanction, that is, they sell seeds that have not been certified by the FSC&RD. The quality of uncertified seeds is variable, and thus performance may or may not be comparable to that of certified seeds. Since the providers of uncertified seeds also regularly supply certified seeds, they may operate simultaneously in regulated and unregulated seed markets.[16]

Lastly, it should be noted that today, both public and private actors play a key role in developing new crop varieties in Pakistan. In the public sector, government research institutions and universities oversee long-standing variety development programmes. These initiatives have been responsible for the release and registration of numerous important crop varieties from several species, including wheat, rice, maize, barley, cotton, pulses, oilseeds, fodders, vegetables, and fruits. As of October 2018, a total of 776 varieties of these crops had been approved for commercial cultivation in Pakistan.[17] In addition to these registered varieties, an unknown number of unregistered crop varieties, including several varieties of genetically modified, insect-resistant cotton, has also been commercialised by plant breeders and seed traders working at public and private institutions.[18]

6.3 The politics of the implementation and oversight of the *Plant Breeders' Rights Act*

As described in the introductory section of this chapter, opposition between the seed industry and civil society groups was one factor that delayed the enactment of the *Plant Breeders' Rights Act* in Pakistan for nearly 17 years. However, there were also other factors that contributed to the slow pace of lawmaking in the country. Among these was the political wrangling that occurred between various actors inside the Pakistani federal government, towards the end of controlling the implementation and oversight of the 2016 *Plant Breeders' Rights Act.*

For example, one of the key challenges that officials faced during the making of the *Plant Breeders' Rights Act* was to obtain separate approvals from the legislatures of the four provinces and two autonomous territories of the country to allow the federal government to legislate the issue of plant breeders' rights. The reason for this is that according to the Pakistani Constitution, agriculture is an area that falls under provincial jurisdiction, i.e., only provincial governments can enact and enforce laws on matters concerning agriculture. In contrast, intellectual property is an issue for which the federal government is responsible. Because plant breeders' rights concern both agriculture and intellectual property, confusion existed over which level of government – i.e., federal or provincial – had the authority to establish and oversee the system of plant breeders' rights.

16 Ibid.

17 Ali, M. A. 2018. 'Seed System in Pakistan: Standards and Procedures.' Paper presented at the International Rice Training Workshop for Agriculture Professionals, Islamabad, October 2. Accessed May 24 2019. www.slideshare.net/anjumalibuttar/seed-system-in-pakistan-standards-and-procedures

18 Rana, et al., note 5.

The strategy that the federal government employed involved seeking and obtaining approval from the various provincial authorities under Article 144 of the Constitution of Pakistan. This constitutional provision allows the provincial assemblies to surrender their regulatory powers to the federal government in relation to matters not enumerated in the Federal Legislative List, including agriculture.[19] However, in such instances, the provincial assemblies retain the authority to annul or amend any federal legislation that relates to the provincial matter that was delegated. It took time for the federal government to obtain approvals from all of the provincial governments, such that it was only in early 2016 that all of the necessary resolutions were passed to enable the enactment of the *Plant Breeders' Rights Act* as a federal law.

Another political challenge that Pakistani lawmakers faced was the need to navigate tensions between two different government departments, each of which claimed that the soon-to-be-established Plant Breeders' Rights Registry should fall under its authority. One department was the FSC&RD, which had spearheaded the making of a national system of plant breeders' rights since the drafting of the 1999 *Plant Breeders' Rights Ordinance*. Furthermore, the FSC&RD had accrued decades of experience regulating similar subject matter, as the authority responsible for overseeing plant variety registration and seed certification under the 1976 Seed Act.

Meanwhile, the Pakistani Intellectual Property Organisation (IPO) also laid claim to the Plant Breeders' Rights registry. The IPO was established in 2005 as an autonomous body whose mandate is to manage all of the local intellectual property offices in Pakistan. This agency asserted that as the principal institution responsible for managing all matters related to intellectual property in the country, it was the natural home for the Plant Breeders' Rights Registry. The FSC&RD countered this argument by declaring that the Registry would be a natural extension of its long-established seed registration programme. Furthermore, the FSC&RD claimed that it already had the necessary infrastructure, expertise, institutional knowledge, and linkages with breeding institutes to manage the Registry effectively and efficiently.

The dispute between the IPO and the FSC&RD lasted for over a decade. In 2007, the federal cabinet declared that the Plant Breeders' Rights Registry would be housed at the IPO. The FSC&RD opposed this decision, as it understood that to lose oversight of the Plant Breeders' Rights Registry meant that it would not have access to the resources and authority that the manager of the Registry would control. In other words, without the Registry, the FSC&RD would exist as an agency for plant variety registration and seed certification only, and not for the

19 The Seed Act was passed in 1976 as a federal law with the intent to harmonise seed sector legislation across all of the provinces of Pakistan. This was only possible because all of the four provincial assemblies previously had passed resolutions under Article 144 of the *Constitution of the Islamic Republic of Pakistan*, thus allowing the federal government to legislate on seed matters.

recognition and enforcement of the rights of breeders, farmers or other stakeholders. Thus, the FSC&RD continued to pursue its claim to the Plant Breeders' Rights Registry within federal governmental channels. Ultimately, the efforts expended by the FSC&RD paid off, when in 2015 the federal cabinet reversed its 2007 decision. This meant that the FSC&RD gained oversight over the Registry, and that the federal government could finally approve the *Plant Breeders' Rights Act* in 2016.

6.4 Key features of the Pakistani *Plant Breeders' Rights Act*

The 2016 *Plant Breeders' Rights Act* aims to 'encourage the development of new plant varieties and to protect the rights of breeders of such varieties.'[20] For this purpose, the Act creates a Plant Breeders' Rights Registry to be housed in the federal Ministry of National Food Security and Research, which is the institution that supervises the FSC&RD.[21] As of May 2019, the *Plant Breeders' Rights Act* had not yet been implemented, and therefore the Registry had not begun to receive applications for plant breeders' rights. Once established, the Registry will perform several tasks, including the registration of new plant varieties and the issuance of plant breeders' rights certificates.[22] The Registry will be managed by a Registrar, whom the federal government will appoint. The Registrar will be an important government official, responsible for performing multiple functions including overseeing the concession of plant breeders' rights certificates.[23]

The 2016 *Plant Breeders' Rights Act* provides that any person may apply to the Registrar for the protection of his/her variety if it is novel, distinct, uniform and stable,[24] and has an acceptable denomination.[25] A variety is novel if it has not been sold in Pakistan for more than one year or in a foreign country for more than four years (six years for vines and trees). A variety is distinct if it differs from varieties of common knowledge by one or more identifiable morphological, physiological, or other characteristics. Lastly, the criteria of uniformity and stability are met where the plants of a variety are sufficiently uniform in their essential characteristics, and where they do not segregate in subsequent propagation. The FSC&RD is responsible for evaluating distinctness, uniformity, and stability, and breeders who apply for protection must submit to the FSC&RD a sufficient quantity of the propagating material of the new variety along with their plant breeders' rights application.[26]

In addition to new plant varieties, essentially derived varieties (EDVs) can be protected under the Pakistani *Plant Breeders' Rights Act.* The Act defines an EDV as a variety derived from a protected variety, which retains the expression of the

20 The *Plant Breeders' Rights Act, 2016* of Pakistan (Act No. L of 2016). Preamble.
21 Ibid, Section 3.
22 Ibid, Section 4.
23 Ibid, Section 6.
24 Ibid, Section 11.
25 Ibid, Section 12.
26 Ibid, Section 16.

essential characteristics of the original variety but is clearly distinguishable.[27] Criteria for how to determine whether an EDV retains the essential characteristics of the initial variety are not specified in the Act, nor are any standards based on which to assess whether the difference between the two varieties is significant or cosmetic. Nevertheless, the Act does elaborate a set of exclusive rights that breeders can exercise over their protected plant varieties, including EDVs. These rights include offering for sale, selling, and marketing; importing and exporting; conditioning or multiplying; and authorising others to produce, sell, market or 'otherwise deal with' a protected variety.[28]

This enumeration of the rights that owners of plant breeders' rights certificates may exercise in relation to protected varieties is consistent with UPOV 1991. For this reason, it is commonly believed that the 2016 *Plant Breeders' Rights Act* is nothing more than a recapitulation of the UPOV Convention model.[29] However, this is not entirely true. The Pakistani plant breeders' rights legislation diverges from UPOV Convention template for a number of reasons. Of these, six are especially noteworthy, as described in subsections 6.4.1 to 6.4.6.

6.4.1 Exception to the requirement of novelty to protect certain extant varieties

In addition to granting rights in relation to new plant varieties, the 2016 *Plant Breeders' Rights Act* contains a mechanism through which extant plant varieties that have been previously registered and released or commercialised in Pakistan may also be protected. This is possible under the Act because these extant varieties are exempted from meeting the requirement of novelty.[30] Although the rationale behind this exception is not mentioned explicitly in the law, it is likely that the intention is to provide intellectual property protection for varieties that have been registered and released or commercialised under the 1976 Seed Act. If a plant breeders' rights application for the registration of an extant variety is successful, the term of the protection will be reduced by the number of years that have elapsed between the registration of the variety under the 1976 Seed Act and the application under the *Plant Breeders' Rights Act.*

6.4.2 Additional requirements for the protection of genetically modified varieties

In addition to all of the other criteria described earlier, the 2016 *Plant Breeders' Rights Act* contains additional requirements for the protection of genetically modified varieties. These include the submission of a certificate from the National Biosafety Committee, which must accompany any application for plant breeders'

27 Ibid, Section 2(x).
28 Ibid, Section 22.
29 For example, see Sadaf, N. 2018. 'Legislative Developments in the Protection of Plant Breeders' Rights in Pakistan.' *IIC-International Review of Intellectual Property and Competition Law* 49 (6): 700–713.
30 The *Plant Breeders' Rights Act, 2016* of Pakistan (Act No. L of 2016). Section 42.

rights that claims a genetically modified plant variety. The purpose of this provision is to certify that the genetically modified variety will not lead to 'any adverse effect on the environment, human, animal or plant life and health.'[31] Furthermore, applicants for plant breeders' rights must submit a declaration that the new variety 'does not contain any gene or gene sequence involving terminator technology.'[32]

6.4.3 Protections for farmers

The protection of new plant varieties under the 2016 *Plant Breeders' Rights Act* grants exclusive commercial exploitation rights to plant breeders, but these rights are subject to certain exceptions that are not commonly found in laws modelled on UPOV 1991. For example, the Pakistani *Plant Breeders' Rights Act* does not authorise the owners of protected plant varieties to prevent farmers from saving, using, sowing, re-sowing, exchanging, sharing, or selling their farm produce.[33] Furthermore, the Act does not permit the owners of protected plant varieties to prohibit 'any exchange of propagating materials among farmers.'[34] The only way in which farmers' use of protected varieties' varieties is limited under the Act is that farmers may not sell the seeds of these varieties on a commercial basis.

6.4.4 Creation of a system for compulsory licensing

The 2016 *Plant Breeders' Rights Act* establishes a framework for compulsory licensing, which can be used to allow third parties to exploit breeders' protected varieties under certain circumstances. For example, the Registrar of the Plant Breeders' Rights Registry is empowered to issue a compulsory licence to a third party if doing so is required to protect the public interest, including public health and nutritional security.[35] The Registrar also can grant a compulsory license to a third party if the owner of a protected breeders' variety engages in anti-competitive practices, or fails to supply adequate quantities of seeds or other propagating material at a reasonable price.[36]

6.4.5 Recognition of access and benefit sharing principles

As discussed in several other chapters of this volume, access and benefit sharing principles are an important feature of both the 1995 *Convention on Biological Diversity* (CBD) and the 2001 *International Treaty on Plant Genetic Resources for Food and Agriculture* (the Plant Treaty). However, these principles are absent

31 Ibid, Section 15.
32 Ibid, Section 15(c).
33 Ibid, Section 25(d).
34 Ibid, Section 25(e).
35 Ibid, Section 33.
36 Ibid.

from standard models of intellectual property for plant varieties. The TRIPS Agreement and the UPOV Convention do not require applicants for intellectual property to adhere to any access and benefit sharing obligations related to the use of plant genetic resources. As a result, various concerns have been raised in relation to the 'unauthorised' access and/or the 'free' use of genetic resources by breeders of new plant varieties.[37] Meanwhile, as a member of the CBD, the Plant Treaty, and the 2010 *Nagoya Protocol on Access to Genetic Resources and the Fair and Equitable Sharing of Benefits Arising from the Utilization* (which is a supplementary agreement to the CBD), Pakistan has assumed obligations to implement laws to recognise the principles of access and benefit sharing.

As a means to synthesise these principles with Pakistan's obligations under the TRIPS Agreement, the 2016 *Plant Breeders' Rights Act* establishes criteria that applicants for plant breeders' rights must meet in relation to the access and use of plant genetic resources. For example, the Act requires applicants for plant breeders' rights to submit evidence that written consent has been obtained from 'the authority representing public sector, private sector or the local community in cases where the plant variety is developed from traditional varieties.'[38] In so doing, the Act also mandates that applicants provide 'documents relating to the compliance of any law regulating access to genetic or biological resources' in Pakistan.[39]

Furthermore, in a separate section on 'Benefit Sharing,' the Pakistani *Plant Breeders' Rights Act* enables relevant stakeholders to file a claim for benefit sharing in cases where a breeder has developed a new plant variety using their plant genetic material. These stakeholders could be individuals or groups of people that are citizens of Pakistan, or private firms, governmental institutions, or non-governmental organisations.[40]

6.4.6 Disclosure requirements

As a means to implement the principles of access and benefit sharing and to ensure that the novelty criterion is met, the 2016 *Plant Breeders' Rights Act* requires applicants for plant breeders' rights to submit 'complete identification data of the parental lines from which the variety has been derived' with their application.[41] In so doing, the Act also obligates breeders to disclose the geographical origin of the source genetic material 'setting forth its novelty, percentage or pedigree, breeding history and a drawing or photograph to understand and evaluate the novelty of the variety.'[42]

37 Adhikari, K. 2018. 'Reconceptualising Access: Moving Beyond the Limits of International Biodiversity Laws.' In *Biodiversity, Genetic Resources and Intellectual Property: Developments in Access and Benefit Sharing,* edited by C. Lawson and K. Adhikari. Abingdon: Routledge, pages 9–32.

38 The *Plant Breeders' Rights Act, 2016* of Pakistan (Act No. L of 2016). Section 15(g).

39 Ibid, Section 15(h).

40 Ibid, Sections 32(2)(a) and 32(2)(b).

41 Ibid, Section 15(f).

42 Ibid, Section 15(f).

Furthermore, unlike standard models for plant breeders' rights laws, the Pakistani regime requires private sector plant breeders to submit a certificate or affidavit as evidence for whether the claimed variety was developed using breeding material from any public sector institution.[43] Although the rationale behind this provision is unclear, in practice it will likely affect benefit sharing arrangements between private breeders who claim intellectual property for new plant varieties, and any public sector breeders who developed the parental lines on which the claimed varieties are based.

6.5 Possible implications of the Pakistani *Plant Breeders' Rights Act*

Similar to standardised models of intellectual property for plant varieties, the primary objective of the 2016 *Plant Breeders' Rights Act* is to encourage the development of new varieties. A secondary but related goal is to create an enabling environment for the creation of new varieties, by granting exclusive commercial exploitation rights to plant breeders, including to produce, reproduce, and market the seeds of the varieties that they develop. These rights are understood to function as an incentive to promote investments in plant varietal improvement. Given these aims, it is likely that once implemented, the Pakistani *Plant Breeders' Rights Act* will have numerous implications for both public and private actors in the national agricultural sector, including local farming communities.

For plant breeders – including those working in both the public and private sectors – and farmers alike, one potential implication that the law could have is the creation of incentives to make 'high quality seeds and planting material' more widely available. The hope is that the proliferation of new plant varieties would help to ensure 'food security,' and to establish 'a viable seed industry' in Pakistan.[44] However, it is notable that the incentives that the law creates for breeders differ depending on whether these individuals are situated in the private or the public sector. This is a unique aspect of the Pakistani framework in comparison to standard plant breeders' rights regimes, including the UPOV Convention.

Where new plant varieties are developed by actors working in the private sector, both the individual breeder or his/her employer institution are entitled to apply for plant breeders' rights, subject to any contractual obligations that may structure their relationship to one another.[45] In contrast, where new varieties are developed in public sector institutions, only the institution itself may apply for plant breeders' rights.[46] In other words, the law requires individual plant breeders working in the public sector to assign their intellectual property rights to their employer institution.

43 Ibid, Section 13(8).
44 Ibid, Preamble.
45 Ibid, Section 13(7).
46 Ibid, Section 13(5).

To counter the argument that this situation could discourage plant breeders working in the public sector to innovate, the 2016 *Plant Breeders' Rights Act* creates a 'Research Incentive Board' designed to create incentives for public sector breeders.[47] Furthermore, the Act stipulates that public sector plant breeders are entitled to a minimum royalty rate of 40 percent of any income generated from the commercialisation of protected varieties that these breeders develop.[48] Furthermore, the Act provides that breeders who formerly worked in the public sector may apply for plant breeders' rights as individuals five years after they retire or leave government service.[49]

Plant breeders working in the public and private sectors alike also could benefit from the fact that the 2016 *Plant Breeders' Rights Act* enables intellectual property to be granted for certain extant varieties that previously have been registered and released or commercialised under the 1976 Seed Act. However, the *Plant Breeders' Rights Act* allows for only a short transition period during which plant breeders could benefit from this provision. Specifically, the *Plant Breeders' Rights Act* requires any applications that claim plant breeders' rights for extant varieties to be filed within two years of the implementation of the Act.

Although the Pakistani *Plant Breeders' Rights Act* aims to protect extant plant varieties that previously have been registered and released or commercialised under the 1976 Seed Act, the law does not recognise any similar form of protection for varieties that are cultivated and developed in farmers' fields. It is possible that the absence of protections for farmers' plant varieties in the Act could jeopardise the vitality of farmers' seed systems, including customary practices for the management of seeds and other planting material. Furthermore, to date no detailed study has been conducted to assess the possible implications that granting intellectual property for new and existing plant varieties (including genetically modified varieties and EDVs) would have for Pakistani farmers, or for their ancestral practices of seed saving, replanting, exchange, and local sale.

Despite these concerns, it should be noted that the *Plant Breeders' Rights Act* does contain other types of protections for Pakistani farmers. For example, the Act creates the obligation that plant breeders obtain written consent from farmers (and other relevant stakeholders) to access and use farmers' plant varieties for the development of new varieties. The law also enables farmers to claim benefit sharing in cases where their varieties have been commercialised by plant breeders or other third parties. Furthermore, the Act prohibits the owners of protected varieties from impeding 'any exchange of propagating materials among farmers,' while also guaranteeing that farmers are permitted 'to save, use, sow, re-sow, exchange, share, or sell [their] farm produce.'[50] Lastly, although the Act prohibits farmers from selling the seeds of protected varieties on a commercial basis, it does not

47 Ibid, Section 45(1).
48 Ibid, Section 45(1).
49 Ibid, Section 13(6).
50 Ibid, Section 25(d).

restrict farmers from selling protected varieties on a non-commercial basis. It is likely that these farmer-friendly provisions will strengthen the customary farming practices of seed saving, use, exchange, and local sale in Pakistan. However, it should be reiterated that the *Plant Breeders' Rights Act* has not yet been implemented, and therefore its provisions remain subject to interpretation by future regulatory regimes.

While questions surrounding the possible implications of the 2016 *Plant Breeders' Rights Act* for Pakistani farmers are important, other stakeholders also have expressed concerns about the provisions of the law in several national workshops and seminars that were organised between 2016 and 2018. These stakeholders include actors representing both private and public interests in the Pakistani agricultural sector. For instance, the domestic seed industry, including the Seed Association of Pakistan, which is a group that represents numerous domestic seed companies, has expressed doubts about whether the Act can be implemented in a meaningful way. The national seed industry is concerned that the Pakistani government lacks both the willingness and the ability to protect plant breeders' rights effectively. Furthermore, domestic seed enterprises worry about the new legal obligations that the Act imposes on plant breeders. These include, for example, requirements related to access and benefit sharing for the use of certain plant genetic resources, and the guarantee that farmers may freely save, use, sow, re-sow, exchange, share, and sell the seeds of protected breeders' varieties.

Likewise, plant breeders working in the public sector also have expressed concerns about the possible impact of the *Plant Breeders' Rights Act* on publicly funded plant breeding and varietal development programmes. Furthermore, as with plant breeders working in the private sector, breeders employed in public institutions also worry about the new obligations that they will be required to fulfil in relation to the access and use of plant genetic resources. Lastly, public sector breeders have voiced concerns about their inability to claim intellectual property on an individual basis for new plant varieties that they develop, which has led to scepticism over whether they would actually benefit from protecting their varieties under the plant breeders' rights regime.

6.6 Areas of intersections and tensions between the *Plant Breeders' Rights Act* and the 1976 Seed Act

There are several areas in which the Pakistani *Plant Breeders' Rights Act* intersects – and in some instances, is in tension – with the national 1976 Seed Act. Furthermore, the prospective enforceability of the *Plant Breeders' Rights Act* depends at least in part on the effectiveness of the 1976 Seed Act. This is because the Pakistani seed market remains characterised largely by customary and unregulated seed management and transaction practices, even though the 1976 Seed Act has been in force for decades. For this reason, prior to exploring the intersections and tensions between the two frameworks, it is important to review the salient features of the 1976 Seed Act, and also of its 2015 amendment.

The stated purpose of the 1976 Seed Act is to control and regulate the quality of seeds that circulate in Pakistan.[51] To achieve this aim, the Act established a set of institutions; introduced procedures for registering new plant varieties and for producing seeds; and enumerated a series of actions that constitute violations of the law, and penalties for committing them. The Seed Act also created several new governmental institutions, including the FSC&RD and national and provincial Seed Councils. Following the implementation of the 1976 Seed Act, the National Seed Council became the institutional body responsible for setting national seed quality standards; regulating the interprovincial circulation of seeds; and advising the government on matters of seed policy.

To obtain registration under the 1976 Seed Act, the law requires the submission of a formal application to the FSC&RD. This application must contain information about the plant variety for which registration is sought, including a detailed description of its physiological and morphological characteristics, and of how it is distinct from other varieties.[52] The application must also propose a specific denomination for the new variety and be accompanied by a sufficient quantity of seeds to enable its evaluation. Upon receipt of an application, the FSC&RD conducts evaluation trials for two or more years at various research stations throughout the country, to assess the suitability of the variety for cultivation in different geographical areas.

Based on these trials, the FSC&RD determines whether it will recommend the variety for registration and submits advice to the Federal Seed Registration Committee, which makes a final decision. If the application is successful, the variety is granted a certificate of registration, which is valid for ten years from the date of issue and is renewable for a period of fewer than five years, except in the case of horticultural plants, whose registration may be extended for up to ten additional years. Upon registration, the name of the variety is entered into a register that is maintained by the FSC&RD. Once inscribed in the registry, the variety can be sold only under the name that it has been assigned. Lastly, the 1976 Seed Act provides a means through which the decisions of the Federal Seed Registration Committee may be contested, which involves an appeal that is heard by the National Seed Council.

The 1976 Seed Act was developed at a time when public institutions were responsible for a majority of the underlying activities that drove the operation of the Pakistani seed sector. However, as discussed earlier in this chapter, over the past several decades the nature of the national seed economy in Pakistan has changed, such that the role of the private sector has expanded while that of the public sector has contracted.[53] As this landscape evolved, the 1976 Seed Act and its accompanying institutional infrastructure became obsolete. The emergent

51 1976 Seed Act. Preamble.

52 Ibid, Section 13.

53 Rana, M. A. 2010. 'Formalising the Informal: The Commercialisation of Bt Cotton in Pakistan.' PhD diss., The University of Melbourne.

private seed industry found this regime to be restrictive, arguing that the law stifled the potential for innovation. Meanwhile, actors in the FSC&RD believed that the provisions of the 1976 Seed Act were no longer adequate to regulate the activities of the private seed sector, including the sale of uncertified seeds.[54]

In 2015, the Pakistani Parliament responded to the concerns that public and private actors in the national seed sector had expressed, by enacting a reform to the 1976 Seed Act. As amended, the Act envisages the enhanced participation of the private sector in seed production. The law allows private firms to establish laboratories for seed accreditation, and to produce basic seed, which under the former version of the law only public sector entities could do.[55] Simultaneously, the 2015 reform to the 1976 Seed Act aims to strengthen the regulatory capacity of the FSC&RD. Towards this objective, the law expressly prohibits the production, sale, or marketing of plant varieties that have not obtained formal approval, and of varieties that have been banned from cultivation in a particular area.[56]

The 2015 reform to the 1976 Seed Act further tightens the Pakistani seed sector by requiring any party that aspires to participate in the seed market to establish its own seed processing plant, or to register with the FSC&RD as a seed dealer.[57] These changes mean that today, no commercial seed sector activities are permitted to be undertaken in Pakistan without official sanction. Furthermore, it is notable that under the reformed 1976 Seed Act, variety registration must be renewed periodically. This implies an increase in the number of bureaucratic transactions that must be undertaken to commercialise seeds in Pakistan. Additionally, the 2015 amendment stipulates that registered dealers are the only entities permitted to sell seeds, which may only be displayed in properly labelled containers. The revised Act also prohibits the sale of 'misbranded' seeds, which it defines as any seed purporting to be what it is not.[58] Lastly, the 2015 amendment to the 1976 Seed Act introduces more severe penalties for violation of the law.[59]

Despite the various changes that the 2015 amendment to the 1976 Seed Act instantiates, there is concern that the revised law still may be an inadequate means to address the needs of the domestic seed sector. Several specific criticisms of the law have been launched. Foremost, according to the framework that the 2015 amendment erects, the regulation of the Pakistani seed sector is situated almost exclusively under the purview of the federal government. Meanwhile, the provincial governments have been relegated to a marginal role. This is problematic for

54 Spielman, D. J. and M. Smale. 2017. 'Policy Options to Accelerate Variety Change among Smallholder Farmers in South Asia and Africa South of the Sahara.' *IFPRI Discussion Paper 1666*. Washington, D.C.: International Food Policy Research Institute (IFPRI). Accessed May 24 2019. http://ebrary.ifpri.org/cdm/ref/collection/p15738coll2/id/131364
55 1976 Seed Act. Section 22(f).
56 Ibid, Section 11(2).
57 Ibid, Section 22(e).
58 Ibid, Section 22(e).
59 Ibid, Sections 23(i) and 23(ii).

two reasons. First, as discussed earlier in the chapter, under the Pakistani Constitution, agriculture is an area that is supposed to be overseen by the provinces. Second, and relatedly, the provincial governments are also responsible for regulating several areas that intersect substantially with agriculture, including research, extension, and water management, among others.

Another criticism of the 2015 amendment to the 1976 Seed Act is that the same basic regulatory procedures apply across all crops species, even though the nature of seed production differs substantially from one species to another. Furthermore, the reproductive biology of the crop matters, such that a different set of commercial incentives apply to the seeds of hybrids versus open-pollinated plants. A final factor is that seed saving is feasible for the repeated propagation of some crops – for instance open-pollinated species – and difficult in others, such as hybrids, whose performance is diminished significantly in subsequent generations. For these and other reasons, seed regulatory regimes should provide testing protocols that are tailored to the various crop species that are cultivated in the relevant territory.

A final concern that has been expressed about the 2015 amendment to the 1976 Seed Act is that the process of variety registration is unnecessarily lengthy and bureaucratic, while also failing to generate any significant benefits for the breeders of new plant varieties. This is because a variety that has been submitted for approval must still undergo at least two years of testing. Furthermore, even after a variety is registered under the reformed 1976 Seed Act, the breeders of that variety would not obtain any kind of exclusive commercial exploitation right.

In this context, the various intersections with and tensions between the 1976 Seed Act and the *Plant Breeders' Rights Act* create a complex situation for actors operating in the Pakistani seed sector. Of these, two are especially relevant for the purpose of this chapter. The first is that following the enactment of *Plant Breeders' Rights Act*, two systems that share a similar purpose exist in parallel within the same organisation. Specifically, a breeder who wishes to obtain exclusive commercial exploitation rights over a new plant variety in Pakistan must submit two separate applications to the FSC&RD: one for plant breeders' rights under the *Plant Breeders' Rights Act* and another for variety registration under the 1976 Seed Act. This situation means that it is possible for a new variety to be protected as intellectual property but not sanctioned for sale, and *vice versa*. It would have been possible to envisage a system in which the submission of an application for plant breeders' rights would automatically confer variety registration.

Second, the criteria of distinctness, uniformity, and stability must be met to obtain both plant breeders' rights and variety registration. However, it is not clear whether these criteria will need to be met separately for applications under the *Plant Breeders' Rights Act* on the one hand, and the 1976 Seed Act on the other hand. It is possible that in cases where a variety has previously been registered under the 1976 Seed Act, the Plant Breeders' Rights Registrar simply could rely on this prior evaluation to determine whether the variety is distinct, uniform, and stable. The *Plant Breeders' Rights Act* does not address this possibility. Instead, the law stipulates only that applicants for plant breeders' rights must submit to the Registrar a sufficient quantity of seeds or propagating material for the realisation of the tests to evaluate distinctness, uniformity, and stability.[60]

6.7 Conclusion

Pakistan took nearly 17 years to introduce its *sui generis Plant Breeders' Rights Act*. In an attempt to comply with the TRIPS Agreement, the 2016 *Plant Breeders' Rights* of Pakistan aims to encourage the development of new plant varieties and to protect the intellectual property of the breeders who develop these varieties. In so doing, the Act also intends to grant breeders' rights for EDVs and genetically modified varieties. Some scholars and development practitioners believe that the *Plant Breeders' Rights Act* is based on UPOV 1991. This is not entirely true. There are a number of provisions in the law that diverge from the UPOV 1991 standard.

For example, the *Plant Breeders' Rights Act* exempts plant varieties that have been previously registered and released or commercialised under the national 1976 Seed Act of Pakistan from meeting the requirement of novelty. Furthermore, the *Plant Breeders' Rights Act* grants several exclusive rights to plant breeders, but these rights are subject to certain exceptions that generally are not found in laws that comply with UPOV 1991. For instance, the Act allows farmers to save, use, sow, re-sow, exchange, share, or sell their farm produce.[61] The Act also does not prohibit any exchange of propagating materials among farmers.[62] Although these exemptions for farmers are subject to certain terms and conditions, these provisions may help to strengthen the customary farming practices of seed saving, use, exchange, and sale in Pakistan.

Another key feature of the *Plant Breeders' Rights Act* is that it creates a mechanism of compulsory licensing to facilitate access to the seeds of protected plant varieties. Additionally, the Act recognises the principles of access and benefit sharing of genetic resources, and requires breeders to disclose the source and origin of the genetic material that has been used to develop new varieties. These 'non-UPOV' provisions have the potential to promote fair and equitable practices of plant breeding and crop varietal development in Pakistan. The unique features of the *Plant Breeders' Act* also provide incentives to plant breeders who work in the public sector. For instance, because public sector breeders must apply for plant breeders' rights through their employer institutions, the Act provides for the creation of a 'Research Incentive Board' to identify and award benefits to these breeders.

Although the *Plant Breeders' Rights Act* contains several unique features, both domestic private and public seed entities have expressed concerns about the law.

60 The *Plant Breeders' Rights Act, 2016* of Pakistan (Act No. L of 2016). Section 16.
61 Ibid, Section 25(d).
62 Ibid, Section 25(e).

Commercial seed enterprises, including the Seed Association of Pakistan, worry that the Pakistani government lacks the necessary willingness and ability to protect plant breeders' rights effectively. Furthermore, domestic firms are concerned about new legal obligations to which they must adhere, and the implications of certain provisions of the law for plant breeding. For example, breeders in the private sector believe that the access and benefit sharing and farmers' privilege provisions of the Act could create obstacles to the development and commercialisation of new plant varieties. Similar concerns have been expressed by breeders who work in the public sector. In particular, public sector breeders have wondered whether new obligations related to the access and use of germplasm for crop varietal development might affect the effective implementation of publicly funded plant breeding programmes.

Lastly, diverse actors in Pakistan have voiced concerns about ways in which the 2016 *Plant Breeders' Rights Act* and the 2015 Seed Act overlap and in some ways are in tension with one another. Because both Acts will be administered by the FSC&RD towards the realisation of similar objectives, appropriate strategies should be developed to address any potential conflict between these regimes.

Chapter 7

The *National Seed Policy* of Timor-Leste

Laying the foundation for the regulation of plant varieties as intellectual property

Pratap Shrestha

7.1 Introduction

Timor-Leste is a small island country located at the eastern end of the Indonesian archipelago, about 550 kilometres north of Australia. Since becoming sovereign[1] in May 2002, Timor-Leste has made a number of international commitments to improve the environment, agriculture, and the governance of biological resources at the national level, and to better integrate the country into global society. For example, Timor-Leste has joined various international treaties, such as the *United Nations Framework Convention on Climate Change* and the *Convention on Biological Diversity* (CBD). Furthermore, the country has sought and acquired membership of international institutions such as the Association of Southeast Asian Nations and the World Intellectual Property Organization. Timor-Leste has also submitted a bid to join the World Trade Organization. One significant future effect of membership of the World Trade Organization will be the requirement to establish a domestic system of intellectual property for plant varieties, pursuant to the *Agreement on Trade-Related Aspects of Intellectual Property* (TRIPS).[2]

Although as of May 2019, Timor-Leste was still not a member of the World Trade Organization, the country has already taken steps to protect plant varieties as intellectual property through a TRIPS-compliant *sui generis* plant variety protection system. This goal is manifested in the *National Seed Policy* of Timor-Leste, which the Ministry of Agriculture, Forestry and Fisheries released in 2013. In 2019, the Ministry was hopeful that the Council of Ministers would approve the *National Seed Policy* in the near future.

1 The country was a colony of Portugal for 455 years and subsequently under Indonesian occupation for 24 years. Timor-Leste is now one of the newest independent nations in the world. The country gained sovereignty in May 2002 and became the 191th member of the United Nations in September of the same year.

2 The TRIPS Agreement obligates all members of the World Trade Organization to provide intellectual property protection for plant varieties through patents, a *sui generis* system, or a combination of both. *Agreement on Trade-Related Aspects of Intellectual Property Rights*. 1995. Article 27.3(b).

In various meetings convened by the National Seed Policy Working Group (which was formed in July 2012) and during personal communications with the author,[3] Ministry officials expressed the view that the effective implementation of the *National Seed Policy* would form the basis for the recognition of intellectual property for plant varieties. These officials also regularly stated that they believed that the establishment of a system for the protection of plant varieties as intellectual property would create incentives for investment in research and the corresponding development of new plant varieties. Furthermore, these officials also hoped that a national framework of plant variety protection would facilitate the production, circulation, and marketing of the seeds of varieties that local farmers prefer and require to ensure food and nutritional security.

This chapter aims to explore how and why the idea of a national policy to regulate holistically the conservation and use of plant varieties materialised in Timor-Leste. The chapter further analyses how this policy lays the foundation for the eventual protection of different categories of plant varieties as intellectual property. There are at least two reasons for why the experience of Timor-Leste is significant in the context of international intellectual property lawmaking. First, most countries elaborate domestic frameworks for the protection of plant varieties either in comprehensive intellectual property policies or in specific patent or plant variety protection laws.[4] In contrast, actors in Timor-Leste have situated the Timorese model for plant variety protection in the *National Seed Policy*. This is noteworthy because the national seed policies and laws that other countries – such as India, Pakistan, and Nepal – have enacted are typically conceived solely as mechanisms to regulate the development, production, circulation, quality control, and marketing of the seeds of new plant varieties. In other words, national seed policies and laws typically do not recognise intellectual property in relation to plant varieties.

The second reason why the Timorese case is unusual is that the *National Seed Policy* expressly rejects both patents and the plant breeders' rights model embodied in the *International Union for the Protection of New Varieties of Plants* (UPOV) as means to grant intellectual property for plant varieties. Instead, Timor-Leste has designed a *sui generis* system that would protect two categories of plant varieties as intellectual property: 'breeders' new varieties' and 'farmers' new varieties.'[5]

Following this introductory section, the chapter is structured as follows. Section 7.2 describes the nature of agriculture in Timor-Leste, while also introducing a series of issues that currently affect the livelihoods of smallholder farmers and the

3 As stated in the Preface of the 2013 *National Seed Policy*, the author served as the International Seed Policy Advisor and thus worked closely with the Ministry of Agriculture, Forestry and Fisheries and other stakeholder groups to develop the Policy and to suggest strategies for implementation. The analyses presented in this chapter are based on the author's personal views and the experiences accrued while working in Timor-Leste.

4 Examples of this approach can be found in other chapters of this volume.

5 *National Seed Policy* of Timor-Leste. 2013. Sections 3.4.1 and 3.4.2.

realisation of food security in the country. Section 7.3 and section 7.4 build on this discussion by analysing the types of cropping and seed systems that characterise Timorese agriculture. Section 7.5 outlines how the formation of the *National Seed Policy* unfolded in 2013. Section 7.6 discusses some key features of the *National Seed Policy* in relation to the conservation and sustainable use of plant genetic resources; rules related to access and benefit sharing and the registration of local plant varieties; and the protection of breeders' and farmers' plant varieties as intellectual property. The conclusion of the chapter, section 7.7, offers a series of recommendations for how the national government, local farming communities, and civil society organisations might work together to ensure that the governance of plant varieties occurs in a sustainable manner in Timor-Leste, thereby ensuring the vitality of agriculture in the country.

7.2 The nature of agriculture in Timor-Leste

The population of Timor-Leste numbers at just over 1.1 million, with an average household size of 5.7 people and a population growth rate of 1.81 percent.[6] While about 72 percent of the population lives in rural areas, approximately 84 percent of the economically active population depends on agriculture for their livelihoods.[7] It is also notable that agriculture contributes about 38 percent of the monthly household income for the average Timorese family,[8] but 42 percent of people still live below the poverty line.[9]

Geographically, Timor-Leste is a hilly country with 44 percent of the land having a slope of 40 percent or greater.[10] Because of this, only 380,000 hectares (25.6 percent) of the total land area is used for agriculture, of which 155,000 hectares (40.8 percent) is dedicated to the cultivation of annual crops, which are principally food grains and vegetables.[11] Timorese agriculture is dominated by smallholder family farms operating on plots whose average size is fewer than 1.2 hectares.[12] Timorese smallholder farmers practice mixed and integrated food

6 General Directorate of Statistics (GDS). 2015. *Population and Housing Census 2015: Preliminary Results.* Díli: GDS, Ministry of Finance, Timor-Leste.

7 General Directorate of Statistics (GDS). 2013. *Timor-Leste Labour Force Survey 2013.* Díli: GDS, Ministry of Finance, Timor-Leste.

8 General Directorate of Statistics (GDS). 2011. *Timor-Leste Household Income and Expenditure Survey 2011.* Díli: GDS, Ministry of Finance, Government of Timor-Leste.

9 General Directorate of Statistics (GDS). 2014. *At-a-glance: Poverty in Timor-Leste 2014.* Díli: GDS, Ministry of Finance, Government of Timor-Leste.

10 Barnett J., S. Dessai, and R. N. Jones. 2007. 'Vulnerability to Climate Variability and Change in East Timor.' *AMBIO: A Journal of the Human Environment* 36 (5): 372–377.

11 Food and Agriculture Organization of the United Nations (FAO). 2019. 'Timor-Leste.' FAOSTAT. Accessed May 23 2019. www.fao.org/faostat/en/#country/176

12 National Directorate of Policy and Planning (NDPP). 2012. *Ministry of Agriculture, Forestry and Fisheries Strategic Plan 2014–20.* Díli: NDPP, Ministry of Agriculture, Forestry and Fisheries, Timor-Leste.

production systems, growing a wide range of crops combined with livestock production, while also depending on forest resources for additional food and fodder for livestock. In general, farming in Timor-Leste is subsistence-oriented, such that food is primarily produced for household consumption, with very little surplus going to market.[13]

Timorese farmers depend heavily on their traditional knowledge, practices, and innovations to sustain food production. Chemical fertilisers are seldom used for food production, and usage is limited to areas that are proximate to market centres and along the border with Indonesian West Timor.[14] Farmers' ability to access and afford chemical pesticides is correspondingly inadequate.[15] Access to irrigation is also low and limited essentially to lowland areas in which rice is cultivated.[16]

Due to the small mean size of landholdings, the low productivity and production of major food crops, and the large average family size, rural households in Timor-Leste regularly experience food and nutritional insecurity.[17] About 64 percent of the population suffers from chronic food insecurity and experiences cyclical food shortages during the lean season.[18] These rural households specifically experience scarcity of maize and rice, which are major staple food crops, for a period of approximately 3.5 months every year.[19] These food shortages are compounded by the generally poor nutritional profile of the average Timorese citizen. Inadequate nutrition is reflected by the fact that of all children under five years of age, 50.2 percent experience stunting, 11 percent experience wasting, and 37.7 percent are underweight.[20]

Notwithstanding these various challenges, it is notable that farmers in Timor-Leste are highly innovative and resourceful. They have developed tactics such as

13 Williams, R. L., S. Bacon, A. Ferreira, and W. Erskine. 2018. 'An Approach to Characterise Agricultural Livelihoods and Livelihood Zones Using National Census Data in Timor-Leste.' *Experimental Agriculture* 54 (6): 857–873.

14 Government of Timor-Leste. 2011. *Timor-Leste Strategic Development Plan 2011–30.* Díli: Government of Timor-Leste; and Lopes, M., and H. Nesbitt. 2012. 'Improving Food Security in East Timor with Higher Yielding Crop Varieties.' In *Food Security in East Timor, Papua New Guinea and Pacific Island Countries and Territories*, edited by D. Templeton. Canberra: Australian Centre for International Agricultural Research (ACIAR), pages 12–26.

15 Government of Timor-Leste. 2011. *Timor-Leste Strategic Development Plan 2011–30.* Díli: Government of Timor-Leste.

16 Food and Agriculture Organization of the United Nations (FAO). 2011. 'Timor-Leste.' AQUASTAT. Accessed May 23 2019. www.fao.org/nr/water/aquastat/countries_regions/TLS/TLS-CP_eng.pdf

17 Lopes, M., A. Ximenes, A. D. R. Ferreira, L. Spyckerelle, R. Williams, H. Nesbitt, and W. Erskine. 2013. 'Household Food Insecurity in Timor-Leste.' *Food Security* 5 (1): 83–94.

18 Government of Timor-Leste. 2005. *Millennium Development Goals - Where Are We Now?* Díli: Government of Timor-Leste.

19 National Directorate of Policy and Planning (NDPP), note 12.

20 Ministry of Health. 2014. *National Nutrition Strategy 2014–2019.* Díli: Government Timor-Leste.

adopting integrated farming (mixing crops, livestock, forest, and aquatic resources) and diversifying their cropping systems.[21] These strategies enable Timorese farmers to feed their families by obtaining a wide range of food types from home gardens and cultivated fields.[22] Uncultivated and wild foods also are gathered from forests, and from areas along streams and waterways to supplement daily nutritional needs, particularly during the food deficit months. Thus, farmers in Timor-Leste maintain and use a significant diversity of both cultivated and uncultivated crops and plant varieties to ensure that their food production system is resilient, and to achieve food and livelihood security for their families.

7.3 Cropping systems and crop diversity in Timor-Leste

Agriculture in Timor-Leste is characterised by three distinct systems of crop production: (1) the lowland irrigated system; (2) the upland rainfed system; and (3) the home garden or homestead agro-forestry system.[23] The lowland irrigated cropping system is prevalent in coastal plains and valleys, and rice is grown as its sole major crop. The upland rainfed cropping system is prevalent on elevated lands and hill slopes without irrigation, and it consists of an array of staple food crops. These include maize, cassava, sweet potato, yams, taro, arrowroot, banana, beans, and peanuts. Farmers also cultivate cash crops such as coffee, coconut, candlenut, cashew, and vanilla for export markets in upland rainfed farming areas. Lastly, in the agro-forestry system, farmers grow a variety of vegetables and fruit trees around the homestead to supplement their daily food requirements. Depending on the season, different sets of vegetables are cultivated consecutively throughout the year. Taro, yam, cassava, and different kinds of spices are also integrated as mixed crops in the homestead agro-forestry system.

Notwithstanding the diverse assortment of crops grown, agriculture is relatively young in Timor-Leste. Historically, people living on the island depended mainly on sea foods and the fruits of wild forest trees. Present day food crops such as upland rice, foxtail millet, yam, taro, and sesame were introduced to the territory only with the arrival of Austronesians about 3,500 years ago.[24] Similarly, it is

21 USC Canada. 2014. *Guidance and Process of Integrating Farmers' Seed System and Community Seed Banking Activities into the National Seed Systems for Released Varieties of Timor-Leste.* Technical Assistance Report submitted to the Ministry of Agriculture, Forestry and Fisheries and the Seeds of Life Programme, Timor-Leste. Ottawa: USC Canada.

22 Ibid. See also Nesbitt, H., W. Erskine, C. J. da Cruz, and A. Moorehead, eds. 2016. *Food Security in Timor-Leste Through Crop Production: Proceedings of TimorAg2016.* Canberra: Australian Centre for International Agricultural Research (ACIAR).

23 National Directorate of Policy and Planning (NDPP), note 12.

24 Williams R. L., H. Nesbitt, C. Nabias, E. Hornai, P. Pereira, L. Almeida, and W. Erskine. 2016. 'Theory, Practice and Results of Food Crop Variety Evaluation and Release in Timor-Leste 2001–2015.' In *Food Security in Timor-Leste Through Crop Production: Proceedings of TimorAg2016*, edited by H. Nesbitt, W. Erskine, C. J. da Cruz, and A. Moorhead. Canberra: Australian Centre for International Agricultural Research (ACIAR), pages 53–63.

believed that Chinese traders brought cotton, mungbean, pigeonpea, sorghum, citrus, and possibly coffee to Timor-Leste about 500 years ago.[25]

Given its situation as an island with a long history of isolation, the genetic base of food crops in Timor-Leste historically remained circumscribed. Correspondingly, agricultural research aimed at enhancing crop diversity and production was limited until the 1990s. The systematic introduction and evaluation of major food crops in Timor-Leste began with the conceptualisation of the Seeds of Life programme in 2000.[26] The programme, which was supported partially by funding from the Australian government, was overseen by the Ministry of Agriculture, Forestry and Fisheries of Timor-Leste from 2000 to early 2016.

Although the inter-species diversity of the major food crops in Timor-Leste is still relatively low, farmers maintain a good varietal (intra-species) diversity for a number of crops at the community level. A 2016 survey that was conducted in Batara and Holarua villages – both of which have rainfed upland cropping systems – found that the maximum number of varieties grown by local farming communities for maize, sweet potato, cassava, taro, and plantain was 10, 11, 9, 7, and 12 respectively.[27] These communities also reported high species and varietal diversity for vegetables and uncultivated or wild food crops, including 32 species and 75 varieties of vegetables, and 47 species and 74 varieties of uncultivated or wild food crops (Table 7.1).

Another study from 2013 found that farming households in the rainfed upland areas of the Manatuto and Aileu municipalities maintain on average 11 species and 35 varieties of staple food crops, eight species and 18 varieties of vegetables, and seven species and 23 varieties of fruit trees per household (Table 7.2). Taken together, Tables 7.1 and 7.2 show that farmers in Timor-Leste maintain and conserve a diverse range of crops, both at the community and the household level.

As mentioned earlier, formal research whose purpose is to develop new crop varieties in Timor-Leste began with the implementation of the first phase of the Seeds of Life programme in 2000.[28] The programme continued in three phases

25 Fox, J. J. 2003. 'Drawing from the Past to Prepare for the Future: Responding to the Challenges of Food Security in East Timor.' In *Agriculture: New Directions for a New Nation—East Timor (Timor-Leste)*. Proceedings of a Workshop 1–3 October 2002, Díli, East Timor, ACIAR Proceedings No. 113. Canberra: Australian Centre for International Agricultural Research (ACIAR), pages 105–114.

26 Seeds of Life. 2019. 'Food Security Begins with Seed Security.' Seeds of Life. Accessed May 23 2019. http://seedsoflifetimor.org/about-us/. For a critical analysis of the Seeds of Life programme, see McWilliam, A., M. Lopes, D. Glazebrook, M. D. J. D. Costa, and A. Ximenes. 2015. 'Seeds of Life: Social Research for Improved Farmer Yields in Timor-Leste.' In *Making a Difference?: Social Assessment Policy and Praxis and its Emergence in China*, edited by S. Price and K. Robinson. New York: Berghahn Books, pages 126–142.

27 USC Canada. 2016. *Technical Report on the Community Seed Banking and Community Variety Registration Procedures for Timor-Leste: Project Completion Report Part II.* Technical Assistance Report submitted to the Ministry of Agriculture, Forestry and Fisheries and the Seeds of Life Programme, Timor-Leste. Ottawa: USC Canada.

28 Seeds of Life, note 26.

Table 7.1 Major staple food crops ranked by their contribution to food production and varietal diversity in the Batara and Holarua villages of Timor-Leste

Crop	*Batara village*		*Crop*	*Holarua village*	
	Rank	*No. of varieties*		*Rank*	*No. of varieties*
Maize	1	10	Maize	1	8
Sweet potato	2	5	Cassava	2	11
Cassava	3	7	Plantain	3	9
Taro	4	8	Sweet potato	4	7
Arrowroot	5	2	Taro	5	3
Plantain	6	11	Arrowroot	6	12

Source: USC Canada. 2016. *Technical Report on the Community Seed Banking and Community Variety Registration Procedures for Timor-Leste: Project Completion Report Part II*. Technical Assistance Report submitted to the Ministry of Agriculture, Forestry and Fisheries and the Seeds of Life Programme, Timor-Leste. Ottawa: USC Canada.

Table 7.2 Average number of crops and varieties maintained by farming households in the Manatuto and Aileu districts of Timor-Leste

Crop	*No. of crops/household*			*No. of varieties/household*		
	Minimum	*Maximum*	*Average*	*Minimum*	*Maximum*	*Average*
Staple food	4	16	11	20	51	35
Vegetables	4	11	8	11	23	18
Fruit trees	4	10	7	14	32	23

Source: USC Canada. 2013. Mid-term Evaluation Survey: Timor-Leste. Ottawa: USC Canada.

until January 2016, contributing to the realisation of the 'Timor-Leste Strategic Development Plan 2011–2030.' One of the goals of this Plan is the achievement of food security through the enhanced production of major food crops.[29] The Seeds of Life programme focused solely on the collection of new crop species and varieties from research centres and gene banks based in other countries, with the aim of identifying high-yielding candidates that could be adapted to local growing conditions in Timor-Leste.

Towards the realisation of this goal, genetic materials from pure line rice and legumes, open-pollinated composite maize, and clonal potato, sweet potato, and cassava were introduced into the country, with the aim to develop suitable crop varieties for local farmers. The ambitiousness of this initiative is evidenced by the fact that about 557 lines of maize, rice, upland rice, cassava, sweet potato, potato, pigeonpea, soybean, mungbean, cowpea, peanut, wheat, and barley were brought

29 Government of Timor-Leste, note 15, page 118.

into Timor-Leste for the purpose of testing their performance under different agro-climatic conditions.[30] Of these, 18 varieties of staple crops, such as wheat, barley, and potatoes were released for commercial cultivation in the country.[31]

Although the Seeds of Life programme succeeded in introducing exotic germplasm as a means to identify potentially beneficial new crop species and varieties, it missed the opportunity to utilise local plant genetic resources and traditional knowledge to develop improved varieties of Timorese staple crops. Areas in which the Seeds of Life programme was particularly weak included the lack of systematic collection, characterisation, assessment, and conservation of local plant genetic resources; the absence of breeding activity utilising local crop varieties; the failure to recognise and promote the nutritional, economic, and socio-cultural values of local crop varieties; and ineffectiveness in strengthening the farmers' seed system.[32]

7.4 Timorese seed systems

Timor-Leste has two distinct seed systems: (1) the State-run seed system, which is characterised by the release and registration of new crop varieties, and the production, quality control, dissemination, and circulation of the seeds of released and registered crop varieties; and (2) the farmers' seed system, in which farmers produce, save, and use their own seeds, in addition to exchanging and selling these seeds with other farmers at the community level.[33] The State-run seed system is coordinated by the National Seed System for Released Varieties, which the Ministry of Agriculture, Forestry and Fisheries established in 2014 to form the primary institutional base for both the development, release, and registration of new plant varieties; and the production, dissemination, and marketing of the seeds of new plant varieties.[34] Additionally, the National Seed Council – which was formed under the *National Seed Policy* of 2013 to develop necessary guidelines for the production of quality seeds and plant varieties – oversees the operations of the National Seed System for Released Varieties.

In order to circulate in the State-run seed system of Timor-Leste, all seeds from all varieties of plants must be produced under close supervision for quality control. Registered seeds are categorised in five groupings, namely breeder, foundation, certified, commercial, and community seeds, with breeder seeds having the highest

30 Williams, et al., note 24.
31 Ibid. See also Seeds of Life, note 26.
32 USC Canada, note 27.
33 Lopes, M. 2018. *Food Security and Sustainable Seed Supply in Timor-Leste: Formal and Informal Seed Systems (Part 1)*. Canberra: Department of Pacific Affairs, Australian National University. Accessed May 23 2019. https://openresearch-repository.anu.edu.au/bitstream/1885/141947/1/ib2018_5_lopes_pt_1_final.pdf
34 Seeds of Life. 2016. *National Seed System for Released Varieties: Providing the Farming Families of Timor-Leste with Secure Access to Quality Seeds*. Díli: Government of Timor-Leste.

degree of genetic and physical purity, and community seeds the lowest.[35] The Directorate of Research and Special Services of the Ministry of Agriculture, Forestry and Fisheries is responsible for the maintenance and production of breeder and foundation seeds. The other three seed categories are managed and regulated by the Directorate of Agriculture and Horticulture.[36]

Contract farmers, who are trained and supervised by the personnel from the Ministry of Agriculture, Forestry and Fisheries, produce all certified seeds in Timor-Leste.[37] Seeds categorised as commercial – which are also termed 'truthful label seeds' – are multiplied by registered commercial seed producers, who themselves are farmers trained in seed production. Commercial seed producers must comply with the quality standards set for this category of seeds, and therefore they test for seed quality (physical purity, germination, and moisture content) and record these data on a truthful label.[38]

Meanwhile, community seeds are produced by Community Seed Producers' Groups for their own use, and for local exchange and marketing. The quality standards for community seeds are not specified or monitored by the National Seed System for Released Varieties or the Ministry of Agriculture, Forestry and Fisheries. Individual Community Seed Producers' Groups work to ensure quality standards, which in turn operate to preserve consumer trust and the group's reputation.[39] A 2015 study estimated that there were 75 contract farmers producing certified seeds, 69 groups producing commercial seeds, and 1,119 Community Seed Producers' Groups producing community seeds in Timor-Leste at that time.[40]

As of mid-2019, the State-run seed system of Timor-Leste included 18 varieties of seven major staple food crops.[41] These varieties have helped to increase the varietal diversity available to farmers in the country. Similarly, different categories of seeds of the varieties that are produced under the Seeds of Life programme have increased farmers' seed security and contributed to increasing food production in Timor-Leste.[42] Despite these positive contributions, the State-run seed

35 Ibid.
36 Kunwar. B., J. Dalton, L. Hornai, and H. Nesbi. 2016. 'Seed Multiplication and Distribution: Selecting the Best Option for Timor-Leste.' In *Food Security in Timor-Leste Through Crop Production: Proceedings of TimorAg2016*, edited by H. Nesbitt, W. Erskine, C. J. da Cruz, and A. Moorhead. Canberra: Australian Centre for International Agricultural Research (ACIAR), pages 64–73. See also Seeds of Life, note 34.
37 Ibid.
38 Ibid.
39 Ibid.
40 Seeds of Life. 2015. *Annual Research Report 2015.* Díli: Ministry of Agriculture, Forestry and Fisheries, Timor-Leste.
41 Williams, et al., note 24.
42 Seeds of Life. 2014. *Adoption Survey 2014.* Díli, Ministry of Agriculture, Forestry and Fisheries, Timor-Leste; and Spyckerelle L., O. Ferreira Agostinho, S. dos Santos, L. V. Branco, and J. Imron. 2016. 'Advances in Food Availability in Timor-Leste.' In *Food Security in Timor-Leste Through Crop Production: Proceedings of TimorAg2016*, edited by H. Nesbitt, W. Erskine, C. J. da Cruz, and A. Moorhead. Canberra: Australian Centre for International Agricultural Research (ACIAR), pages 38–45.

system has not been able to meet the varietal diversity and quantity needs of local farmers. The seeds produced under the State-run seed system are able to provide less than 10 percent of the country's total seed requirement.[43] This means that farmers themselves must manage the seeds of a large number of crops and varieties under the second major seed system, i.e., the farmers' seed system.

The farmers' seed system in Timor-Leste, also known as the local seed system or traditional seed system, is characterised by the production, saving, and use by farmers of their own seeds, and by the exchange and sale of these seeds by farmers at the local or community level.[44] Farmers mobilise their personal social networks to obtain, exchange, and sell seeds. These networks include relatives, friends, neighbours, other farmers, and local markets, both within and outside particular farming communities.[45]

The farmers' seed system in Timor-Leste includes the seeds of different kinds of plant varieties, including landraces, local varieties, adapted varieties, and new varieties, all of which farmers cultivate and maintain on their own holdings. Furthermore, traditional knowledge plays an important role in the farmers' seed system of Timor-Leste. This knowledge pertains to customary seed management practices such as selection, cleaning, drying, and storage. It should also be noted that small quantities of commercial seeds, which are usually imported, are sometimes marketed by private traders and local agricultural shops (*Loja Agrikultura*) in Timor-Leste without going through the variety registration and release process. These seeds also become part of the farmers' seed system.

As mentioned earlier, the farmers' seed system constitutes the major source of seeds for farmers, supplying more than 90 percent of the total seed requirement in Timor-Leste.[46] The local crops that farmers cultivate and circulate under the farmers' seed system are significant to local communities because of the contributions that they make to livelihood enhancement and food security. Furthermore, local plant species and varieties are also well adapted to the Timorese climate and the country's low input production system.

Despite this, no systematic research or effort has been made to conserve, document, or enhance local plant species or varieties in Timor-Leste, or to control their replacement by a less genetically diverse set of higher-yielding commercial crops. This possibility is evidenced by a recent study on seed diversity in the Batara and Holarua villages,[47] which reported the loss of local varieties of sorghum, pearl millet, and foxtail millet in these communities. Farmers in Batara also reported the loss of four varieties of maize, two varieties of sweet potato, and two varieties of potato.

43 CRS, Mercy Corps, MAF/Seeds of Life, CARE, CIAT and UEA/Dev. 2013. *Seed System Security Assessment, Timor-Leste*. An Assessment Funded by the United States Agency for International Development/US Office of Foreign Disaster Assistance. Díli, Timor-Leste. Accessed May 23 2019. http://seedsystem.org/wp-content/uploads/2014/05/SSSA-Timor-Leste-report-final.pdf

44 USC Canada, note 21.

45 Ibid.

46 CRS, Mercy Corps, MAF/Seeds of Life, CARE, CIAT and UEA/Dev., note 43.

47 USC Canada, note 27.

If the farmers' seed system were to receive the required investments in research and development – in addition to adequate policy support – it could contribute significantly to national seed and food security in Timor-Leste. Strengthening the farmers' seed system could yield substantial benefits in the form of an enhanced national seed system. Early evidence for this possibility is found in a consultation that the Seeds of Life programme commissioned following the adoption of the *National Seed Policy* of 2013. This consultation developed recommendations for how the farmers' seed system and community seed banking activities could support the National Seed System for Released Varieties of Timor-Leste.[48]

Based on the recommendations of the consultation, in 2015 the Seeds of Life programme initiated a collaboration with USC Canada – an international development organisation – and Resilient Agriculture and Economy through Biodiversity in Action (RAEBIA) – a local non-governmental organisation – to pilot a community seed banking system in the Batara and Holarua villages. The initiative involved the creation and mobilisation of community seed banks for the conservation, collection, documentation, characterisation, assessment, and enhancement of local crop varieties, including the production and circulation of their seeds. Subsequent to the initial trial, RAEBIA has continued to scale up its community seed banking activities, which include the collection, conservation, and production of the seeds of local plant varieties. However, RAEBIA has not been able to implement other activities such as the characterisation, assessment, and enhancement of local crop varieties due to lack of resources for scientific and plant breeding work. According to the officials of RAEBIA, the characterisation, assessment, and enhancement of these varieties would require additional investment and support from other agencies, such as the Ministry of Agriculture, Forestry and Fisheries.[49]

7.5 The making of the *National Seed Policy*

The gestation of the *National Seed Policy* of 2013 began when the Ministry of Agriculture, Forestry and Fisheries, in collaboration with the Seeds of Life programme, created a National Seed Policy Working Group in July 2012. The National Seed Policy Working Group consisted of 13 members,[50] including leaders from the Ministry, civil society organisations, international non-governmental

48 USC Canada, note 21.

49 Personal communication with Xisto Martins, Executive Director of RAEBIA in July 2017.

50 These members specifically included key officials of the Ministry of Agriculture, Forestry and Fisheries such as the National Director Agriculture and Horticulture, the National Director Research and Special Services, the National Director Policy and Planning, the National Director of Agriculture and Community Development. The members of this committee also included the USC Canada Timor-Leste Country Director; a Representative of CARE Timor-Leste; a Representative of La'o Hamutuk; a Representative of the Rural Development Programme IV (RDP4) at the Ministry of Agriculture, Forestry and Fisheries; development partners; private sector representatives; and advisors and experts involved in the Seeds of Life programme.

organisations, private industry, and experts from the Seeds of Life programme. The National Director of the Agriculture and Horticulture Division of the Ministry chaired the Working Group, the mandate of which was to coordinate and oversee the drafting and adoption of the *National Seed Policy*. To assist with the formulation of the Policy, the Working Group contracted the author to serve as the Policy Advisor.

As the Policy Advisor, the author suggested that the National Seed Policy Working Group should utilise a participatory strategy to formulate the *National Seed Policy*. Thus, the National Seed Policy Working Group divided the drafting process into several smaller stages, each of which garnered participation from concerned stakeholders, including local farming communities and local seed production groups (Table 7.3). Through this process, smallholder farmers and small-scale seed producers were consulted directly, and the concerns and issues that they raised were thoroughly addressed at different stages during the making of the *National Seed Policy*. Civil society organisations that advocated for food sovereignty and the protection of farmers' rights – including *La'o Hamutuk* (The Timor-Leste Institute for Development Monitoring and Analysis) and *Hasatil* (Strengthening Agriculture Sustainability in Timor-Leste) – were also given the opportunity to provide suggestions for how to accommodate their interests in different versions of the *National Seed Policy*. Participating civil society organisations were granted unrestricted access to the draft documents at all stages of the policy formulation process.

Following approval by the Minister for Agriculture, Forestry and Fisheries in March 2013, the *National Seed Policy* was adopted within the Ministry of Agriculture, Forestry and Fisheries to guide its seed research and development programme. As of May 2019, several key institutional bodies, including the National Seed Council and the Variety Approval, Release and Registration Committee already have been formed and operationalised pursuant to the terms of the *National Seed Policy*. In addition, the Variety Approval, Release and Registration Committee and the National Seed Council approved the release and registration of seven new crop varieties in April 2016.[51] However, despite the successes that the *National Seed Policy* has already achieved surrounding the administration of Timorese seed systems, the Council of Ministers has not yet approved the framework. This means that the policy is not yet binding. Moreover, the framework continues to evolve, having recently undergone revisions and refinements within the Ministry of Agriculture, Forestry and Fisheries in preparation for re-submission to the Council of Ministers.

7.6 Key features of the *National Seed Policy*

The Timor-Leste *National Seed Policy* of 2013 is a comprehensive framework whose purpose is to govern the conservation and sustainable use of plant genetic resources; the breeding and development of plant varieties; the registration and protection of plant varieties as intellectual property; and the production, quality

51 Seeds of Life, note 40.

Table 7.3 Stages of the making of the *National Seed Policy* of Timor-Leste

Stages	*Activities*	*Outcomes*
Stage 1: Understanding and identifying seed systems and seed security issues	Assessment of the situation of national seed systems and seed security, including the review of the Timor-Leste Strategic Development Plan 2011–2030 by the Policy Advisor. Organisation of the first meeting of the National Seed Policy Working Group in August 2012. Organisation of consultation meetings with Staff of the Ministry of Agriculture, Forestry and Fisheries and Suco (village) Chiefs of Manatuto District; the Community Seed Producers' Group in Liquica District; and *Hasatil* members.	Understanding of seed issues relevant for the *National Seed Policy*. Collection of concerns and issues such as food sovereignty, seed security, and farmers' rights over seeds. Agreement on the process and plan of action for the formulation of the *National Seed Policy*.
Stage 2: Developing the policy framework	Formulation of a policy framework by the Policy Advisor. Discussion on the policy framework with the National Seed Policy Working Group. Continuation of the consultation meetings with government entities, farming communities, and civil society organisations.	Agreement on a policy framework that provided the basis for drafting the *National Seed Policy* (e.g., achieving seed sovereignty was accepted as a guiding principle).
Stage 3: Drafting of the policy in consultation with the National Seed Policy Working Group	Development of the draft *National Seed Policy* by the Policy Advisor. Organisation of the meeting to discuss the draft *National Seed Policy* with the National Seed Policy Working Group in August 2012.	Revision of the draft *National Seed Policy* and its submission to the Ministry of Agriculture, Forestry and Fisheries for further consultations and inputs.
Stage 4: Collection of feedback from stakeholder groups	Organisation of policy consultation workshops in various districts to collect feedback on the draft *National Seed Policy*. Organisation of five other workshops to cover 12 districts (in total, 670 participants representing government agencies, non-governmental organisations, village chiefs, farmers' groups, the private sector, and academia attended these workshops).	Collection of feedback and inputs for further refinement of the Policy. Increased awareness about the draft *National Seed Policy* among the district government agencies, farming communities, non-governmental organisations, the private sector, and academia.

	Organisation of a separate workshop for academics to obtain their feedback on the draft *National Seed Policy*. Based on inputs from local civil society organisations, submission of additional inputs by *La'o Hamutuk*.	
Stage 5: Finalisation of the *National Seed Policy* and endorsement from the Ministry of Agriculture, Forestry and Fisheries	Incorporation of relevant feedback and inputs from Stage 4 consultations and development of a revised *National Seed Policy*. Organisation of a meeting in March 2013 to build consensus among all members of the National Seed Policy Working Group to propose for the endorsement of the Policy by the Ministry of Agriculture, Forestry and Fisheries.	Approval of the *National Seed Policy* of 2013 by the National Seed Policy Working Group, and its endorsement by the Ministry of Agriculture, Forestry and Fisheries.

control, and marketing of the 'seeds of all plants used for food and agriculture and for any commercial purpose.'[52] The Policy adopts 'national seed sovereignty [as] the overarching guiding principal.'[53] The aspiration to achieve national seed sovereignty is reinforced through the requirement that the national seed system focus on the seeds of plant varieties that can be grown locally to achieve self-sufficiency in seed production and supply, and which are adapted to the socio-cultural, economic, and environmental conditions that Timorese farmers face. Subsections 7.6.1 to 7.6.3 discuss some of the key features of the Policy that are relevant for the governance of plant varieties in Timor-Leste.

7.6.1 Conservation and sustainable use of plant genetic resources

The *National Seed Policy* acknowledges the important roles that farmers play in the conservation and sustainable utilisation of plant genetic resources and the development of plant varieties in Timor-Leste, including through the application of the local knowledge, practices, and innovations that they have passed from generation to generation. In recognition of the contributions that farmers have made as both individuals and collectives, the Seed Policy requires the deployment of a community-based approach to the governance of plant genetic resources in the country. Some of the key features of this strategy include:

- documentation and characterisation of local plant genetic resources, and establishment of a Community Biodiversity Register to catalogue these resources at the local level;
- active engagement of farmers and farming communities in on-farm, *in-situ* conservation and sustainable use of plant genetic resources;
- support for the efforts and practices of local and indigenous peoples in the protection of natural habitats (e.g., forests, bodies of water, and other public lands), towards the conservation and sustainable use of crop wild relatives and wild plant species used for food;
- encouragement for farmers and farming communities to register local plant genetic resources to establish their ownership rights; and
- support for farming communities to establish Community Seed Banks as a mechanism to govern their plant genetic resources and ensure local seed security.

The *National Seed Policy* is also concerned with bolstering the national system of *ex situ* conservation. This is done, for instance, through the establishment of a National Gene Bank of plant genetic resources and associated local knowledge.[54]

52 *National Seed Policy of Timor-Leste*. 2013. 'Scope,' page 5 (the Policy does not cover the seeds of forest species that have not been cultivated by farmers in Timor-Leste).
53 Ibid, 'Objectives,' page 5.
54 Ibid, Section 1.2.3.

The Seed Policy further mandates the creation of a national database of Timorese plant genetic resources and associated traditional knowledge, which is to be populated with information collected from the Community Biodiversity Register.[55] As a whole, the provisions are designed to bolster conservation efforts both within particular communities and at the national level.

7.6.2 Access and benefit sharing, prior informed consent, and the registration of local plant varieties

The *National Seed Policy* is consistent with the obligations that Timor-Leste has assumed under a treaty to which the country is party, namely the CBD. The Policy expressly states, 'the sovereign right of Timor-Leste over its plant genetic resources will be protected as prescribed in the CBD and national biodiversity policy of the country.'[56] In order to realise the goals of the CBD, the Policy contains a series of guidelines for the development of a national framework to govern access and benefit sharing. For instance, the Policy stipulates that access to plant genetic resources may only be granted after negotiating mutually agreed terms with, and obtaining prior informed consent from the relevant national authority and the farming communities that hold the resources in question.

Furthermore, in an attempt to create a farmer-friendly access and benefit sharing regime and to incentivise the continued conservation and sustainable use of local plant genetic resources by farming communities, the Policy calls for the establishment of a National Biodiversity Fund and the provision of Biodiversity Conservation Awards. With the objective of enabling farmers to benefit from the conservation and use of local plant varieties, the Policy also states that legal arrangements should be made to develop a simple mechanism for farmers to register local plant varieties without cost, and without the requirement to meet the standard registration criteria of novelty, distinctness, uniformity, and stability.[57] The registration of local plant varieties is expected to strengthen the farmers' seed system and to ensure that third parties obtain prior informed consent and execute benefit-sharing agreements before they are able to access and use local plant varieties.[58]

7.6.3 Registration and protection of breeders' and farmers' plant varieties as intellectual property

Another key feature of the *National Seed Policy* is its framing of how the country should institutionalise a system to grant protections for different kinds of plant varieties. On the one hand, the National Policy envisages offering a form of plant

55 Ibid, Section 1.2.1.
56 Ibid, Section 1.4.
57 Ibid, Sections 1.3.1 and 1.3.2.
58 Ibid, Sections 1.4.2 and 1.4.5.

breeders' rights as a means to stimulate investment in crop development and to facilitate the growth of the domestic seed sector. On the other hand, the framework expressly rejects the UPOV model, and it also specifies that Timor-Leste should not allow for plant varieties to be patented.[59]

Instead, the *National Seed Policy* outlines a *sui generis* system of intellectual property for plant varieties designed to grant rights to plant breeders and farmers alike, which would be implemented by subsequent legislation.[60] In so doing, the Policy states that the future framework for plant variety protection should incorporate a set of 'special provisions [and relaxed] criteria and procedures' for the registration of new plant varieties that farmers breed and develop at the local level.[61] This means that the criteria and procedures for the protection of farmers' new varieties as intellectual property would diverge from the novelty, distinctness, uniformity, and stability requirements that professional plant breeders would need to follow.[62]

The *National Seed Policy* also specifies that the prospective intellectual property law for plant varieties should incorporate a mechanism through which compulsory licenses would ensure that protected varieties are available broadly to farmers. Compulsory licenses could be granted, for instance, if protected varieties are not being supplied in sufficient quantities or at fair prices for various reasons, including lack of organisational capacity to produce seeds according to appropriate quantity or quality standards, or with the intent to monopolise the seed market.[63]

While the draft of the national intellectual property law for plant varieties has not yet been elaborated, the *National Seed Policy* stipulates that the future bill should provide at least two specific exemptions from infringement of the rights granted. The first would allow farmers to use protected plant varieties for personal purposes.[64] Meanwhile, the second exception would allow for the use of protected varieties in research and academic training.[65] These provisions evidence the intention of Timorese policymakers to incorporate multiple aspirations into a future intellectual property law for plant varieties.

Important goals that the *National Seed Policy* aims to achieve include to develop national industries for plant breeding and seed production, and to ensure that smallholder farmers remain seed sovereign. The Policy also endeavours to create a legal framework to enable farmers to save, use, reproduce, share, exchange, and sell farm-produced seeds of all plant varieties, including intellectual property protected plant varieties.[66] The *National Seed Policy* further grants farmers the right to participate in decision making in relation to the conservation

59 Ibid, Section 3.4.1.
60 Ibid, Section 3.4.2.
61 Ibid, Section 3.1.4.
62 Ibid, Section 3.1.2.
63 Ibid, Section 6.8.
64 Ibid, Section 3.4.4.
65 Ibid, Section 3.4.5.
66 Ibid, Section 3.4.4.

and sustainable use of plant genetic resources. This right is substantiated by requiring the participation of two farmers (one woman and one man) as delegates to the National Seed Council.[67]

7.7 Conclusion

Given that the local-level production of crops and seeds is the primary source of food and seed security in Timor-Leste, the creation of conducive environments to govern plant varieties is critical for the improvement of the livelihoods of many citizens. Meanwhile, the relatively low diversity of the species and varieties of staple food crops in Timor-Leste presents both challenges and opportunities for the local and the national food systems. On the one hand, additional research and development programmes are required to conserve and enhance local plant varieties. On the other hand, it would be possible to introduce new varieties from overseas, as a means to broaden the genetic base of the agricultural crops grown in the country. Furthermore, in addition to the proper governance of widely cultivated plants, many of which pertain to exotic species, it is critical that the native plant diversity of Timor-Leste be conserved and used sustainably.

As of mid-2019, Timor-Leste did not have any binding laws related to issues including agrobiodiversity conservation, the registration of local plant varieties, or intellectual property for breeders' and farmers' plant varieties. In fact, the only policy framework that the country has developed in relation to this subject matter is the *National Seed Policy* of 2013. The Policy was built around the concept of seed sovereignty, which involves a focus on plant species and varieties that are adapted to local farming and climatic conditions, and that meet the socio-cultural, economic, food, and nutritional needs of Timorese farmers.

The institutionalisation of the notion of seed sovereignty, coupled with the adaptation of the aims of the CBD to fit the context of Timorese agriculture, together provide a series of foundational guidelines for how local plant varieties should be governed in Timor-Leste. The *National Seed Policy* further lays the groundwork for future domestic legislation that would regulate intellectual property for plant varieties. According to the parameters of the Policy, this prospective law should grant different sets of rights to plant breeders on the one hand, and to farmers on the other hand, surrounding the use of different categories of plant varieties. The typology that the *National Seed Policy* elaborates specifically includes breeders' new plant varieties, farmers' new plant varieties, and local plant varieties.

It is likely that the system of governance for these different categories of plant varieties will continue to evolve in Timor-Leste in the near future. Membership of the CBD requires that the country enact a binding national law on access and benefit sharing, a mandate that ostensibly will be achieved when the Council of Ministers of Timor-Leste formally approves the *National Seed Policy*. However, a greater shift will likely occur when the country joins the World Trade

67 Ibid, Section 9.3.12.

Organization. Membership of this Organization may incentivise the Timorese government to expedite the development of laws and regulations related to the recognition of intellectual property for plant varieties. While a more rapid pace of policy formation could beget benefits for Timor-Leste, it could also diminish the ability of farmers to participate in this process. Therefore, in anticipation that Timor-Leste will be required to adhere to the TRIPS Agreement, it is crucial that farmers' organisations and other civil society groups proactively establish strategies for responding to the country's prospective membership of the World Trade Organization.

Building upon their experiences in developing the *National Seed Policy*, farming communities and civil society organisations could continue to work with government authorities to oppose certain changes related to the governance of plant varieties, which might occur in the future. These groups should be aware that legislators in Timor-Leste could face pressure to harmonise their country's laws with those of other World Trade Organization members, including via the adoption of a framework modelled on the UPOV Convention. Meanwhile, in the immediate term, it will be important to monitor the status of the *National Seed Policy*, given that as of May 2019 the framework was still undergoing review by the Council of Ministers. The eventual enactment of the *National Seed Policy* is expected to provide a foundation for the governance of different types of plant varieties in the country. However, the transformation of the *National Seed Policy* into a binding Timorese Seed Law is likely to represent the beginning rather than the end of developments surrounding the legal regulation of breeders' new plant varieties, farmers' new plant varieties, and local plant varieties in Timor-Leste.

Chapter 8

A fresh look at the protection of 'domestic' and 'wild' plant varieties in Thailand

Pawarit Lertdhamtewe and David J. Jefferson

8.1 Introduction

In scholarship about intellectual property for plants, the Thai system often is touted as an example that other countries could follow.[1] Rather than simply adopt a standardised model of intellectual property to protect the new plant varieties that professional breeders develop, Thailand elected to follow an independent approach. The country was the first in the world to enact modern *sui generis* plant variety protection legislation,[2] predating the Indian system by two years. One of the features of the Thai framework – which has drawn both significant praise and criticism – is the protection that it offers for different categories of plant varieties. Specifically, in addition to granting intellectual property for new plant varieties, the Thai regime enables 'local domestic,' 'general domestic,' and 'wild' plant varieties to obtain some form of protection.

The approach to intellectual property for plant varieties in Thailand has been recognised as innovative and laudable because it attempts to balance the interests of diverse actors in the national agricultural sector, including plant breeders, researchers, farmers, and local communities. Nevertheless, in practice the system of protection for domestic and wild varieties has proven difficult to implement. One reason for this may be traced to the law itself, and the way that it conceptualises local domestic, general domestic, and wild plant varieties. However, as Adhikari also discusses in Chapter 10 of this volume, there has also been significant confusion in the way that legal scholars have interpreted these categories of plant varieties. The aim of this chapter is to identify and analyse problems related to how the Thai regime defines and regulates domestic and wild plant varieties, and to

1 See, for example, Correa, C. M., with contributions from S. Shashikant and F. Meienberg. 2015. *Plant Variety Protection in Developing Countries. A Tool for Designing a Sui Generis Plant Variety Protection System: An Alternative to UPOV 1991*. Bonn: Association for Plant Breeding for the Benefit of Society (APBREBES). Accessed May 28 2019. www.apbrebes.org/files/seeds/ToolEnglishcompleteDez15.pdf

2 In the context of the present chapter, a 'modern *sui generis* system' means an independent, national intellectual property law for plant varieties that was created following the entry into force of the *Agreement on Trade-Related Aspects of Intellectual Property Rights* (TRIPS) in 1995.

offer suggestions for how the law might be reformed to render the protection of these types of varieties more effective.

The structure of the chapter is as follows. Section 8.2 explains why, even in the context of rapid economic transformation, customary agriculture – and by extension, domestic and wild plant varieties – remain fundamental in Thailand. Section 8.3 describes the making of the national framework of intellectual property for plant varieties in Thailand, with emphasis on how diverse actors were able to participate in this process. Section 8.4 introduces the substance of the Thai plant variety protection regime, describing some of the primary ways in which it converges with and diverges from the standard model embodied in the *International Convention for the Protection of New Varieties of Plants* (UPOV Convention). Section 8.5 delves into the form of protection for local domestic plant varieties that the Thai regime offers, while also identifying areas of concern. Similarly, section 8.5 focusses on the conceptualisation of general domestic and wild plant varieties in Thailand, and on problems associated with the way that the law protects these varieties. Lastly, section 8.6 concludes the chapter with a series of recommendations for how the Thai system of intellectual property for plants could be improved, centring on the protection of domestic and wild varieties.

8.2 The continued importance of customary agriculture in Thailand

The recent history of Thailand has been cited widely as a case study in successful economic development. Nationally, poverty declined from 67 percent in 1986 to 7 percent in 2015, on a wave of rising prices for agricultural exports.[3] Nevertheless, rural areas in the country remain economically marginal compared to urban centres, with two-thirds of Thai poor concentrated in rural regions.[4] While the contribution of agriculture to the gross domestic product of Thailand has declined in recent years, the country is still one of the largest exporters in the world of various commodity crops, including rice, sugarcane, rubber, fish, and seafood.[5] Furthermore, although the population is increasingly urbanising, it is estimated that more than one-third of the 60 million people that comprise the Thai population (nearly 22 million people) identify as farmers.

Notwithstanding the diminished contribution of agriculture to Thai gross domestic product and the corresponding decrease in the share of the labour force working in farming, the average farm size in the country has remained small. In fact, the proportion of small to large holdings actually increased from 1978 to 2013, while the average size of smallholdings has declined. The persistence of smallholder farmers in Thailand in the face of rapid economic growth has been

3 The World Bank. 2018. 'The World Bank in Thailand: Overview.' The World Bank. Accessed May 15 2019. www.worldbank.org/en/country/thailand/overview

4 Food and Agriculture Policy Decision Analysis. 2018. *Socio-Economic Context and the Role of Agriculture: Thailand*. Rome: The Food and Agriculture Organization of the United Nations.

5 Ibid.

characterised as 'one of the most enduring agrarian puzzles of the development era.'[6] In other words, smallholder farming in Thailand persists despite deep socio-economic transformation.

However, Thai small-scale farming itself is undergoing significant changes. The amount of land that in the past may have been sufficient to provide for household livelihoods is no longer adequate, given increased pressures associated with participation in consumer capitalist economies.[7] In the context of widening market and spatial integration in Thailand, farming has ceased to provide the major source of income for many households. Nevertheless, many adults in rural areas continue to farm and to identify themselves as farmers, retaining a strong attachment to land and place.[8]

In this context, it is important to note that in Southeast Asia in general and Thailand specifically, in recent decades there has been an upsurge in smallholder production of export commodities. Scholars have argued that the willingness of smallholders to participate in cash crop production potentially could offer a more inclusive development pathway than large-scale plantation farming.[9] According to this logic, an intellectual property system for plant varieties should offer forms of protection for diverse categories of varieties. Doing so could enable farmers to register the varieties that they develop, thereby incentivising their participation in market economies. Furthermore, such a regime could compensate farmers for their intergenerational work as stewards of native and traditional types of plants, and thus more accurately account for the resources that are used in the production of commercial products. In essence, this is what the Thai framework of intellectual property for plant varieties attempts to do.

8.3 The making of the Thai system of intellectual property for plant varieties

Similar to the experience of many of the countries whose stories this book recounts, the notion of protecting plant varieties as intellectual property gained visibility in Thailand only after the *Agreement on Trade-Related Aspects of Intellectual Property Rights* (TRIPS) entered into force in 1995. As a member of the World Trade Organization, Thailand was required to enact intellectual property legislation for plant varieties, either through the national patent law, or via an 'effective *sui generis* system.'[10] Motivated by the obligations that the country assumed under the TRIPS Agreement, in the mid-1990s, the Thai government

6 Rigg, J., A. Salamanca, M. Phongsiri, and M. Sripun. 2018. 'More Farmers, Less Farming? Understanding the Truncated Agrarian Transition in Thailand.' *World Development* 107 (2018): 327–337, 327.

7 Ibid, 328.

8 Ibid, 330.

9 Cramb, R., V. Manivong, J. C. Newby, K. Sothorn, and P. S. Sibat. 2017. 'Alternatives to Land Grabbing: Exploring Conditions for Smallholder Inclusion in Agricultural Commodity Chains in Southeast Asia.' *The Journal of Peasant Studies* 44 (4): 939–967, 940.

10 *Agreement on Trade-Related Aspects of Intellectual Property*. 1995. Article 27.3(b).

initiated a comprehensive campaign to update the national intellectual property regime, which included the enactment of a system of protection for plant varieties.

The process of developing the Thai plant variety protection law began in 1994, when the National Assembly mandated two government agencies, namely the Ministry of Commerce (MoC) and the Ministry of Agriculture and Cooperatives (MoAC), to study the possible impact and implications of enacting legislation to grant intellectual property for plant varieties in Thailand.[11] Curiously, rather than collaborate these ministries developed two separate yet similar bills for plant variety protection, both of which were submitted to the National Assembly for consideration. The only notable difference between the two proposed bills was that the administration of the prospective national plant variety protection regime would fall under the oversight of either the MoC or the MoAC, depending on which version the National Assembly decided to accept.[12]

Significantly, neither of these two proposals was developed in isolation. Instead, the MoC and MoAC bills both were drafted with the support of representatives from the International Union for the Protection of New Varieties of Plants (UPOV). Specifically, in 1994, UPOV organised a 'capacity building' workshop in Thailand to promote the UPOV model of intellectual property for plant varieties. This event was underwritten with the financial support of the Ministry of Agriculture, Forestry and Fisheries of Japan.[13] As a result of this foreign influence, both the initial bills that the MoC and MoAC proposed were based on the 1978 Act of the UPOV Convention (UPOV 1978).[14]

This association with UPOV sparked substantial controversy and provoked vigorous debate in Thai civil society.[15] Thus, multiple stakeholder groups, including the legal academy, research institutions, non-governmental organisations, and farmers' groups protested against the adoption of the MoC and MoAC bills.[16] In response, in 1997 the government of Thailand appointed a Drafting Committee

11 For a brief account of the historical background of Thailand's PVP Act, see Compeerapap, J. 1997. 'The Thai Debate on Biotechnology and Regulations.' *Biotechnology and Development Monitor* 32: 1315.

12 Ibid.

13 Kanniah, R. 2005. 'Plant Variety Protection in Indonesia, Malaysia, the Philippines and Thailand.' *Journal of World Intellectual Property* 8 (3): 283–310, 285–287.

14 *International Convention for the Protection of New Varieties of Plants*, 33 UST 2703, 815 UNTS 109 (1961); revised by 33 UST 2703 (1978).

15 For a brief overview discussion, see Janchitfah, S. 1998. 'Patenting Mother Nature Provokes Outrage.' *Bangkok Post*, January 4.

16 See, for example, Kuanpoth, J. 2009. 'Protection of Traditional Knowledge in the Face of Globalisation: Balancing Mechanism between CBD and TRIPS.' *Thailand Journal of Law and Policy* 12 (1). www.thailawforum.com/articles/Legal-Protection-Of-Traditional-Knowledge.html (describing the two main arguments made by domestic interest groups against the adoption of the initial PVP bills. First, the author argues that the bills favoured demands made by foreign corporations. Second, the author argues that the bills failed to adequately recognise the rights of farmers, and that the draft frameworks would have a detrimental effect on local plant breeders and the well-being of poor farmers in the country).

to generate a new plant variety protection bill. The Drafting Committee was designed expressly to create consensus between diverse social actors, and thus it was comprised of a broad spectrum of civil society, including plant breeders, farmers, academics, and representatives of non-governmental organisations and private industry.[17]

The Drafting Committee made several significant modifications to the original MoC and MoAC bills. Foremost, the Committee combined the two proposals to create a unified Plant Variety Protection Bill, which deviated in several ways from the UPOV model of intellectual property for plant varieties.[18] One of the most substantial departures from the UPOV standard was the inclusion of provisions to substantiate the concept of 'farmers' rights.' This innovation included the invention of new forms of intellectual property for different categories of domestic plant varieties, as discussed in detail in subsequent sections of this chapter. Thus, the final version of the Bill represented an attempt to assuage concerns expressed by both the Thai civil society and actors from the domestic and foreign private sector. In so doing, the Thai Plant Variety Protection Bill incorporated protections for

17 Lianchamroon, W. 1998. 'Community Rights and Farmers' Rights in Thailand.' *Biotechnology and Development Monitor*, 36: 9, 11 (noting that the government of Thailand formed a national committee comprised of diverse representatives, including plant breeders and farmers, to redraft these two bills).

18 A large body of literature argues that under the terms of the TRIPS Agreement, the definition of *sui generis* is broad. This means that World Trade Organization member countries can create any form of intellectual property for plant varieties, according to their particular needs and priorities. See, for example, Kuanpoth, note 16; Mosoti, V. and A. Gobena. 2007. *International Trade Rules and the Agriculture Sector: Selected Implementation Issues.* Rome: The Food and Agriculture Organization of the United Nations. Accessed May 29 2019. www.fao.org/3/a1477e/a1477e00.pdf; Ragavan, S. and J. Mayer O'Shields. 2007. 'Has India Addressed Its Farmers' Woes? A Story of Plant Protection Issues.' *Georgetown International Environmental Law Review* 20: 97, 100–101; Lertdhamtewe, P. 2013. 'Asian Approaches to International Law: Focusing on Plant Protection Issues.' *Journal of Intellectual Property Law and Practice* 8 (5): 388–398; Cullet, P. 2004. 'Intellectual Property Rights and Food Security in the South.' *Journal of World Intellectual Property* 7 (3): 261–286, 269; Cottier, T. and M. Panizzon. 2004. 'Legal Perspectives on Traditional Knowledge: The Case for Intellectual Property Protection.' *Journal of International Economic Law* 7 (2): 371–399, 375–76; Raustialia, K. 2000. 'Compliance and Effectiveness in International Regulatory Cooperation.' *Case Western Reserve Journal of International Law* 32 (3): 387–440, 393–394; Dutfield, G. 1999. 'Intellectual Property Rights, Trade and Biodiversity: The Case of Seeds and Plant Varieties.' The World Conservation Union Intersessional Meeting on the Operation of the Convention. Montreal, Canada, June 1999; Straus, J. 1996. 'Implications of the TRIPS Agreement in the Field of Patent Law.' In *From GATT to TRIPS-The Agreement on Trade-Related Aspects of Intellectual Property Rights*, edited by F. K. Beier and G. Schricker. Munich: Max Planck Institute for Foreign and International Patent, Copyrights and Competition Law, page 160; Blakeney, M. 1996. *Trade-Related Aspects of Intellectual Property Rights: A Concise Guide to the TRIPS Agreement.* London: Sweet & Maxwell; and Correa, C. M. 1994. 'The GATT Agreement on Trade-Related Aspects of Intellectual Property Rights.' *European Intellectual Property Review* 8: 327–335.

both breeders' and farmers' plant varieties.[19] The Bill was adopted by the National Assembly in 1999, and the new law was published under the title *Plant Variety Protection Act B.E.2542 (1999)* (Thai PVP Act). Section 8.4 briefly discusses some of the key features of this Act.

8.4 Convergence with and divergence from the UPOV model

In comparison to standard models of intellectual property for plant varieties such as UPOV, the most notable distinguishing feature of the Thai PVP Act is its provision of protection for different categories of plant varieties. Thus, the law creates a typology that includes: (1) new plant varieties; (2) local domestic plant varieties; (3) general domestic plant varieties; and (4) wild plant varieties. Notwithstanding this differentiation, the Act also elaborates a general definition of the term 'plant variety,' which means 'a plant grouping of similar or identical genetic or botanical characteristics, with particular features which are uniform, stable, and distinct from other grouping[s] in the same species of plant.'[20] The re-inscription of the criteria of distinctness, uniformity, and stability – which essentially date to the original delineation of requirements for protection in the first (1961) version of the UPOV Convention – have important implications for the protection of domestic and wild plant varieties, as discussed in section 8.5 and section 8.6.

Meanwhile, the form of protection that the Thai PVP Act establishes for new plant varieties essentially tracks the UPOV model. In addition to meeting the criteria of distinctness, uniformity, and stability, to be protected a new plant variety must also be novel in a commercial sense. This means that the propagating material of the new variety may not have been exploited, whether through sales or other means of distribution, for more than one year prior to the date of application for intellectual property protection.[21] Parties who obtain protection for new plant varieties under the Thai PVP Act enjoy the exclusive right to produce, sell, or distribute in any manner, import, export, or possess for any of these acts, the propagating material of the protected variety.[22] These provisions all recapitulate the UPOV model of intellectual property for the kinds of new varieties that professional plant breeders develop.

19 Kanniah, note 13, page 285; Compeerapap, note 11, page 1315; Changtavorn, T. 2011. 'Law on Plant Variety Protection in Thailand.' In *Textbook on Intellectual Property Law in Thailand*, edited by the Thai Bar Association. Bangkok: The Thai Bar Association, page 294; Lertdhamtewe, P. 2013. 'Plant Variety Protection in Thailand: The Need for a New Coherent Framework.' *Journal of Intellectual Property Law and Practice* 8 (1): 33–42, 34; Kuanpoth, note 16; Janchitfah, note 15; Lianchamroon, note 17, page 11; and Lianchamroon, W. 1996. 'Intellectual Property Rights on Genetic Resources: Case Study of Thailand.' Southeast Asian meeting of the Crucible Group, May 7–9. Cited in GRAIN. 1996. 'UPOV: Getting a Free TRIPS Ride?' GRAIN. Accessed May 29 2019. www.grain.org/seedling/?id+161

20 *Plant Variety Protection Act B.E.2542 (1999)* of Thailand (Thai PVP Act). Section 3.

21 Ibid, Section 12(1).

22 Ibid, Section 33.

Notably, however, the Thai PVP Act deviates from the UPOV standard for the protection of new plant varieties in certain ways. For instance, the Thai law contains provisions that specifically address situations in which plant breeding was conducted pursuant to an employment agreement or other contract whose purpose was to create a new plant variety. In such cases, the Act stipulates that the right to apply for plant variety protection vests in the employer rather than the breeder, but in some instances the breeder may be entitled to special remuneration.[23]

Another important difference from the UPOV standard surrounds the period of protection granted for new plant varieties. Specifically, the Thai PVP Act provides for 12 years of exclusivity for plants that are capable of bearing fruits within a period of fewer than two years after planting; and for 17 years of exclusivity for plants that will only fruit after more than two years.[24] Meanwhile, the Thai legislation grants a substantially longer period of protection for varieties of trees, at 27 years.[25] In the 1991 Act of the UPOV Convention (UPOV 1991), the duration of exclusivity is set at 25 years for trees, and 20 years for all other species.

These divergences from the UPOV model are intended, ostensibly, to customise its standardised form of intellectual property for new plant varieties to accommodate the realities of plant breeding in Thailand. Similarly, the Thai PVP Act also expands on the UPOV framework by incorporating a series of provisions that are designed to balance the exclusive rights granted to plant breeders with other important interests. For instance, the authorisation of the right holder is not required to use a protected new plant variety: (1) for purposes other than as propagating material; (2) education, study, experimentation, or research for the purpose of breeding or developing new plant varieties; (3) for acts committed in 'good faith'; and (4) by farmers, under certain circumstances.[26]

Although these exceptions to the exclusive proprietary rights granted for new plant varieties are broader than those contained in UPOV 1978 and UPOV 1991, it is important to recognise that the Thai conceptualisation of the 'farmer's privilege'[27] is narrower than in other countries that have enacted *sui generis* laws. This is because the Thai PVP Act permits farmers to cultivate or propagate protected new plant varieties only in cases where the Minister of Agriculture and Cooperatives, with the approval of the Plant Variety Protection Commission, names the

23 Ibid, Section 16.
24 Ibid, Section 31(1–2).
25 Ibid, Section 31(3).
26 Ibid, Section 33.
27 This concept refers to the recognition that farmers historically have relied on the ability to reproduce planting material – including from plant varieties that are protected under intellectual property laws – for personal and non-commercial uses without requiring permission from the right holder. Salazar, R., N. P. Louwaars, and B. Visser. 2006. 'On Protecting Farmers' New Varieties: New Approaches to Rights on Collective Innovations in Plant Genetic Resources.' *CGIAR Systemwide Program on Collective Action and Property Rights*, CAPRi Working Paper No. 45, page 13.

protected new variety as a 'promoted plant variety.'[28] Furthermore, even where a variety is designated as 'promoted,' farmers are permitted to cultivate or propagate it only in an amount not exceeding three times the quantity obtained from the rightsholder.[29] These limitations contrast with the approach taken in countries such as India, for example, where farmers are entitled to save, use, sow, re-sow, exchange, share, or sell their farm produce, including the seeds of protected new varieties, without restriction.[30]

Nevertheless, the Thai PVP Act transcends the UPOV model by recognising other limitations to the ability of the owners of protected new plant varieties to exercise the rights that the law grants. For instance, the Act enables the Minister of Agriculture and Cooperatives to prohibit the production, sale, distribution, importation, or exportation of new plant varieties on numerous grounds, which include for the prevention of diseases, the promotion of health, the maintenance of public welfare, the preservation and conservation of the environment and biological diversity, or for other public interests.[31] Conversely, the Minister is also empowered to issue compulsory licences to make the protected new variety broadly available, when motivated by reasons of national security, the maintenance of 'nutritious stability,' the prevention of monopoly, or to otherwise protect the public.[32] Lastly, the Thai PVP Act effectively requires diligence on the part of rightsholders, such that if they do not commercialise their protected new varieties within three years following registration, third parties may apply to obtain usage rights for these varieties.[33] The same provision applies if owners of new varieties do not make propagating material available in sufficient quantities to satisfy national demand, or if they sell this material at an 'exorbitant' price.[34]

In addition to the various ways in which the Thai PVP Act circumscribes the rights granted for new plant varieties, the law is also significant for its amalgamation of aspects of UPOV with the framework of the 1992 *Convention on Biological Diversity* (CBD). This latter treaty is concerned with regulating access to biological resources, and the sharing of benefits derived from the commercial exploitation of these resources. One of the ways in which the Thai Act gives effect to the CBD is through a disclosure of origin requirement. Specifically, the Act requires that applications for the protection of new plant varieties must contain information including the name of the variety and its essential features; details about its origin or the genetic materials used to develop the variety, including in relation to the breeding process; and a 'profit-sharing agreement' in the case where a domestic or wild plant variety has been used to create the new variety.[35] The purpose of these

28 Thai PVP Act. Section 33(4).
29 Ibid.
30 *Protection of Plant Varieties and Farmers' Rights Act, 2001* of India. Section 39(1)(iv).
31 Thai PVP Act. Section 36.
32 Ibid.
33 Ibid, Section 37.
34 Ibid.
35 Ibid, Section 19.

requirements is to ensure transparency and prevent 'biopiracy,'[36] while providing a 'passport' or permit for the transfer of Thai biological resources.[37]

A final feature of the Thai PVP Act that distinguishes it from the UPOV model is embodied in the 'Plant Varieties Protection Fund,' whose purpose is to support and subsidise activities related to the conservation, research, and development of plant varieties.[38] Among other functions, this Fund is meant to serve as a mechanism for benefit sharing, as imagined in the CBD. The resources that the Fund accrues come from various sources, including profit-sharing agreements executed for the use of general domestic or wild plant varieties for the purpose of breeding. Distributions from the Fund may be made to support the conservation, research, and development activities that communities or local government organisations undertake. The creation of the Plant Varieties Protection Fund represents an innovative approach to integrating intellectual property for plant varieties with other policy goals. However, in practice it is questionable whether the benefits that the Fund is intended to provide ever actually reach farmers.[39]

Although the form of protection that the Thai PVP Act recognises for new plant varieties generally reinscribes the UPOV model, representatives of domestic and foreign firms have criticised the law as insufficient to incentivise the development and commercialisation of new varieties. One area of concern surrounds the term of protection that the Act grants, which at between 12 and 17 years for plants other than tree species is shorter than the 20 years that UPOV 1991 provides. Furthermore, the Thai PVP Act currently requires that new varieties derived from genetic modification may be protected only after the Department of Agriculture or another competent authority conducts a safety appraisal focussed on possible environmental, health, and public welfare impacts.[40] The Thai regime also does not currently recognise 'essentially derived varieties,' which in contrast are able to be protected in frameworks that comply with UPOV 1991.

In part to address the criticisms launched by representatives of civil society and industry alike, a draft amendment to the Thai Act was published in October 2017. One of the key changes that this amendment proposed was that new plant varieties not based on existing Thai varieties (i.e., local domestic, general domestic, or wild varieties) would be exempted from the profit-sharing requirements that the

36 The notion of 'biopiracy' may be understood as the misappropriation or unauthorised exploitation of a country's national biodiversity. See, for example, Robinson, D. F. 2010. *Confronting Biopiracy: Challenges, Cases and International Debates.* New York: Earthscan.

37 Lertdhamtewe, note 18, page 397; Robinson, D. F. 2007. *Exploring Components and Elements of Sui Generis Systems for Plant Variety Protection and Traditional Knowledge in Asia.* Geneva: International Centre for Trade and Sustainable Development (IISD), page 22.

38 Ibid, Section 54.

39 Robinson, D. 2008. '*Sui Generis* Plant Variety Protection Systems: Liability Rules and Non-UPOV Systems of Protection.' *Journal of Intellectual Property Law and Practice* 3 (10): 659–665, 663.

40 Ibid, Section 13.

Act currently mandates.[41] If enacted, this change could have the effect of limiting the revenue that accrues to the Plant Varieties Protection Fund, which as noted earlier may already suffer from ineffectiveness.

Meanwhile, other reforms that the amendment proposes would align the Thai regime more closely with the UPOV model. These include extending the periods of protection for new plant varieties so that they are consistent with UPOV 1991, and introducing protections for essentially derived varieties.[42] Furthermore, the draft amendment proposes restricting the farmers' privilege, such that the Minister of Agriculture and Cooperatives would have the discretion to limit all or partial cultivation or propagation by farmers of certain selected varieties.[43]

Public comments on proposed draft amendment to the Thai PVP Act were received in October and November 2017, but since that time, officials have not taken any formal action to modify the law. Nevertheless, given the apparent willingness of the Thai government to consider alterations to the national system of intellectual property for plant varieties, it is an opportune time to take a fresh look at how the law conceptualises and protects domestic and wild varieties. Section 8.5 centres on the embodiment of local domestic plant varieties in the Thai PVP Act, while section 8.6 focusses on general domestic and wild plant varieties.

8.5 Definition and protection of local domestic plant varieties in the Thai PVP Act

This chapter has already observed that one of the key features that distinguishes the Thai system of intellectual property for plants from international standards such as UPOV is its creation of a form of protection for varieties that farmers develop. There are many issues and concerns associated with how laws have conceived of farmers' plant varieties as intellectual property,[44] and as the first example worldwide of a modern *sui generis* system, it is understandable that the Thai regime might not operate as originally envisaged. However, before exploring the criticisms that have been launched in relation to the form of protection for local

41 Prasertsri, P. 2017. 'Thai Plant Variety Protection Act Amendment Update.' *United States Department of Agriculture Foreign Agricultural Service GAIN Report No. TH7147.* November 2. Accessed May 15 2019. https://gain.fas.usda.gov/Recent%20GAIN%20Publications/Thai%20Plant%20Variety%20Protection%20Act%20Amendment%20Update_Bangkok_Thailand_11-2-2017.pdf

42 For instance, it has been reported that the Amendment would align the periods of protection for the breeder's right with UPOV 1991; introduce protections for essentially derived varieties; and restrict the farmers' privilege. Sujintaya, S. 2018. 'First Draft Amendment to the Plant Varieties Protection Act.' *Insight, Baker McKenzie*, January 23. Accessed May 15 2019. www.bakermckenzie.com/en/insight/publications/2018/01/first-draft-amendment-plant-varieties/

43 Ibid.

44 For a detailed analysis of the issues and concerns associated with the conceptualisation of farmers' varieties as intellectual property, see Chapter 10 of this volume.

domestic plant varieties, it is crucial to scrutinise exactly how this category of varieties is framed in the Thai PVP Act.

The Thai regime stipulates that a plant variety may be protected as a local domestic variety if: (1) it exists only in a particular locality of the country; and (2) it is not already registered as a new variety.[45] The registration of a local domestic variety entitles the owner, which may be an individual or a 'community' of people who take part in the conservation or development of the variety,[46] to exercise a set of exclusive rights. These rights are similar to those granted for new plant varieties under the Thai PVP Act, including rights to develop, study, conduct an experiment or research in, produce, sell, export, or distribute by any means the propagating material of the registered local domestic variety.[47]

The Act also specifies several exceptions to the exclusive rights that owners of local domestic plant varieties may obtain. Thus, authorisation from the right holders is not required for the use of the protected local domestic variety: (1) for purposes other than use as propagating material; (2) for acts committed in good faith; (3) for the cultivation and propagation realised by individual farmers in amounts not exceeding three times the quantity of propagating material obtained; and (4) for non-commercial activities.[48] These exceptions are analogous to those that the Thai PVP Act recognises for the unauthorised use of new plant varieties.

While these provisions are sufficiently clear, it remains important to disentangle a more basic question: what exactly is a 'plant variety' in a general sense, according to the Thai PVP Act? The definitions section of the law clarifies that the term 'means a plant grouping of similar or identical genetic and botanical characteristics, *with particular features which are uniform, stable, and distinct* from other grouping[s] in the same species of plant.'[49] This conceptualisation of 'plant variety' is significant, because it means that local domestic varieties must meet the same basic criteria as new varieties, except for novelty.

The requirement that local domestic plant varieties conform to the same distinctness, uniformity, and stability standards that UPOV devised for professional plant breeders' varieties may not serve the best interests of farmers. The plant varieties that farmers develop typically are more genetically heterogeneous – and therefore less uniform and stable – than the varieties that professional breeders create.[50] The fact that the Thai PVP Act requires uniformity and stability for these varieties may explain why in the 20 years during which the Act has been in force, not a single local domestic variety has been registered under the law.

45 Thai PVP Act. Section 43.
46 Ibid, Section 44.
47 Ibid, Section 47.
48 Ibid.
49 Ibid, Section 3 (emphasis added).
50 Louwaars, N. and F. Burgaud. 2016. 'Variety Registration: The Evolution of Registration Systems with a Special Emphasis on Agrobiodiversity Conservation.' In *Farmers' Crop Varieties and Farmers' Rights: Challenges in Taxonomy and Law*, edited by M. Halewood. Abingdon: Routledge, pages 184–211.

An alternative explanation for the lack of utilisation of the Thai PVP Act by individual farmers and local communities can be found in the requirement that by definition, a local domestic variety 'only exists in [a] particular locality and has been conserved or developed exclusively by a particular community.'[51] For years, critics have argued that this provision is inappropriate, given the way that plants, people, and knowledge tend to circulate among different geographical locations.[52] However, few have considered the implications that the definition of the term 'locality' may have for the protection of local domestic varieties in Thailand.

The Thai PVP Act conceptualises 'locality' as 'a group of people residing and commonly inheriting and passing over culture continually and registered under this Act.'[53] Two aspects of this rather confusingly worded definition are especially striking. First, the law does not conceive of locality in expressly geographic terms. Instead, locality in this sense refers to a group of people who relate to one another through the medium of a shared culture. A broad interpretation of this provision would suggest that local domestic plant varieties need not be confined to a specific space, but rather that their use should be conditioned culturally in certain ways by a particular group of people.

The second part of the locality definition that merits discussion is the phrase 'registered under this Act.' This means that, according to the plain language of the law, localities do not exist – legally speaking – unless they are inscribed as such in the plant variety protection system. Furthermore, there is slippage in the Act between the terms 'locality' and 'community.' For instance, the law provides that 'a *sui juris* person, residing and commonly inheriting and passing over culture continually, who takes part in the conservation or development of the [local domestic] plant variety … may register as a community under this Act.'[54] The Thai PVP Act then enumerates a series of protocols that must be followed to register as a community. However, no parallel procedures are specified to explain how localities should be registered. So, if a locality is a group of people registered under the Act, but no registration procedures are provided, can it be inferred that the terms 'locality' and 'community' are synonymous for the purposes of the Thai PVP Act? If so, this would reinforce the supposition that locality does not necessarily refer to physical space, thereby potentially affording greater latitude for farmers to register local domestic varieties.

A final issue that the conceptualisation of local domestic plant varieties in the Thai PVP Act raises, and which to date has received little scholarly attention, is related to the profit-sharing agreement requirements that the law mandates. Specifically, the Act stipulates that a person who:

51 Thai PVP Act. Section 45.

52 Bandyopadhyay, D. 2018. *Securing Our Natural Wealth: A Policy Agenda for Sustainable Development in India and its Neighboring Countries*. Singapore: Springer Nature; and Thathong, S. 2009. 'Rethinking Strategies in Legal Protection of Traditional Knowledge – A Case Study of Thailand.' *Journal of the Thai Justice System* 2 (2): 97, 111.

53 Thai PVP Act. Section 3.

54 Ibid, Section 44.

> collects, procures, or gathers a local domestic plant variety or any part thereof for the purposes of variety development, education, experiment or research for commercial interest shall make a profit-sharing agreement in relation to the profits derived from the use of such local domestic plant variety.[55]

The parameters of the profit-sharing agreement are elaborated in greater detail in the Act in relation to general domestic plant varieties, and thus they are discussed in section 8.6 of the chapter.

However, it should be noted here that when the subject matter is a local domestic plant variety, the law specifies the exact profit-sharing terms that the agreement should contain. Thus, 20 percent of the profits is allocated to the persons who conserve or develop the plant variety; 60 percent is designated to the community as its common revenue; and a final 20 percent is provided to the local government organisation, the farmers' group, or the cooperative that executes the agreement with the user of the local domestic variety. This profit-sharing distribution plan probably was intended to provide clarity and therefore encourage communities and third-party users to negotiate and execute profit-sharing agreements. However, in practice the rigidity of these terms could stifle the development of relationships between providers and users, and between the different individuals and institutions that act as providers.

For instance, the allocation of 60 percent of any profits to the community as common revenue could be controversial where a specific group of farmers develop a local domestic variety without the involvement of other members of that community. Likewise, given the ambiguities discussed above in relation to the definition of community, it may be difficult to delimit the sharing of common revenue. If communities are not necessarily confined to particular geographical spaces, then how can it be ensured that all members are identified properly for the purposes of profit sharing?

Given these various uncertainties and limitations, perhaps it is unsurprising that to date, no local domestic plant varieties have been registered under the Thai PVP Act. In contrast, and as section 8.6 discusses, the conceptualisation of general domestic plant varieties in the Act may afford greater opportunities for farmers to benefit from the intellectual property system. Nevertheless, there are also several reasons why the Thai framework for the protection of general domestic and wild varieties is also due for reform.

8.6 Definition and protection of general domestic and wild plant varieties in the Thai PVP Act

The Thai PVP Act defines 'general domestic plant variety' to mean 'a plant variety originating or existing in the country and commonly exploited,'[56] which does not fall into one of the other categories of plant varieties that the law enumerates. Some

55 Ibid, Section 48.
56 Ibid, Section 3.

confusion exists about the criteria that must be met to protect general domestic varieties. On the one hand, scholars have claimed that general domestic plant varieties do not need to meet the requirements of distinctness, uniformity, and stability.[57] However, this interpretation ignores the fact that the global term 'plant variety' is defined in the Thai PVP Act as having 'particular features which are uniform, stable, and distinct.'[58]

On the other hand, this situation may be contrasted with the definition of 'wild plant variety' in the Act, which is understood to mean 'a plant variety which currently exists or used to exist in the natural habitat and has not been commonly cultivated.'[59] While this conceptualisation also subsumes the global term 'plant variety,' a separate section of the Thai PVP Act stipulates that the requirement of uniformity does not apply to wild plant varieties.[60] Thus, the clearest interpretation of the plain text of the Thai law is that the criteria of distinctness, uniformity, and stability apply to general domestic plant varieties, whereas wild varieties only need to meet the standards of distinctness and uniformity. The rationale for these differential requirements is unclear, and it is particularly unusual for uniformity and stability to be decoupled from one another. As a practical matter, uniformity and stability are typically linked, in that examiners who evaluate intellectual property applications for plant varieties generally take stability for granted once uniformity has been established.[61]

One of the advantages of the way in which the Thai PVP Act defines general domestic plant varieties in comparison to local domestic varieties is that it is clear that lawmakers assumed that the former category would be in use throughout the country. However, other aspects of the conceptualisation of general domestic varieties have proven controversial. For instance, scholars have noted that the word 'existing' in this definition is contentious. Specifically, Thai government officials have debated the merits of allowing protection for plant varieties that are not native to the country but rather were introduced from other locations in the past.[62] While this may be the case, science on plant genetics has long questioned the validity of the concept of 'centres of origin' for certain species of plants.[63] Thus, the fact that the Thai PVP Act enables general domestic plant varieties to be protected regardless of whether they would be considered to be 'native' to Thailand should be regarded positively.

57 Gagné, G. and C. Ratanasatien. 2016. 'Commentary on Thailand's Plant Varieties Protection Act.' In *Farmers' Crop Varieties and Farmers' Rights: Challenges in Taxonomy and Law*. In *Farmers' Crop Varieties and Farmers' Rights: Challenges in Taxonomy and Law*, edited by M. Halewood. Abingdon: Routledge, pages 310–318.

58 Thai PVP Act. Section 3.

59 Ibid.

60 Ibid, Section 11.

61 Janis, M. D. and S. Smith. 2007. 'Technological Change and the Design of Plant Variety Protections Regimes.' *Chicago-Kent Law Review* 82 (3): 1557–1615, 1583.

62 Robinson, note 39.

63 Harlan, J. T. 1971. 'Agricultural Origins: Centers and Noncenters.' *Science* 174 (4008): 468–474.

In contrast to the system that the Thai PVP Act establishes for new and local domestic plant varieties, the law does not provide a mechanism to register general domestic or wild varieties. This means that the sole form of protection available under the Act for these latter categories of plant varieties is contractual rather than statutory in nature, since the use of a profit-sharing agreement is mandated. In other words, the type of protection available for general domestic and wild varieties does not follow a proprietary logic. Instead, as Robinson (2008) suggested, this system might be better understood as a set of 'liability rules.'[64] This approach 'entails a regulatory system that allows 'users' to access materials without necessarily gaining prior permission, provided that they provide some compensation to those that are the 'providers' of, in this case, a plant variety that has been developed or improved.'[65]

Another way to think about the provisions on general domestic and wild plant varieties in the Thai PVP Act is to recall the access and benefit sharing principles of the CBD. In effect, the Act functions in a manner similar to that envisaged by the CBD, such that parties who collect, procure, or gather general domestic or wild plant varieties must obtain permission from the competent governmental official (i.e., access), and conclude a profit-sharing agreement, pursuant to which revenue will accrue to the Plant Varieties Protection Fund (i.e., benefit sharing). While the Thai PVP Act is silent on the information that should be included in profit-sharing agreements for local domestic varieties, the law specifies a series of details that need to be incorporated into any agreement whose subject matter includes general domestic or wild varieties. Specifically, the agreement must contain a description of why the plant variety is being collected; the quantity of samples obtained; the obligations of the user; terms related to the prospective intellectual property protection of creations derived from the plant variety that was collected; the rate of profit sharing; the term of the agreement and how it can be revoked; and the procedures to be used for dispute resolution.[66]

In this way, the Thai PVP Act was ahead of its time, as it anticipated provisions that later were solidified in the 2010 *Nagoya Protocol on Access to Genetic Resources and the Fair and Equitable Sharing of Benefits Arising from their Utilization to the Convention on Biological Diversity* (Nagoya Protocol). For instance, the Nagoya Protocol requires that users of genetic resources obtain prior informed consent from resource providers, and negotiate mutually agreed terms to secure the fair and equitable sharing of benefits arising from the utilisation of genetic resources. However, in comparison to the Nagoya Protocol, the Thai PVP Act is limited in several respects.

First, and most importantly, the framework for access and benefit sharing that the Nagoya Protocol establishes extends beyond physical materials, to grant protection for traditional knowledge associated with the use of genetic

64 Robinson, note 39.
65 Ibid, page 660.
66 Thai PVP Act. Section 52.

resources. In contrast, the system of protection for general domestic and wild plant varieties in Thailand does not include traditional knowledge within its purview. Furthermore, under the Thai PVP Act, profit-sharing agreements should be negotiated between the prospective user of the plant variety in question and the relevant governmental authority. In contrast, the Nagoya Protocol requires that where traditional knowledge is associated with the use of particular genetic resources, prior informed consent must be sought, and mutually agreed terms must be negotiated with the indigenous or local communities that hold this knowledge.[67]

Another distinction between the Nagoya Protocol system of access and benefit sharing and the Thai framework for the protection of general domestic and wild plant varieties is that the former regime expressly imagines that benefit sharing may assume diverse forms. Thus, according to the Nagoya Protocol benefits may be monetary (e.g., access fees, up-front payments, milestone payments, royalty payments, licence fees, etc.) or non-monetary (e.g., sharing of research results, education and training, participation in product development, capacity building, social recognition, etc.). In 2011, a Ministerial Regulation adopted by the Council of State of Thailand clarified that benefit sharing pursuant to the Plant Varieties Protection Fund may include non-monetary benefits, such as technology transfer and capacity building.[68]

However, it is important to note that the terms of the Thai PVP Act still apply only to the commercial use of general domestic and wild plant varieties. This means that no access and benefit sharing provisions – or in the language of Robinson (2008), liability rules – are triggered when general domestic and wild plant varieties are used by third parties for non-commercial purposes, such as research, experimentation, or education. Furthermore, as described earlier, the official recognition of non-monetary benefits does not extend to the use of traditional knowledge associated with general and wild plant varieties, even if this use is commercial in nature. Because the law does not require prospective users of general and wild varieties to obtain prior informed consent from or negotiate mutually agreed terms with the communities from which plant materials are obtained, in practice it may be difficult to ensure that benefits are distributed properly to local custodians of these types of varieties.

8.7 Conclusions and recommendations

Ironically, one of the primary reasons for which the Thai system of intellectual property for plant varieties is praised is also one of its greatest weaknesses. That is, since its enactment in 1999, the Thai PVP Act has been lauded as an innovative

67 *Nagoya Protocol on Access to Genetic Resources and the Fair and Equitable Sharing of Benefits Arising from their Utilization to the Convention on Biological Diversity (2010).* Article 7.

68 Gagné and Ratanasatien, note 57.

approach to meet the obligations mandated by the TRIPS Agreement, while also attending to other policy goals such as those embodied in the CBD. This holistic strategy means that the Thai framework is both an intellectual property law and something more, encompassing rules to govern the access and use of different categories of plant varieties, and in so doing, departing from the logic of property.

However, the compromise that the Thai law represents has failed to satisfy fully any of the stakeholder groups whose actions the law regulates. On the one hand, commercial interests complain that the Thai PVP Act does not offer a sufficiently robust form of intellectual property for new plant varieties.[69] Thus, since the entry into force of the Act, domestic and foreign plant breeders have lobbied for reforms that would effectively reproduce the model embodied in UPOV 1991 in Thailand. On the other hand, civil society organisations – including especially groups representing smallholder farmers – and academics have called for the Thai PVP Act to be amended in a way that would protect domestic and wild plant varieties more effectively.

The draft amendment to the Act that was published in 2017 appears mainly to address the concerns launched by the domestic and foreign seed industry and plant breeders, without proposing corresponding changes that would bolster protections for domestic and wild plant varieties. For instance, the amendment would introduce a longer term of protection for new plant varieties; reduce the regulatory burden for genetically modified varieties; allow for the protection of essentially derived varieties; lower the number of varieties that would be subject to prior informed consent and mutually agreed terms requirements; and restrict the farmers' privilege. While it does not appear likely that the draft amendment will be enacted in the near future, many factors are compelling Thailand to shift increasingly towards the model of intellectual property for plant varieties embodied in UPOV 1991.[70]

In the context of this dynamic, it is difficult to recommend a simple solution for how Thailand might reform its system of governance for different categories of plant varieties. Since the country is not currently a member of UPOV, it retains a large measure of flexibility surrounding how to protect plant varieties as intellectual property. However, whether or not Thailand elects to join UPOV in the future, it is important to recognise that its system of plant variety protection does not presently provide many benefits to farmers. To date, farmers have not taken advantage of the possibility to obtain rights over local domestic varieties. Furthermore, the extent to which disbursements from the Plant Varieties Protection Fund have actually benefitted farmers is unclear.

69 Donavanik, J. 2013. *Plant Variety Protection Law in Thailand.* Bangkok: Nititham Publishing, page 29; Changtavorn, note 19, page 294; Masarek, A. 2010. 'Treetop View of the Cathedral: Plant Variety Protection in South and Southeast Asian Least-Developed Countries.' *Emory International Law Review*, 24: 433–467; and Lertdhamtewe, P. 2012. 'Thailand's Plant Protection Regime: A Case Study in Implementing TRIPS.' *Journal of Intellectual Property Law and Practice* 7 (3): 186–193, 191.

70 See Chapter 2 of this volume.

For these reasons, it is important that any prospective reform to the Thai system of plant variety protection does not focus solely on how to create broader exclusive rights for the new varieties that plant breeders develop. Instead, lawmakers should identify strategies to incentivise farmers to register their local domestic varieties, which could include, for example, modifying the uniformity and stability requirements for protection. Furthermore, changes should be considered to the framework for the governance of general domestic and wild plant varieties, such that traditional knowledge associated with the use of these varieties would also be included within the scope of access and benefit sharing. When it was developed over two decades ago, the Thai PVP Act was a paragon of innovative lawmaking, operating as a means to uphold international obligations while simultaneously catering to the interests of diverse local stakeholders. While the implementation of this regime has yielded certain insights, the time has arrived to conduct a new experiment with intellectual property for plant varieties in Thailand.

Chapter 9

From neglect to protection

Recognising the importance of farmers' varieties in Sri Lanka

Asanka Perera and Kamalesh Adhikari

9.1 Introduction

Sri Lanka, a small tropical island nation in the Indian Ocean, is known for its high levels of crop genetic diversity. With more than 6,000 varieties of native food crops and their wild relatives, Sri Lanka offers a valuable repository of agrobiodiversity, which could be leveraged to benefit agriculture and food production at local, national, and global levels.[1] For example, Sri Lanka's diverse range of traditionally grown varieties of crops such as rice, finger millet, maize, and vegetables possesses traits that could enhance food and nutritional security, and enable adaptation to climate change, both within the country and across the world.[2]

Although Sri Lanka is endowed with a wide range of crop genetic diversity, in recent decades the traditional crop varieties that farmers have historically grown have largely been neglected in the country. The primary reason for this is that Sri Lankan institutions have relied predominantly on the import of foreign germplasm for plant breeding and crop improvement. Specifically, the material used by professional plant breeders in Sri Lanka is typically sourced from the *ex situ* collections of the CGIAR (Consultative Group for International Agricultural Research) and agricultural research centres of other countries. Thus, imported, foreign germplasm is regularly used in Sri Lanka to develop 'modern' crop varieties, which are then released or registered for dissemination and sale in local seed markets.

In contrast, 'farmers' varieties,' which also are referred to as 'traditional varieties' in this chapter, have been used rarely in Sri Lankan plant breeding

1 Gunatilleke, N., R. Pethiyagoda, and S. Gunatilleke. 2008. 'Biodiversity of Sri Lanka.' *Journal of the National Science Foundation of Sri Lanka* 36 (25): 25–61; and Bossuyt, F., M. Meegaskumbura, N. Beenaerts, D. Gower, R. Pethiyagoda, K. Roelants, and A. Mannaert, et al. 2004. 'Local Endemism within the Western Ghats-Sri Lanka Biodiversity Hotspot.' *Science* 306 (5695): 479–481.

2 Rebeira, S. P., H. A. M. Wickramasinghe, W. L. G. Samarasinghe, and B. D. R. Prashantha. 2014. 'Diversity of Grain Quality Characteristics of Traditional Rice (Oryza sativa L.) Varieties in Sri Lanka.' *Tropical Agricultural Research* 25 (4): 470–478; Carew-Reid, J., ed. 2002. *Biodiversity Planning in Asia.* Cambridge: The World Conservation Union (IUCN); and Rajapaksha, U. 1998. *Traditional Food Plants in Sri Lanka.* Colombo: Hector Kobbekaduwa Agrarian Research and Training Institute.

programmes. It is notable that this is the case even though the public sector – including especially the Sri Lanka Council for Agricultural Research Policy and the Sri Lankan Department of Agriculture – remains the most important source of improved crop varieties in the country.[3] Although it might be expected that private sector plant breeders – especially those working in multinational firms – would primarily utilise parental lines that were developed outside Sri Lanka, it is surprising that government-run institutions have not taken greater advantage of the country's national agrobiodiversity in their breeding programmes.

The neglect of farmers' varieties over the past several decades in Sri Lanka has resulted in a number of challenges that threaten to jeopardise the lives and livelihoods of the country's citizens. For instance, the genetic diversity on which Sri Lankan breeders can draw has diminished, which could limit the ability to isolate favourable traits. Meanwhile, farmers' traditional knowledge, which is critical for agricultural innovation, including in relation to climate change adaptation, is disappearing. The decrease in agrobiodiversity has also resulted in degraded ecosystems, a fact that could imperil both the environment and human well-being.[4] Lastly, the neglect of farmers' varieties, coupled with the increased demand for modern varieties in Sri Lankan markets, has posed special challenges for the nearly 1.8 million smallholder farmers that comprise the rural population.[5] This is because, historically, these farmers have depended on the conservation and cultivation of traditional varieties on small holdings of approximately 0.5 hectares or less.[6] For smallholder farmers in Sri Lanka, modern varieties are typically unattainable due to the need to purchase planting material from the market, or the high cost associated with the inputs needed to grow these varieties.

In recent years, national stakeholders have raised several concerns surrounding the neglect of farmers' varieties in Sri Lanka.[7] A principal area of apprehension relates to the 2001 *Draft Bill on the Protection of Plant Varieties (Breeder's Rights)*

3 For detailed data on the use of foreign and domestic plant materials in Sri Lankan breeding programmes, see Muthukuda, D. H. and P. M. Wijerathne, eds. 2010. *Country Report on the State of Plant Genetic Resrouces for Food and Agriculture: Sri Lanka*. FAO/Government Cooperative Programme: The Status of the PGRFA in Sri Lanka. Colombo: Department of Agriculture, Sri Lanka. Accessed May 24 2019. www.fao.org/3/i1500e/SriLanka.pdf

4 Bandaratillake, H. M., ed. 2014. *Sri Lanka's Fifth National Report to the Convention on Biological Diversity 2014*. Colombo: Biodiversity Secretariat, Ministry of Environment and Renewable Energy, Sri Lanka. Accessed May 24 2019. www.cbd.int/doc/world/lk/lk-nr-05-en.pdf

5 Weerasekara, P., C. Withanachchi, G. Ginigaddara, and A. Ploeger. 2018. 'Nutrition Transition and Traditional Food Cultural Changes in Sri Lanka during Colonization and Post-Colonization.' *Foods* 7 (7): 111.

6 Ginigaddara, G. A. S. and S. P. Disanayake. 2018. 'Farmers' Willingness to Cultivate Traditional Rice in Sri Lanka: A Case Study in Anuradhapura District.' *IntechOpen*, pages 229–240. Accessed May 24 2009. http://dx.doi.org/10.5772/intechopen.73082

7 Hirimuthugodage, D. 2011. 'The Trade Related Intellectual Property Rights (TRIPs) Agreement and Agriculture in South Asia: A Sri Lankan Perspective.' *South Asia Economic Journal* 12 (2): 287–305.

(PVP Bill), which is the focus of the present chapter. This framework represents the effort of Sri Lankan lawmakers to comply with obligations that the country has assumed under the *Agreement on Trade-Related Aspects of Intellectual Property Rights* (TRIPS) of the World Trade Organization.[8] Critics of the PVP Bill argue that the regime is problematic because it does not enable local farming communities to obtain the protections that they need to incentivise the conservation, use, and development of traditional plant varieties.

The objective of this chapter is to analyse why it is in the interest of Sri Lanka to enable farmers to obtain legal protection for the plant varieties that they traditionally cultivate. Following this introductory section, the chapter is divided into five sections. Section 9.2 provides an overview of the current Sri Lankan intellectual property framework, while also describing the evolution of the PVP Bill. Section 9.3 presents a series of arguments to explain why Sri Lanka should introduce protections for farmers' varieties in a new version of the PVP Bill. Section 9.4 offers two potential approaches that Sri Lanka could follow to protect farmers' varieties. Section 9.5 concludes the chapter by arguing that the Sri Lankan PVP Bill should be revised to incorporate protections for farmers' varieties. There are several strategies that Sri Lankan lawmakers could consider to accomplish this goal, but any future regime should, at minimum, establish a system of access and benefit sharing for the use of farmers' varieties.

9.2 The evolution of the Sri Lankan system of intellectual property for plant varieties

In 1979, the enactment of the *Code of Intellectual Property Act No. 52* marked an important milestone, as the first 'modern' intellectual property law in Sri Lanka.[9] The overall aim of the Code was to foster economic development through increased commercial activity in the country. Notwithstanding this goal, the Code did not meet the minimum standards mandated by the TRIPS Agreement, which entered into force in 1995. Thus, in 2003, the Sri Lankan Parliament passed the *IP Act No. 36*. This Act was designed to fulfil the requirements of the TRIPS Agreement, for instance by making patents available for inventions in all fields of

8 Sri Lanka has been a member of the World Trade Organization since 1 January 1995. For further information about Sri Lanka's participation in the World Trade Organization and specific commitments under the TRIPS Agreement, see World Trade Organization. 2019. 'Sri Lanka and the WTO.' World Trade Organization. Accessed May 24 2019. www.wto.org/english/thewto_e/countries_e/sri_lanka_e.htm

9 However, it is important to note that *The British Investor's Ordinance* of 1859 was the first statute on intellectual property in Sri Lanka. The first Sri Lankan patent was granted under this regime in 1860. For further discussion, see Karunaratna, D. M. 2006. 'Issues Related to the Enforcement of IP Rights: National Efforts to Improve Awareness of Decision Makers and Education of Consumers.' *Advisory Committee on Enforcement, Third Session (May 15–17, 2006)*. Geneva: World Intellectual Property Organization. Accessed May 24 2019. www.wipo.int/edocs/mdocs/enforcement/en/wipo_ace_3/wipo_ace_3_5.doc

technology.[10] However, the 2003 *IP Act No. 36* stopped short of allowing plant varieties to be protected with patents. Instead, Sri Lankan lawmakers opted to create a separate, *sui generis* system of intellectual property for plant varieties, focusing on the new varieties that professional breeders develop. This intention manifested in the PVP Bill, a framework that complies with the TRIPS Agreement.

The development of the PVP Bill was the result of a collaboration between the National Intellectual Property Office of Sri Lanka and the Sri Lankan Department of Agriculture.[11] On July 24 2001, these governmental entities organised a national seminar to provide a platform through which relevant stakeholder groups could discuss the provisions of the PVP Bill. The hope was that this event would lead to a national consensus on the contents of the proposed intellectual property system for plant varieties. The audience was diverse, comprised of representatives of civil society organisations, law firms, and relevant industries.

At the seminar, industry representatives expressed support for the PVP Bill and for the kind of exclusive exploitation rights that it would grant to plant breeders. In contrast, experts from civil society organisations and law firms voiced concerns about the possible implications that the PVP Bill could have for farmers and traditional agricultural systems. Because the PVP Bill was designed to grant intellectual property protection for breeders' new varieties in a form that tracked the 1991 Act of the *International Convention for the Protection of New Varieties of Plants* (UPOV 1991), critics argued that the law would not address the needs of Sri Lankan farmers. A specific concern was that PVP Bill did not contain parallel protections for the conservation, use, and exchange of traditional plant varieties.[12]

Soon after the conclusion of the national seminar, in late 2001 a group of non-governmental organisations, including the Law and Society Trust and the Institute of Policy Studies, decided to collaborate and to submit a set of recommendations to the National Intellectual Property Office of Sri Lanka. Because Sri Lanka was not – and as of May 2019, is still not – a member of the *International Convention for the Protection of New Varieties of Plants* (UPOV Convention), these organisations advocated for the Sri Lankan government not to follow the UPOV model of intellectual property for plant varieties. Instead, these groups recommended that the scope of the PVP Bill be revised to recognise the rights of local farmers over their varieties. Furthermore, the non-governmental organisations argued that the Sri Lankan system of plant variety protection should promote the conservation, use, and improvement of traditional varieties, including those that are bred by public entities such as the Department of Agriculture.[13]

10 *Agreement on Trade-Related Aspects of Intellectual Property Rights* (TRIPS). 1995. Article 27.1.
11 Perera, A. 2011. 'Plant Variety Protection in Sri Lanka and its Impact on Sri Lanka's Agricultural Economy: A Critical Analysis.' *Journal of World Intellectual Property* 14 (4:3): 301–333.
12 For a detailed analysis of the UPOV Convention and its implications for countries such as Sri Lanka, see Chapter 2 in this volume.
13 Perera, A. 2010. *Protection of Plant Varieties in Sri Lanka*. Colombo: Law and Society Trust.

From the period of 2001 to 2010, the Sri Lankan government convened several consultations in an attempt to address the concerns that civil society organisations and other stakeholder groups raised about the possible implications that the proposed plant breeders' rights regime could have for customary agricultural systems. In an attempt to accommodate the interests of diverse stakeholders, in 2011, the Sri Lankan government released a revised version of the PVP Bill. Compared to the 2001 draft, the revised framework recognises certain privileges and safeguards for farmers. For example, the 2011 PVP Bill would permit farmers to 'save, use, sow, re-sow, exchange, share or sell [their] farm produce including [the seed of a protected variety].'[14] The 2011 version of the Bill would also exempt farmers from penalties associated with the infringement of plant breeders' intellectual property rights, under certain circumstances. For instance, farmers would not be considered to have infringed plant breeders' rights if they were not aware that a particular variety was protected as intellectual property at the time of infringement.[15]

Another key feature of the 2011 PVP Bill is that it recognises the role that farmers play in the cultivation and conservation of crop genetic diversity, including that of wild species and traditional plant varieties. Thus, the 2011 PVP Bill defines 'farmer' as any individual who: (1) grows crops by cultivating the land himself/herself; (2) oversees the cultivation of crops by another person; (3) is a 'tenant cultivator'; or (4) conserves and preserves – whether individually or collectively – any wild species or traditional variety, or adds value to these plants through the selection and identification of useful properties.[16] Furthermore, the revised PVP Bill provides a definition of 'farmers' variety,' which is conceptualised as a variety that has been 'traditionally cultivated and evolved by [...] farmers in their fields' or that is a 'wild relative or landrace of a variety about which [...] farmers possess the common knowledge.'[17]

Although these changes may be understood as improvements over the 2001 version of the Sri Lankan PVP Bill, it is notable that the revised draft framework has been stalled since 2011. Part of the reason for this inertia is that certain stakeholder groups have continued to express concerns over the contents of the Bill. For instance, notwithstanding its express recognition of farmers and farmers' varieties, the 2011 PVP Bill fails to create an enabling environment for farmers to obtain legal rights over their traditional varieties. Section 9.3 discusses a series of reasons why Sri Lanka should develop a new version of its proposed *sui generis* framework that would include protections for farmers' varieties.

14 *Draft Bill on the Protection of Plant Varieties (Breeder's Rights)* of Sri Lanka. 2011. Section 34(ii).

15 Ibid, Sections 35(i) and 35(ii).

16 Ibid, Section 4.

17 Ibid.

9.3 Why should Sri Lanka recognise legal protections for farmers' varieties?

More than 70 percent of the Sri Lankan population lives in rural areas, and a majority of these people depend on subsistence farming.[18] A key feature of Sri Lankan agriculture is that thousands of traditionally cultivated varieties of crop species – including rice, finger millet, maize, and a range of vegetables – have evolved in farmers' fields. This has occurred across a wide range of agro-ecological regions, leading to substantial agrobiodiversity. The crop varieties that Sri Lankan farmers have customarily cultivated did not merely evolve through mutation or natural selection. Instead, many of these varieties have been developed through the contributions that numerous generations of farmers have made based on their traditional knowledge. For example, farmers have routinely identified favourable characteristics that wild and other plants display, and have selected for traits that are useful for economic, environmental, and food security reasons.[19]

Another important feature of customary farming systems in Sri Lanka is the importance of the production, reproduction, and circulation of the seeds and other propagating material of different crop species. For example, customary practices of seed saving, use, exchange, and sale together supply approximately 80 percent of the propagating material that farmers require for food production in Sri Lanka.[20] Nevertheless, the country faces a number of challenges in relation to the conservation, use, and development of farmers' plant varieties. Furthermore, because the current version of the Sri Lankan PVP Bill solely focusses on establishing protections for the new plant varieties that professional breeders develop, it is likely that additional issues would emerge if this framework were enacted. Specific problems could be the disincentivisation of the conservation, use, and improvement of farmers' varieties. Subsections 9.3.1 to 9.3.4 discuss specific reasons to explain why Sri Lanka should incorporate a form of protection for farmers' varieties into its plant variety protection regime.

9.3.1 To advance the interests of farmers

As described earlier, the 2011 PVP Bill of Sri Lanka reinscribes the UPOV Convention model of intellectual property for new plant varieties. Thus, the framework would grant a set of exclusive exploitation rights to plant breeders, including to produce, reproduce, sell, export, and import the seeds and other propagating material of their protected plant varieties.[21] The criteria that breeders must satisfy

18 FAO. 2018. *Country Gender Assessment of Agriculture and the Rural Sector in Sri Lanka*. Colombo: Food and Agriculture Organization of the United Nations. Accessed May 24 2019. www.fao.org/3/CA1516EN/ca1516en.pdf

19 Weerasekara, et al., note 5.

20 Samaratunga, P. A. and D. Hirimuthugodage. 2014. *Intellectual Property Rights in Protecting New Plant Varieties and Farmers' Traditional Knowledge: The Case of Rice in Sri Lanka*. Colombo: Institute of Policy Studies.

21 *Draft Bill on the Protection of Plant Varieties (Breeder's Rights)* of Sri Lanka. 2011. Section 23.1.

to obtain protection for their varieties are identical to those that UPOV enumerates, namely novelty, distinctness, uniformity, and stability.[22] Similar to UPOV 1991, new varieties from all genera and species would be able to be protected as intellectual property under the Sri Lankan regime, provided that they meet the requirements for protection. This means that plant breeders could potentially breed or discover and develop new plant varieties using 'extant' plant varieties – including farmers' varieties – as source breeding material.[23] These provisions have a number of implications for how the 2011 PVP Bill, if enacted, could affect the lives of Sri Lankan farmers.

Foremost, it is notable that the 2011 PVP Bill does not create a separate category of protection for farmers' plant varieties. Although it could be argued that farmers might apply for protection when they act as breeders of new varieties, there are a number of reasons why this possibility is an insufficient means to advance the interests of farmers. First, the requirements of novelty, distinctness, uniformity, and stability are typically difficult for farmers to meet, thus rendering it difficult for them to obtain rights as breeders over traditionally cultivated or farmer-bred varieties. Specifically, it is unlikely that farmers could claim that their traditional varieties are novel because these varieties have typically been sold 'or otherwise disposed of' for periods of time greater than one year prior to the date of application.[24] Furthermore, it would likely be challenging for Sri Lankan farmers to meet the criteria of uniformity and stability. Because traditional varieties are often characterised by genetic heterogeneity, it is unlikely that these varieties would be understood as 'sufficiently uniform'[25] and that the essential characteristics of these varieties would 'remain unchanged after repeated propagation.'[26]

Notably, the TRIPS Agreement does not specify the criteria that countries should set as requirements for plant varieties to be protected as intellectual property. Thus, some countries that are members of the World Trade Organization but not the UPOV Convention have devised systems of intellectual property for plant varieties with different requirements for the protection of breeders' varieties on the one hand, and farmers' varieties on the other hand. For instance, farmers' varieties are not required to meet the criterion of novelty in India or Thailand. Likewise, the Indian plant variety protection regime relaxes the requirements of uniformity and stability, such that a greater number of off-types are permitted for farmers' varieties than for breeders' varieties.[27]

In addition to creating a system that would better enable farmers to protect their plant varieties as intellectual property, Sri Lankan lawmakers should also consider other strategies to advance the interests of farmers. This is because Sri Lanka has committed to implement the guarantees of the 2001 *International*

22 Ibid, Section 9.1.
23 Ibid, Section 15.1.
24 Ibid, Section 10.
25 Ibid, Section 12.
26 Ibid, Section 13.
27 For further details about the criteria for the protection of farmers' varieties in India and Thailand, see Chapter 10 in this volume.

Treaty on Plant Genetic Resources for Food and Agriculture (the Plant Treaty), which the country ratified in December 2013. Article 9 of the Plant Treaty requires Sri Lanka to develop national measures to 'protect and promote' a series of 'farmers' rights.' These include the right to the protection of farmers' traditional knowledge; the right to save, exchange, reuse and sell farm-saved seeds; and the right to equitable participation in benefits that accrue from the use of farmers' plant genetic resources for food and agriculture, and their traditional knowledge.[28] Other countries, such as India and Thailand, have incorporated some of these guarantees into their national systems of intellectual property for plant varieties. There is no reason why Sri Lanka could not also adopt such an approach.

9.3.2 To create a system of access and benefit sharing for the use of farmers' varieties

The current draft of the prospective system of intellectual property for plant varieties in Sri Lanka could lead to unjust outcomes where farmers' varieties are used in plant breeding and development. There are two reasons for this. First, as discussed in subsection 9.3.1, the 2011 PVP Bill does not create a mechanism through which farmers' varieties could easily be protected. Second, it is possible that plant breeders could use farmers' varieties as source germplasm, without any obligation to obtain prior informed consent from farmers. Likewise, the Bill does not require breeders to share any benefits that may result from the use of farmers' varieties with the providers of this source germplasm.

The 2011 PVP Bill would require applicants for plant variety protection to declare that 'the genetic material or parent material was lawfully acquired for [the] breeding [of the new variety].'[29] However, it is not explicit if this provision would require applicants to seek prior informed consent or to conclude access and benefit sharing agreements with the providers of the genetic or parent material used to develop the new variety. Given that the 2011 PVP Bill does not contain any access and benefit sharing language, and that there is no other legal regime in Sri Lanka to govern this subject matter, 'lawfully acquired' in this context would likely be interpreted merely to mean not in violation of any private contract or criminal law. Breeders of new plant varieties could exploit this ambiguity to appropriate farmers' varieties for use as parent material, without the need to fulfil any access and benefit sharing obligations.

Sri Lankan lawmakers should be concerned about the potential appropriation of farmers' varieties. Evidence indicates that Sri Lanka is extremely vulnerable to biopiracy,[30] a concept that may be understood as the misappropriation or

28 *International Treaty on Plant Genetic Resources for Food and Agriculture*. 2001 (the Plant Treaty). Article 9.

29 *Draft Bill on the Protection of Plant Varieties (Breeder's Rights)* of Sri Lanka. 2011. Section 17.2(x).

30 Akurugoda, C. L. 2013. 'Biopiracy and Its Impact on Biodiversity: A Critical Analysis with Special Reference to Sri Lanka.' *International Journal of Business, Economics and Law* 2 (3): 48–52.

unauthorised exploitation of a country's national biodiversity.[31] One example is found in the case of Kotala-himbutu (*Salacia reticulata*), which is a plant that traditionally is used in Sri Lanka for different health benefits, including to control hyperglycaemia (high blood sugar).[32] As of May 2019, numerous parties already had exploited this plant for different commercial purposes without obtaining prior informed consent from the providers of Kotala-himbutu, and without executing benefit sharing agreements with these providers. A 2006 estimate suggested that there existed a number of patents claiming the use of different properties of Kotala-himbutu.[33] Because local stakeholders believed that biopiracy had occurred, in 2006, the Sri Lankan government banned the export of all planting material of Kotala-himbutu and other related species, such as Heen-himbutu (*Salacia chinensis*) and Himbutu (*Salacia oblonga*).[34]

However, this export ban does not go far enough. Instead, to mitigate the risk of biopiracy or the misappropriation of traditional plant varieties, Sri Lanka should incorporate provisions on access and benefit sharing into its PVP Bill. In so doing, the country should follow the principles that have been articulated in the 1992 *Convention on Biological Diversity* (CBD) and the 2010 *Nagoya Protocol on Access to Genetic Resources and the Fair and Equitable Sharing of Benefits Arising from their Utilization to the Convention on Biological Diversity* (Nagoya Protocol).[35] Sri Lanka is a Contracting Party to both of these treaties, and the Sri Lankan government has expressed its commitment to implement national rules to regulate the access and utilisation of genetic resources and associated traditional knowledge. However, as of May 2019, the country had still not created a system of fair and equitable benefit sharing.

9.3.3 To generate incentives for the conservation, use, and development of farmers' varieties

As described in the introduction to this chapter (section 9.1), the rapid loss of traditional plant varieties, caused mainly by the growing dependence on modern varieties, is a significant concern for Sri Lanka.[36] As a result of the erosion of local plant genetic diversity, traditionally grown plant varieties have been disappearing

31 Robinson, D. F. 2010. *Confronting Biopiracy: Challenges, Cases and International Debates.* New York: Earthscan.

32 Li, Y., T. H. W. Huang, and J. Yamahara. 2008. 'Salacia Root, A Unique Ayurvedic Medicine, Meets Multiple Targets in Diabetes and Obesity.' *Life Sciences* 82 (21–22): 1045–1049.

33 Gunawardena, J. 2006. 'Kothala-Himbutu: Decisive Victory over Bio-piracy.' *The Island*, July 12. Accessed May 24 2019. www.island.lk/2006/07/12/midweek4.html

34 Ibid; Rodrigo, M. 2013. 'Biopiracy on Rise.' *The Sunday Times*, February 24. Accessed May 24 2019. www.sundaytimes.lk/130224/news/biopiracy-on-the-rise-34295.html

35 Samaratunga and Hirimuthugodage, note 20. See also Kariyawasam, K. 2005. 'The Recent Law Reforms and Plant Intellectual Property Law in Sri Lanka: Compliance with the TRIPS and CBD.' *Australian Journal of Asian Law* 7 (2): 169–186.

36 Weerasekara, et al., note 5.

from farmers' fields at an increasing rate in recent years. This has significant implications for future plant breeding, food security, climate change adaptation, and issues that are fundamental to Sri Lankan agriculture. In addition, traditional knowledge associated with the use of locally cultivated plant varieties – which is also critical for agricultural innovation – has been disappearing due to the growing use of imported and modern varieties.[37] To address these challenges, Sri Lankan policymakers should find ways to reverse the trend of the replacement of traditional varieties by modern varieties, and correspondingly to create incentives for the conservation, use, and development of farmers' varieties.

Furthermore, to achieve these goals, the 2011 PVP Bill should be revised in a way that would create an enabling environment for Sri Lankan governmental plant breeding institutions and the domestic private sector to collaborate with local farmers. This could take the form of, for example, varietal development research and participatory breeding programmes that focus on the use and improvement of traditional varieties for commercial cultivation. Furthermore, the prospective Sri Lankan intellectual property system for plant varieties should recognise and reward farmers as innovators and the breeders of traditionally cultivated plant varieties. This could be done by following strategies similar to those implemented in India, for instance by creating a system of awards to recognise individual farmers and communities as 'plant genome saviours.'[38] Evidence from other countries suggests that farmers would be motivated to conserve and develop traditional varieties, including crop wild relatives, if they were able to obtain economic incentives and/or social or legal recognition for their contributions.[39]

9.3.4 To ensure food security

Over time, many traditional varieties that historically formed the basis of food security in Sri Lanka have been destroyed as 'weeds.'[40] The traditional varieties that have survived suffer from marginalisation, given that both public and private seed entities in Sri Lanka have focussed solely on modern crop varieties in their breeding and commercialisation programmes. Together, these factors have resulted in the loss of a large number of traditional varieties that farmers historically grew to meet their food security needs. For example, many traditional rice varieties such as Kuruluthuda, Dahanala, Dik Wee, Suwandel, and Pokalli have already disappeared from most farmers' fields.[41] Different traditional varieties of finger millet, which in the past contributed significantly to local food security in Sri Lanka, have also been lost, mainly due to their gradual replacement by other crop

37 Ibid.
38 See Chapter 5 in this volume.
39 Ibid.
40 Rajapaksha, note 2.
41 Daniel, S. 2018. 'Twelve Traditional Varieties of Rice That Used to be Popular in Sri Lanka.' *Roarmedia*, May 24. Accessed May 24 2019. https://roar.media/english/life/history/twelve-traditional-varieties-of-rice-that-used-to-be-popular-in-sri-lanka/

species such as maize.[42] The Field Crop Research and Development Institute of the Sri Lankan Department of Agriculture estimates that the total national land area devoted to finger millet cultivation in Sri Lanka decreased from 21,000 hectares in the late 1980s to 7,000 hectares in 2016.[43]

Although in theory, the cultivation of modern, 'improved' crop species and varieties should offer benefits such as higher yield or greater nutritional value, to date Sri Lanka has not been able to achieve its food security goals. The 2019 Global Hunger Index, which is a comprehensive tool that is designed to measure and track hunger at global and national levels, ranked Sri Lanka 67th out of 119 countries studied.[44] It is important to emphasise that food insecurity in Sri Lanka was not a concern in the past, and that farmers were once self-reliant in meeting their food production needs. For instance, researchers have found that in the past, the Sri Lankan diet was so diverse that food 'was consumed according to the type of person (child, adult, elder), physiology (sick, pregnant, nursing), degree of activity (less active, energetic), and the type of meal (breakfast, lunch, dinner).'[45] While rural people in Sri Lanka generally relied on rice as their staple food, numerous different varieties of this crop were consumed for different purposes. Thus, '[v]arious rice varieties were served to pregnant and lactating women, as well as to sick people and the monks [...] There are records that in ancient Sri Lanka, there were more than 2442 different varieties of rice.'[46]

Given that Sri Lanka has not been able to achieve past levels of food security through the emphasis on modern crop varieties, Sri Lankan policymakers should devise and adopt strategies to ensure food security through the development and cultivation of traditional varieties. In contrast to modern varieties, which are typically derived from foreign germplasm, farmers' varieties have traits that local people prefer for agronomic, gastronomic, nutritional, cultural, religious, and other reasons. Traditional varieties also adapt well to different local climatic and agronomic conditions, require few or no inputs, and display superior performance when grown in marginal soils.[47]

The Sri Lankan system of intellectual property for plant varieties could recognise the importance of traditional varieties to the realisation of food and nutritional security by broadening its current focus on the incentivisation of the development of breeders' new varieties. Thus, the 2011 PVP Bill should be expanded to create incentives to support the conservation, use, and development

42 Rajapaksha, note 2.
43 Field Crop Research and Development Institute, Department of Agriculture, Sri Lanka. 2019. 'Finger Millets (*Eleusine coracana*) Kurakkan.' Field Crop Research and Development Institute, Department of Agriculture, Sri Lanka. Accessed May 24 2019. www.doa.gov.lk/FCRDI/index.php/en/crop/45-finger-millets-e
44 *The Economist*. 2019. 'The Global Food Security Index: Ranking and Trends.' *The Economist*. Accessed May 24 2019. https://foodsecurityindex.eiu.com/Index
45 Weerasekara, et al., note 5.
46 Ibid.
47 Rajapaksha, note 2.

of traditional plant varieties. For example, the 2011 PVP Bill could include provisions that are designed to support the implementation of participatory plant breeding programmes. Doing so would recognise the value of traditional varieties as a means to 'reverse the historical trend of separation between farmers and plant breeders, bringing them together in the process of developing new crop varieties or improving existing ones.'[48]

9.4 How should Sri Lanka protect farmers' varieties in its intellectual property law?

The first strategy that Sri Lanka could consider to protect farmers' plant varieties in a revised version of the 2011 PVP Bill would be to establish requirements for the protection of these varieties that would differ from those which breeders' varieties must meet. This is because it is unlikely that most Sri Lankan farmers would be able to demonstrate that their traditionally grown varieties meet the criteria of novelty, distinctness, uniformity, and stability. Thus, the Sri Lankan framework should relax these criteria for farmers' varieties, or alternatively, establish other mechanisms through which farmers' varieties would receive legal protection. Based on a model proposed by Correa (2015),[49] there are two distinct approaches that Sri Lankan policymakers could consider to revise the 2011 PVP Bill.

The first approach would involve the creation of a 'dual system' of intellectual property for plant varieties. Under this dual system, breeders' and farmers' plant varieties alike would be eligible for protection as intellectual property. To obtain exclusive exploitation rights, breeders' plant varieties would need to meet the criteria of novelty, distinctness, uniformity, and stability. These requirements are the same as those that standard models of intellectual property for plants, such as the UPOV Convention, mandate. Meanwhile, farmers' varieties would be eligible for protection based on relatively less stringent criteria, similar to those that other countries' *sui generis* plant variety protection laws define.

For instance, farmers' varieties could be exempted from the requirement of novelty. Countries including India and Thailand have adopted this approach, by allowing farmers to register their varieties even where they are not new in a commercial sense.[50] Similarly, the Sri Lankan regime could relax the criteria of

48 As quoted in Dawson, J. C. and J. R. Goldberger. 2008. 'Assessing Farmer interest in Participatory Plant Breeding: Who Wants to Work with Scientists?' *Renewable Agriculture and Food Systems* 23 (3): 177–187, 178.

49 Correa, C. M., with contributions from S. Shashikant and F. Meienberg. 2015. *Plant Variety Protection in Developing Countries. A Tool for Designing a Sui Generis Plant Variety Protection System: An Alternative to UPOV 1991*. Bonn: Association for Plant Breeding for the Benefit of Society (APBREBES). Accessed May 24 2019. www.apbrebes.org/files/seeds/ToolEnglishcompleteDez15.pdf

50 For further discussion on the registration of farmers' varieties, see Chapter 10 in this volume.

uniformity and stability for farmers' varieties, while still complying with the TRIPS Agreement. The *sui generis* laws of India and Malaysia could serve as examples when drafting these provisions. For instance, in India up to double the number of off-types is permitted for farmers' varieties compared to breeders' varieties when evaluating uniformity.[51] Meanwhile, Malaysia does not require farmers' varieties to demonstrate uniformity or stability. Instead, farmers' varieties are eligible for protection under the Malaysian law if they meet the criterion of 'identifiability.' This concept is easier for farmers to meet than uniformity and stability, because it only requires the identification of at least one special characteristic that differentiates the variety from others.[52]

Although Sri Lankan lawmakers could take advantage of the 'policy space' available under the TRIPS Agreement to define the criteria based on which farmers' varieties may be protected as intellectual property, it is important to recognise that several issues may still need to be resolved. Foremost, there is the question of whether rights should be granted to individual farmers, to groups of farmers, or both. In Sri Lanka, farmers often work collectively and form cooperative entities. This collaboration takes the form of, for example, preparation of land for cultivation, sowing seeds, harvesting crops, and conserving and improving traditional plant varieties. Because Sri Lankan farmers tend to collaborate when conserving, using, and developing traditional plant varieties, it might be difficult or inappropriate to identify an individual farmer, or even a single farming community, as the legal owner of a traditional plant variety. Similarly, it might be improper to require other farming communities to pay royalties for the use of a traditional variety to which one particular community has obtained exclusive intellectual property rights.[53] Such a requirement could jeopardise the realisation of farmers' rights as conceptualised in the Plant Treaty.

The second approach that Sri Lankan policymakers could consider to reform the 2011 PVP Bill relates to the idea of protecting farmers' varieties based on principles that would fall outside the logic of intellectual property. According to this approach, farmers' varieties would not be protected by exclusive rights that an individual farmer or groups of farmers would 'own.' Thus, one individual farmer or farmers' group would not be able to prevent other Sri Lankan farmers from producing, reproducing, saving, exchanging, or selling the propagating material of the protected variety. Instead, the second approach would operate outside the realm of intellectual property, focussing instead on preventing the misappropriation of farmers' varieties through a system of access and benefit sharing. This strategy would have the advantage of implementing one of the major objectives of the CBD and the Nagoya Protocol at the national level.

A key feature of the access and benefit sharing approach is that farmers would be able to exercise a collective right to equitable participation in monetary or non-

51 Ibid.
52 Ibid.
53 Ibid.

monetary benefits that accrue from the commercial use of traditional varieties.[54] Meanwhile, all third parties, including plant breeders, would be required to obtain prior informed consent from farmers before they access farmers' varieties for commercial purposes, which could include, for example, the development of new plant varieties.[55] By following this approach, the Sri Lankan intellectual property system for plant varieties should also require all applicants for rights over new varieties to declare in their applications that parental materials were obtained from legitimate providers, based on mutually agreed terms that include access and benefit sharing arrangements. Countries including Thailand, India, and Malaysia have already incorporated similar provisions into their *sui generis* plant variety protection laws.[56]

9.5 Conclusion

With more than 6,000 varieties of traditional food crops, Sri Lanka is home to a valuable repository of crop germplasm, which could be leveraged to enhance plant breeding, food security, and agricultural development. However, despite the tremendous agrobiodiversity that characterises the country, Sri Lanka has not capitalised on the policy space available in the TRIPS Agreement to create a *sui generis* system of intellectual property for plant varieties that would enable traditional varieties to be protected. The lack of legal protections for farmers' plant varieties in Sri Lanka could have serious negative implications for the livelihoods of farming communities, including their ability to utilise traditional varieties to achieve food and nutritional security, and to adapt to climate change impacts. Furthermore, without a system through which traditional varieties could be protected, Sri Lankan farmers remain vulnerable to the misappropriation of both farmers' plant varieties and associated traditional knowledge.

54 For further discussion on access and benefit sharing, see Beck, E. 2019. 'Access and Benefit Sharing—The Perspective of Basic Research.' *Phytomedicine* 53 (2019): 302–307. See also Siebenhüner, B. and J. Suplie. 2005. 'Implementing the Access and Benefit-Sharing Provisions of the CBD: A Case for Institutional Learning.' *Ecological Economics* 53 (4): 507–522.

55 For further discussion on prior informed consent, see Wynberg, R., D. Schroeder, and R. Chennells, eds. 2009. *Indigenous Peoples, Consent and Benefit Sharing: Lessons from the San-Hoodia Case.* Berlin: Springer.

56 See, for example, Antons, C. 2016. 'Article 27(3)(b) TRIPS and Plant Variety Protection in Developing Countries.' In *TRIPS Plus 20: From Trade Rules to Market Principles,* edited by H. Ullrich, R. M. Hilty, and M. Lamping. Berlin: Springer, pages 389–414; Lertdhamtewe, P. 2012. 'Thailand's Plant Protection Regime: A Case Study in Implementing TRIPS.' *Journal of Intellectual Property Law and Practice* 7 (3): 186–193; Ranjan, P. 2009. 'Recent Developments in India's Plant Variety Protection, Seed Regulation and Linkages with UPOV's Proposed Membership.' *The Journal of World Intellectual Property* 12 (3), 219–243; and Kanniah, R. 2005. 'Plant Variety Protection in Indonesia, Malaysia, the Philippines and Thailand.' *The Journal of World Intellectual Property* 8 (3): 283–310.

It is critical that Sri Lankan lawmakers establish a framework through which farmers could obtain legal protection for the plant varieties that they traditionally cultivate, both as a means to address local needs, and to comply with the CBD, the Nagoya Protocol and the Plant Treaty. Doing so would also introduce new economic and social incentives, such that farmers would be recognised and rewarded for the contributions that they make to the conservation, development, and circulation of local plant genetic resources. Due to the significance of traditional varieties for Sri Lankan agriculture, the 2011 PVP Bill should broaden its current narrow focus on the new plant varieties that professional breeders develop. Thus, the 2011 PVP Bill should establish mechanisms to ensure that Sri Lankan traditional varieties are conserved, used, and developed. In so doing, the 2011 PVP Bill could be revised in a way that would support the establishment of participatory breeding programmes, through which professional breeders and farmers would collaborate to improve traditional Sri Lankan varieties.

This chapter has suggested two potential approaches that Sri Lankan lawmakers could follow to incorporate a system of protection for farmers' varieties into the national plant variety protection law. The first would be to establish a dual system of intellectual property for plant varieties. Under this paradigm, breeders' and farmers' plant varieties alike could be protected as intellectual property. However, the dual system would mandate separate criteria for the protection of breeders' varieties on the one hand, and farmers' varieties on the other hand. While breeders' varieties would be required to demonstrate novelty, distinctness, uniformity, and stability, farmers' varieties would be exempted from the requirement of novelty. Furthermore, the criteria of uniformity and stability could be relaxed for farmers' varieties, for instance by allowing a greater number of off-types during field trials than would be permitted for breeders' varieties. Another option would be to substitute the criterion of 'identifiability' for uniformity and stability. Doing so would allow Sri Lankan farmers to obtain protection for their varieties provided that they are able to identify one special characteristic that differentiates the variety from others.

Even if Sri Lanka elects to develop a framework through which farmers' varieties could obtain legal protection, it will still be important to resolve several issues. For instance, lawmakers should carefully consider whether to recognise exclusive rights in relation to traditional plant varieties. This is because Sri Lankan farmers customarily work collaboratively, making it difficult to identify an individual farmer, or even a single farming community, as the 'owner' of a traditional variety. If exclusive rights were granted for traditional varieties, it is possible that disputes could arise between different individual farmers or farmers' cooperatives surrounding the use of protected varieties.

In addition to the dual system of intellectual property for plant varieties, this chapter outlined a second approach that Sri Lanka could follow to protect farmers' varieties based on non-proprietary principles. According to this strategy, farmers – whether as individuals or collectives – would not be able to exclude other farmers from the production, reproduction, saving, exchange, or sale of the propagating material of any traditional varieties that they register. Instead, the non-proprietary approach would focus on preventing the misappropriation of farmers' varieties by non-farmers. This would be done by implementing a national system of access and benefit sharing that would follow the objectives articulated in the CBD and the Nagoya Protocol.

Whichever approach Sri Lanka elects to follow, the country should act to reverse the current neglect of traditional crops and varieties. Agrobiodiversity is one of the most valuable natural features of the country, and Sri Lankan farmers possess an analogously rich reserve of traditional knowledge related to the use of traditional plants. By establishing a form of protection for farmers' plant varieties, Sri Lankan lawmakers could achieve multiple policy goals, including those related to plant breeding, food security, and agricultural development. Furthermore, protecting traditional plant varieties could simultaneously improve the livelihoods of Sri Lankan rural peoples, and assure the future vitality of national plant genetic diversity.

Chapter 10

What does it mean to protect farmers' varieties as intellectual property?

Kamalesh Adhikari

10.1 Introduction

Over the past two decades or so, much has been written about the merits of the unique, *sui generis* plant variety rights laws that countries such as India, Thailand, and Malaysia have developed to comply with the 1995 *Agreement on Trade-Related Aspects of Intellectual Property Rights* (TRIPS).[1] Research that evaluates *sui generis* plant variety rights legislation helps to address a number of questions and concerns. These include: Why and how should countries design TRIPS-compatible *sui generis* plant variety rights systems to provide for the protection of breeders' and farmers' plant varieties? Why should countries, especially developing and least-developed ones, reject the model outlined in the '*Guidance for the Preparation of Laws Based on the 1991 Act of the UPOV Convention*'?[2] Lastly, how should countries ensure that their plant variety rights laws support the access and benefit sharing principles contained in the 1992 *Convention on Biological Diversity* (CBD) and the 2001 *International Treaty on Plant Genetic Resources for Food and Agriculture* (the Plant Treaty)? The aim of this chapter is not to focus further on these questions and concerns or the merits of TRIPS-compatible *sui generis* plant variety rights laws; instead, the chapter considers a question that to date

1 See, for example, Antons, C. 2016. 'Article 27(3)(b) TRIPS and Plant Variety Protection in Developing Countries.' In *TRIPS Plus 20: From Trade Rules to Market Principles*, edited by H. Ullrich, R. M. Hilty, and M. Lamping. Berlin: Springer, pages 389–414; Andersen, R. and T. Winge, eds. 2013. *Realising Farmers' Rights to Crop Genetic Resources: Success Stories and Best Practices.* New York: Routledge; Tansey, G. and T. Rajotte, eds. 2008. *The Future Control of Food: A Guide to International Negotiations and Rules on Intellectual Property, Biodiversity and Food Security.* London: Earthscan; Dhar, B. 2002. *Sui generis Systems for Plant Variety Protection: Options under TRIPS.* Geneva: Quaker United Nations Office; and Correa, C. M. 2000. *Intellectual Property Rights, the WTO and Developing Countries: The TRIPS Agreement and Policy Options.* New York: Zed Books.

2 For the most recent version of this guidance document, see International Union for the Protection of New Varieties of Plants (UPOV). 2017. *Guidance for the Preparation of Laws Based on the 1991 Act of the UPOV Convention.* UPOV/INF/6/5. Geneva: UPOV. Accessed May 28 2019. www.upov.int/edocs/infdocs/en/upov_inf_6.pdf

has not received any real, sustained attention by scholars. That is, what does it mean to protect farmers' varieties as intellectual property?

Addressing this question is important for a number of reasons. Of these, three stand out. The first is that although prior scholarly analyses have focussed on ways, options, and model laws to protect farmers' varieties, there exists little clarity about what farmers' varieties actually are.[3] To the extent that scholars have considered the meaning of farmers' varieties, it is generally assumed that farmers' varieties have 'no fixed, internationally recognized taxonomic or legal definition,' that the concept of 'farmers' varieties' is still evolving, and that the use of a plethora of other terms complicates the conceptualisation of farmers' varieties as an object of legal rights.[4] For example, the term 'farmers' varieties' is used variously to refer to many different categories of plants, including native varieties, traditional varieties, local varieties, autochthonous varieties, indigenous varieties, folk varieties, heirloom varieties, local cultivars, landraces, and crop wild relatives.[5] Scholars also claim that some of these plant varieties may be owned or controlled – either individually or jointly – by farmers and breeders (e.g., landraces and local varieties), or farmers and the State (e.g., native varieties and wild crop relatives).[6]

3 See, for example, Correa, C. M., with contributions from S. Shashikant and F. Meienberg. 2015. *Plant Variety Protection in Developing Countries. A Tool for Designing a Sui Generis Plant Variety Protection System: An Alternative to UPOV 1991.* Bonn: Association for Plant Breeding for the Benefit of Society (APBREBES). Accessed May 28 2019. www.apbrebes.org/files/seeds/ToolEnglishcompleteDez15.pdf; Zerbe, N. 2007. 'Contesting Privatization: NGOs and Farmers' Rights in the African Model Law.' *Global Environmental Politics* 7 (1): 97–119; and Sahai, S. 2003. 'CoFaB: A Developing Country Alternative to UPOV.' In *Farmers' Rights to Livelihood in the Hindu-Kush Himalayas*, edited by R. Adhikari and K. Adhikari. Kathmandu: South Asia Watch on Trade, Economics and Environment, pages 26–32.

4 Halewood, M. and I. Lapeña 2016. 'Farmers' Varieties and Farmers' Rights: Challenges at the Crossroads of Agriculture, Taxonomy and Law.' In *Farmers' Crop Varieties and Farmers' Rights: Challenges in Taxonomy and Law*, edited by M. Halewood. New York: Routledge, pages 1–24, 3.

5 See, for example, Berg, T. 2009. 'Landraces and Folk Varieties: A Conceptual Reappraisal of Terminology.' *Euphytica* 166 (3): 423–430; Saxena, S. and A. K. Singh. 2006. 'Revisit to Definitions and Need for Inventorization or Registration of Landrace, Folk, Farmers' and Traditional Varieties.' *Current Science* 91 (11): 1451–1454; and Zeven, A. C. 1998. 'Landraces: A Review of Definitions and Classifications.' *Euphytica* 104 (2): 127–139.

6 For an argument that landraces may belong to both breeders and farmers, see, for example, Casañas, F., J. Simó, J. Casals, and J. Prohens. 2017. 'Toward an Evolved Concept of Landrace.' *Frontiers in Plant Science* 8 (145): 1–7. An example of a country that recognises indigenous communities, private persons, and the State as the rightsholders of native resources is Australia. See Department of the Environment and Heritage. 2002. *Nationally Consistent Approach for Access to and the Utilisation of Australia's Native Genetic and Biochemical Resources.* Canberra: Department of the Environment and Heritage, Australian Government. Accessed May 28 2019. www.environment.gov.au/system/files/resources/bbfbde06-d13a-4061-b2f9-c115d994de2d/files/nca.pdf

Although the academic literature has not been able to create a unified definition of farmers' varieties, *sui generis* laws in countries such as India, Thailand, and Malaysia have operationalised this term by recognising farmers' intellectual property for different categories of plant varieties. However, to date no comprehensive study has examined the process through which the meanings of these various categories of plant varieties were debated, negotiated, and understood in a country-specific context. Furthermore, research has not explored how different national stakeholders have participated in delimiting the scope of the intellectual property granted for farmers' varieties in countries that have enacted *sui generis* laws. Thus, the question remains of how local debates, negotiations, and understandings shaped the conceptualisation of various types of plant varieties as farmers' intellectual property in national legal frameworks.

The second reason to explore what it means to protect farmers' varieties as intellectual property concerns the ambiguities associated with the legal status of these varieties after the period of protection ends. Farmers' varieties are eligible to be protected for a specified period of time in countries such as India,[7] Thailand,[8] and Malaysia.[9] However, in their analyses of the Indian regime, some scholars have argued that the protection of farmers' varieties '[modifies] the intellectual property ideal that at the end of the intellectual property term (or when the exclusive rights exhaust) the plant materials become available for any and all uses without restrictions as part of a public domain.'[10] In other words, this argument holds that even after the period of exclusivity for farmers' varieties ends in India, these varieties would receive a kind of *de facto* perpetual protection. This is because the law requires that breeders must always 'establish a social license to use' farmers' varieties as source germplasm, and 'account for any benefit sharing claims' that the registrants of farmers' varieties may make.[11]

Notwithstanding the claims made by scholars, conversations with officials at the Plant Variety Protection and Farmers' Rights Authority of India and other stakeholders in India and Thailand, with whom the author met during fieldwork for this project,[12] revealed that the Indian and Thai governments have not clarified the legal status of farmers' varieties after the periods of protection end.[13] In

7 *Protection of Plant Varieties and Farmers' Rights Act* of India. 2001. Section 24(6)(ii).
8 *Plant Varieties Protection Act* of Thailand. 1999. Sections 31 and 50.
9 *Protection of New Plant Varieties Act* of Malaysia. 2004. Section 32(1)(b).
10 Trustum-Behan, E. and C. Lawson. 2016. 'The Protection of Plant Varieties and Farmers Rights Act 2001 (In) and New Plant Varieties, Extant Varieties and Farmers' Varieties: A New Form of Property?' *Australian Intellectual Property Journal* 27 (2): 73–87, 82.
11 Ibid, page 83.
12 The author conducted fieldwork in India, Thailand, and Nepal from November to December 2018. The fieldwork helped in gathering relevant information and data from three focus group discussions and 44 personal interviews with stakeholders representing government agencies, publicly funded agricultural research organisations, private seed entities, farmers' groups, and non-governmental organisations.
13 Personal interviews with policymakers and other stakeholders in India and in Thailand (December 2018).

Thailand, this issue may not lead to any immediate impact, given that to date no farmers' varieties have been registered under the Thai *Plant Varieties Protection Act* of 1999. In contrast, in India it is likely that the uncertainties surrounding the possible inclusion of farmers' varieties in the public domain could emerge as a significant concern in the near future. This is because from 2009 to 2018, the Plant Variety Protection and Farmers' Rights Authority of India granted intellectual property protection to 1,586 farmers' varieties.[14] Given that the period of protection for farmers' varieties in India is 15 years, it is unclear whether protected farmers' varieties would begin to enter the public domain beginning in 2024.

The third factor that motivates the investigation of what it means to recognise farmers' varieties as intellectual property relates to an ongoing debate about how 'farmers' rights' should be conceptualised to enable farmers to control the use, circulation, and commercialisation of their varieties. In this debate, some scholars have suggested that farmers' varieties should be protected through the same kind of exclusive rights that plant breeders receive in standard models of intellectual property for plant varieties.[15] Meanwhile, other scholars have rejected the idea of protecting farmers' varieties based on the logic of plant breeders' rights.[16] These scholars have advocated for the protection of farmers' varieties based on the principles of social recognition, unfettered exchange and circulation of plant varieties, and equitable participation in the benefits that arise from the access and commercial use of farmers' varieties.[17]

The underlying arguments behind these competing ideas are rendered explicit in the two most prominent proposals for recognising farmers' rights: the 'stewardship' approach and the 'ownership' approach.[18] According to the stewardship

14 Based on the data collected from the official records of the New Delhi-based Protection of Plant Varieties and Farmers' Rights Authority of India (December 2018).

15 For an analysis of why farmers' varieties should not be treated as less valuable than breeders' varieties, see Mooney, P. 2011. 'International Non-governmental Organizations: The Hundred Year (or so) Seed War – Seeds, Sovereignty and Civil Society – A Historical Perspective on the Evolution of the "Law of the Seed".' In *Plant Genetic Resources and Food Security: Stakeholder Perspectives on the International Treaty on Plant Genetic Resources for Food and Agriculture*, edited by C. Frison, F. López, and J. Esquinas-Alcazar. Abingdon: Routledge, pages 135–148.

16 See, for example, Salazar, R., N. P. Louwaars, and B. Visser. 2007. 'Protecting Farmers' New Varieties: New Approaches to Rights on Collective Innovations in Plant Genetic Resources.' *World Development* 35 (9): 1515–1528.

17 For an analysis of why varieties developed by farmers should not be protected as intellectual property, and why a collective mechanism of access and benefit sharing should be developed, see Santilli, J. 2012. *Agrobiodiversity and the Law: Regulating Genetic Resources, Food Security and Cultural Diversity*. Abingdon: Routledge. For an analysis of open access principles, see Kloppenburg, J. 2014. 'Re-purposing the Master's Tools: The Open Source Seed Initiative and the Struggle for Seed Sovereignty.' *Journal of Peasant Studies* 41 (6): 1225–1246.

18 For an analysis of how countries such as India and Brazil have adopted 'ownership' and 'stewardship' approaches to protect farmers' rights, see, for example, Peschard, K. 2017. 'Seed Wars and Farmers' Rights: Comparative Perspectives from Brazil and India.' *The Journal of Peasant Studies* 44 (1): 144–168; and Santilli, J. 2013. 'Genetic Resources Common Pools in Brazil.' In *Common Pools of Genetic Resources: Equity and*

approach, it is assumed that farmers should have the collective right to conserve and use their plant varieties, and to obtain rewards and benefits for making their varieties available for research and breeding. A major feature of the stewardship approach is that it aligns with the principle of common heritage. This precept holds that farmers' varieties should be available in the public domain for the common good of humankind. In contrast, the ownership approach would recognise the collective or individual right of farmers to protect their varieties according to the logic of exclusive rights to private intellectual property. Thus, according to the ownership approach, farmers' varieties would not constitute the common heritage of humankind or form part of the public domain.[19]

This chapter argues that this binary way of thinking about farmers' rights is limited by certain assumptions. The dichotomisation of farmers' rights suggests that farmers should be either the 'exclusive' owners or the 'socially-recognised' stewards of their varieties. In other words, there is an assumption that farmers' rights should be based on either a proprietary logic or the non-proprietary principles of unfettered exchange and circulation of plant varieties. These kinds of assumptions ignore the fact that the question of how to protect farmers' rights is not confined to how and why farmers should own or circulate their varieties. As this chapter demonstrates, this question must also grapple with the fact that farmers play different roles, for example, as conservers, breeders, producers, and consumers of different types of locally cultivated plant varieties. These include: varieties that are indigenous or traditionally grown, varieties that adapt to local growing conditions through decades of selection by farmers, varieties that farmers breed and develop for commercialisation, and varieties that external agencies make available for farmers to cultivate.

Given the complex nature of the roles that farmers play in relation to different types of locally cultivated varieties, the author does not take a side in the proprietary versus non-proprietary debate. Instead, this chapter explores how local needs and dynamics related to the conservation, use, breeding, and commercialisation of plant varieties may complicate the conceptualisation of farmers' varieties as intellectual property. In so doing, a case study from Nepal is presented where over the past two decades, significant developments have taken place to reshape understandings of 'farmers' varieties' and 'the protection of farmers' varieties as intellectual property.'

In contrast to existing *sui generis* frameworks that other countries have enacted, Nepal's evolving plant variety rights regime does not recognise native, indigenous,

Innovation in International Biodiversity Law, edited by E. C. Kamau and G. Winter. Abingdon: Routledge, pages 135–158.

19 For a detailed analysis of the 'ownership' and 'stewardship' approaches and whether these two can be combined to protect farmers' rights, see Andersen, R. 2018. 'The International Treaty on Plant Genetic Resources for Food and Agriculture: Toward the Realization of Farmers' Rights as a Means of Protecting and Enhancing Crop Genetic Diversity.' In *Routledge Handbook of Biodiversity and the Law*, edited by C. R. McManis and B. Ong. Abingdon: Routledge, pages 135–153.

traditional, or local varieties of common knowledge as farmers' varieties. Rather, the Nepali scheme conceptualises native, indigenous, traditional, and local varieties of common knowledge as 'source germplasm' and varieties that are developed from the use of such germplasm as farmers' intellectual property, that is, 'farmers' varieties.' In so doing, the Nepali framework requires that farmers' varieties be distinguishable from other varieties by at least one characteristic (distinctness) and that they reproduce true to form across individual plants (uniformity) and across generations (stability).

A key feature of the Nepali scheme is that it proposes to grant farmers the right to register and obtain a certificate to claim ownership for farmers' varieties. However, in contrast to the plant variety rights laws of India, Thailand, and Malaysia, the Nepali regime does not explicitly recognise farmers' exclusive rights to produce, reproduce, and market the seeds of protected farmers' varieties. Furthermore, the Nepali draft law is also unique in that it does not specify any period of protection for farmers' varieties.

Although the Nepali draft law contains many interesting provisions, in Nepal as in other countries, little is understood about the local needs and dynamics related to the protection of farmers' varieties as intellectual property, let alone the implications of such protection. The analysis in this chapter of the case of *Jethobudho* – a traditionally grown rice cultivar that a group of farmers in the Pokhara valley of Nepal developed into a commercial variety in 2006 – reveals that there are many questions and concerns that still need to be resolved in relation to the conceptualisation of farmers' varieties as intellectual property.

This chapter is structured as follows. Section 10.2 explains how and why farmers' varieties evolved as a legal construct in countries such as India, Thailand, and Malaysia, and how the approach that these countries have taken to recognise farmers' varieties as intellectual property is different to that of Nepal. Section 10.3 describes the context in which Nepal created protections for farmers' varieties under its evolving plant variety rights regime. Section 10.4 explores how farmers' understandings of different categories of native, indigenous, traditional, and local plant varieties were discussed by the drafting committee members when developing the notion of farmers' varieties into a legal concept in Nepal's *Draft Bill on Plant Variety Protection and Farmers' Rights*. Section 10.5 analyses how the *Jethobudho* rice cultivar that farmers traditionally grow evolved to be recognised as the *Pokhareli Jethobudho* variety under Nepali law. Section 10.6 identifies and discusses a number of questions and concerns that the case of the commercialisation of *Pokhareli Jethobudho* raises in relation to the conceptualisation of farmers' varieties as intellectual property in Nepal. Section 10.7 concludes the chapter.

10.2 Farmers' varieties as an international legal construct

From the adoption of the *Plant Patent Act*[20] by the United States in 1930 to the enactment of the TRIPS Agreement in 1995, intellectual property laws for plant

20 The 1930 *Plant Patent Act* of the United States is the first intellectual property law to grant a specialised form of protection for plant varieties (the protection was, however, confined to 'new' and 'distinct' ornamental plants and fruits that were reproduced from

varieties focussed only on varieties that were novel and that met certain specific criteria. To be protected with patents, plant varieties need to meet the criteria of 'novelty,' 'inventive step,' and 'industrial application.'[21] To obtain plant breeders' rights – which emerged as an alternative to patents after the advent of the 1961 *International Convention for the Protection of New Varieties of Plants* (UPOV Convention) – a variety must be 'novel,' 'distinct,' 'uniform,' and 'stable.'[22] Today, countries that provide patent protection for plant varieties continue to focus on – to a greater or lesser extent – varieties that are new, involve an inventive step, and are capable of industrial application.[23] However, in parallel, over the past two decades or so, *sui generis* laws have emerged in a number of countries to reshape the way that plant varieties are protected as intellectual property. Examples include the plant variety rights laws that countries such as India, Thailand, and Malaysia introduced in the late 1990s and early 2000s to comply with Article 27.3 (b) of the TRIPS Agreement. This provision obligates all members of the World Trade Organization to provide intellectual property protection for plant varieties through patents, a *sui generis* system, or both.

A striking feature of the *sui generis* plant variety rights laws of India, Thailand, and Malaysia is that they move beyond the logic of the conventional UPOV-based plant breeders' rights model. In so doing, these legal instruments do not limit their scope to the protection of plant breeders' novel, distinct, uniform, and stable varieties. Instead, these national laws – which in this chapter are termed 'UPOV-plus' – also recognise exclusive rights that farmers may obtain in relation to the different categories of plant varieties that they conserve, cultivate, and develop under local growing conditions. The categories of plant varieties for which farmers may obtain protection include: varieties that traditionally have been cultivated and developed by farmers in their fields, or that are landraces or wild relatives of crop varieties about which farmers possess common knowledge (India);[24] local domestic plant varieties that exist in a particular geographic area of the country (Thailand);[25] and traditional varieties that have been bred or discovered and developed by farmers (Malaysia).[26]

Another important feature of the UPOV-plus plant variety rights laws of India, Thailand, and Malaysia is that they establish criteria for the protection of farmers' varieties that diverge from the requirements that breeders' varieties must meet.

'asexual propagation'). See Pottage, A. and B. Sherman. 2007. 'Organisms and Manufactures: On the History of Plant Inventions.' *Melbourne University Law Review* 31 (2): 539–568.

21 *Agreement on Trade-Related Aspects of Intellectual Property Rights* (TRIPS). 1995. Article 27.1.

22 1991 Act of the *International Convention for the Protection of New Varieties of Plants* (UPOV 1991). Articles 5, 6, 7, 8 and 9.

23 An example is the *Patents Act 1990* of Australia.

24 *Protection of Plant Varieties and Farmers' Rights Act* of India. 2001. Section 2(l).

25 *Plant Varieties Protection Act* of Thailand. 1999. Section 43(1).

26 *Protection of New Plant Varieties Act* of Malaysia. 2004. Sections 2 and 14(2).

For example, under the 1999 *Plant Varieties Protection Act* of Thailand, local domestic plant varieties are not required to be novel for farmers to protect these varieties. The Thai law provides for the protection of local domestic varieties if they have existed in a particular geographical location of the country and if they have been conserved and developed exclusively by a particular farming community.[27] The form of protection granted for local domestic plant varieties includes the right to produce, sell, export, or distribute the seeds of these varieties[28] for a specified period.[29]

Similar to the Thai law, the 2001 *Protection of Plant Varieties and Farmers' Rights Act* of India also exempts farmers' varieties from the requirement of novelty. Furthermore, although farmers' varieties must meet the requirements of distinctness, uniformity, and stability,[30] the *2009 Protection of Plant Varieties and Farmers' rights (Criteria for DUS for Registration) Regulations* of India relax the rules based on which these varieties are assessed. Compared to other varieties that can be protected under the law, up to double the number of off-types/mixtures is permitted for farmers' varieties to meet the threshold of uniformity.[31] In addition, once farmers' varieties have met the uniformity criterion, there is no need for these varieties to pass any stability test.[32] The registration of farmers' varieties in India enables owners to exercise exclusive rights that are similar to those granted to plant breeders.[33]

The Malaysian system for the protection of farmers' varieties diverges from the laws of India and Thailand in one key area. Under the 2004 *Protection of New Plant Varieties Act* of Malaysia, traditional varieties that farmers improve through the selection and identification of useful properties must be new and distinct, but they are not required to be uniform and stable to be protected as intellectual property.[34] Instead, the Malaysian plant variety rights law introduces the criterion of 'identifiability'[35] for improved traditional varieties. The rationale behind the inscription of this concept is that identifying one special characteristic of an improved traditional variety should be easier for Malaysian farmers than to pass a rigorous test for uniformity and stability. Another unique aspect of the Malaysian law is that if improved traditional varieties meet the criteria of novelty, distinctness, and identifiability, they may be registered as new breeders' varieties. This means

27 *Plant Varieties Protection Act* of Thailand. 1999. Sections 43, 44 and 45.
28 Ibid, Section 47.
29 Ibid, Sections 31 and 50.
30 *Protection of Plant Varieties and Farmers' Rights Act* of India. 2001. Section 15(2).
31 *Protection of Plant Varieties and Farmers' Rights (Criteria for DUS for Registration) Regulations* of India. 2009. Section 5(6).
32 Ibid, Section 5(7).
33 Ibid, Sections 24(6)(ii) and 24(6)(iii).
34 *Protection of New Plant Varieties Act* of Malaysia. 2004. Section 14(2).
35 Ibid, Section 14(3)(e).

that Malaysian farmers can exercise exclusive breeders' rights[36] to exploit protected varieties for a specific period of time.[37]

In addition to the protection of farmers' varieties based on a unique set of criteria, the plant variety rights laws of India, Thailand, and Malaysia share other salient features. For example, all of these UPOV-plus laws ensure that farmers have the ability – to a greater extent than what is available under the 1991 Act of the UPOV Convention (UPOV 1991)[38] – to save, exchange, reuse, and sell seeds that are harvested from protected plant varieties.[39] Furthermore, the Indian, Thai, and Malaysian laws all require breeders of new plant varieties to meet the condition of disclosure, which contrasts with the UPOV model. This means that the applicant for plant breeders' rights must demonstrate evidence that prior informed consent was obtained from, and/or a benefit sharing agreement was negotiated with, the provider of the source germplasm. This might occur, for example, in cases where the breeder has used a farmers' variety to develop a new variety.[40]

A close examination of these countries' legislation suggests that India, Thailand, and Malaysia opted to develop UPOV-plus laws for three main reasons. The first is that the UPOV Convention created a system that grants a temporary commercial monopoly to reward the efforts of the breeders of new plant varieties, but it did not obligate breeders to seek consent to access and exploit – or to share benefits obtained through the use of – farmers' genetic resources.[41] To some extent, the CBD addressed how access and benefit sharing concerns could be incorporated into the process of plant breeding and the commercial use of farmers' plant genetic resources.[42] However, to date these issues have not been addressed in the UPOV system, or in negotiations for the review Article 27.3(b) of the TRIPS

36 Ibid, Section 14(2).
37 Ibid, Section 32(1)(b).
38 UPOV 1991. Articles 15.1 and 15.2.
39 *Protection of Plant Varieties and Farmers' Rights Act* of India. 2001. Section 39(iv); *Plant Varieties Protection Act* of Thailand. 1999. Sections 33(4) and 33(5); and *Protection of New Plant Varieties Act* of Malaysia. 2004. Section 31.
40 *Protection of Plant Varieties and Farmers' Rights Act* of India. 2001. Sections 24, 26 and 40; *Plant Varieties Protection Act* of Thailand. 1999. Sections 19(3), 19(4), and 19(5); and *Protection of New Plant Varieties Act* of Malaysia. 2004. Sections 12(10)(f) and 12(10)(g).
41 Medaglia, J. C., C. Oguamanam, O. Rukundo, and F. Perron-Welch. 2019. *Comparative Study of the Nagoya Protocol, the Plant Treaty and the UPOV Convention: The Interface of Access and Benefit Sharing and Plant Variety Protection*. Montreal: Centre for International Sustainable Development Law. Accessed May 28 2019. www.cisdl.org/wp-content/uploads/2019/04/Final-Report-Nagoya-Protocol-Plant-Treaty-and-UPOV.pdf
42 See, for example, Adhikari, K. 2018. 'Reconceptualising Access: Moving Beyond the Limits of International Biodiversity Laws.' In *Biodiversity, Genetic Resources and Intellectual Property: Developments in Access and Benefit Sharing*, edited by C. Lawson and K. Adhikari. Abingdon: Routledge, pages 9–32.

Agreement.[43] The UPOV-plus laws of India, Thailand, and Malaysia rectify this oversight.

The second reason that explains why India, Thailand, and Malaysia pursued UPOV-plus plant variety rights laws relates to the gradual strengthening of the scope of plant breeders' rights under the UPOV Convention. The prior, 1961 and 1978 Acts of the UPOV Convention contained certain flexibilities for farmers to save, use, exchange, and sell the farm-saved seeds of protected plant varieties. This latitude was restricted in UPOV 1991, which prevents farmers from selling the seeds of protected plant varieties.[44] The reduction of the policy space available for farmers under the principle of the 'farmers' privilege' raised concerns, especially because a significant number of farming communities in India, Malaysia, and Thailand – as in many other developing countries – still rely on traditional agricultural systems and the customary farming practices of seed saving, exchange, and sale. The UPOV-plus laws of these countries protect these practices, while expanding the notion of the farmers' privilege into an enforceable right.

The third and final reason that motivated India, Thailand, and Malaysia to introduce UPOV-plus plant variety rights laws concerns the notion of 'farmers' rights' over crop genetic resources. The concept of farmers' rights gained international recognition in the 1980s through a resolution that was annexed to the 1983 *International Undertaking on Plant Genetic Resources for Food and Agriculture*. This non-binding resolution stated that 'farmers' rights mean rights arising from past, present, and future contributions of farmers in making available plant genetic resources.'[45]

In 2001, the Plant Treaty further substantiated the concept of farmers' rights. In so doing, the Plant Treaty recognised a set of rights to which farmers are entitled, including the right to the protection of their traditional knowledge; the right to save, exchange, reuse and sell farm-saved seeds; and the right to equitable participation in benefit sharing related to the use of their plant genetic resources and

43 For detailed information about the review of Article 27.3(b) of the TRIPS Agreement, see World Trade Organization. 2019. 'TRIPS: Reviews, Article 27.3(b) and Related Issues: Background and the Current Situation.' World Trade Organization. Accessed May 28 2019. www.wto.org/english/tratop_e/trips_e/art27_3b_background_e.htm

44 See, for example, Netnou-Nkoana, N. C., J. B. Jaftha, M. A. Dibiloane, and J. Eloff. 2015. 'Understanding of the Farmers' Privilege Concept by Smallholder Farmers in South Africa.' *South African Journal of Science* 111 (1–2): 1–5; and Sahai, S. 2002. 'India's Plant Variety Protection and Farmers' Rights Legislation.' In *Global Intellectual Property Rights*, edited by P. Drahos and R. Mayne. New York: Palgrave Macmillan, pages 214–223.

45 Food and Agriculture Organisation of the United Nations. 1989. 'E. Commission on Plant Genetic Resources and the International Undertaking: Progress Report.' *Twenty-fifth Session of the Conference of the Food and Agriculture Organisation of the United Nations.* Accessed May 28 2019. www.fao.org/3/x5588E/x5588e06.htm#e.%20commission%20on%20plant%20genetic%20resources%20and%20the%20international%20undertaking:%20prog

traditional knowledge.[46] These farmers' rights were negotiated to address the concerns that developing and least-developed countries had raised in international forums in the 1980s and the 1990s. Therefore, it is unsurprising that the international recognition of farmers' rights has influenced the form of intellectual property for plant varieties that has been recognised in the UPOV-plus laws of India, Thailand, and Malaysia.

The reasons that inspired Nepal to pursue a UPOV-plus framework of plant variety rights parallel those that drove lawmaking in India, Thailand, and Malaysia. As such, there are many similarities between the plant variety rights laws of these three countries and the Nepali framework. Nevertheless, the approach that Nepal has taken to recognise farmers' varieties as intellectual property is distinct from the way that India, Thailand, and Malaysia have conceived of protections for farmers' varieties. Section 10.3 describes the unique aspects of the Nepali regime, while also providing an historical overview of how the idea of creating a UPOV-plus plant variety rights law originated in Nepal.

10.3 The making of the UPOV-plus plant variety rights regime in Nepal

In 1965, Nepal introduced the *Patent, Design and Trademark Act* as its first modern intellectual property law. Although the Nepali public sector already had started to breed and introduce a number of improved varieties, this Act did not contain any specific provision to regulate the development and protection of new crop varieties and seeds in Nepal. The legal regulation of new crop varieties and seeds became possible only after Nepal promulgated the 1988 *Seeds Act*. In consideration of the growing involvement of the public sector in crop varietal development and the gradual expansion of the private domestic seed industry in the 1980s, the *Seeds Act* primarily aimed to regulate the production, marketing, export, and import of quality seeds.[47] The infrastructure necessary to meet this objective also accompanied the legislation. The Act created a National Seed Board to release and register improved plant varieties and to certify seeds; to test the distinctness, uniformity, and stability of improved plant varieties; and to grant the right of ownership to plant breeders based on certain prescribed rules.[48]

Over time, the implementation of the *Seeds Act* led to the release and registration of hundreds of plant varieties of cereal, vegetable, and other crops in Nepal.[49]

46 *International Treaty on Plant Genetic Resources for Food and Agriculture* (the Plant Treaty). Article 9.
47 *Seeds Act* of Nepal. 1988. Section 5(4) and 5(5).
48 Ibid, Section 5(6).
49 For detailed information about all of the varieties that have been released and registered in Nepal, see Joshi, B. K., M. R. Bhatta, K. H. Ghimire, M. Khanal, S. B. Gurung, R. Dhakal, and B. R. Sthapit. 2017. *Released and Promising Crop Varieties of Mountain Agriculture in Nepal (1959–2016)*. Kathmandu: Local Initiatives for Biodiversity, Research and Development, the Nepal Agriculture Research Council, and Bioversity International.

However, the National Seed Board never developed any rules to specify what kinds of ownership rights, if any, the breeders of new plant varieties could exercise under the law. According to the Nepali seed authorities, because there was no legal dispute over the ownership of plant varieties, neither the 1997 *Seeds Regulations* nor the 1999 *National Seed Policy* explained the nature and scope of breeders' ownership right over plant varieties.[50]

It was only after Nepal applied to join the World Trade Organization in 1998 that intellectual property protection for plant varieties emerged as a national concern. Between 1998 and 2003, numerous consultations were held to explore the possibility of enacting a TRIPS-compliant plant variety rights law. The majority of Nepali people are poor subsistence farmers who hold fewer than 0.5 hectares of land and who rely on customary practices of seed saving, exchange, and sale to obtain over 90 percent of their cereal crop seeds and 35 percent of their vegetable crop seed requirement.[51] Consultations with the Nepali public led to the formation of a national consensus: in Nepal, any prospective plant variety rights should recognise the rights and interests of farmers. Furthermore, it was agreed that the law would respond to the needs of the domestic private sector – whose presence in the national seed economy was limited to the marketing of new seeds – and the domestic public sector – which had been leading plant breeding and crop varietal development projects since the 1960s.[52]

Another major outcome of these dialogues manifested during the final stages of accession negotiations at the World Trade Organization. Nepal did not agree to join the UPOV Convention as a means to comply with the TRIPS Agreement.[53] The Nepali delegates stated that their government would not accede to the World Trade Organization if membership were made contingent on ratifying the UPOV Convention.[54] Ultimately, negotiators on both sides agreed that the Nepali government would enact 'a separate, free-standing Plant Variety Protection Act [to] protect the rights of relevant stakeholders in accordance with the needs of the

50 Personal interviews with the authorities of the former and current seed officials of the National Seed Quality Control Centre (November 2018).

51 Central Bureau of Statistics. 2011. *Nepal Living Standards Survey 2010/2011*. Kathmandu: Central Bureau of Statistics, Government of Nepal.

52 For a detailed historical analysis of the role of public and private sectors in the development, release, and registration of plant varieties in Nepal, see, for example, Adhikari, K. 2016. 'Shaping Seed Regulation in Nepal: The Role of Networks, Informality and Community.' PhD diss., The Australian National University.

53 In August 2003, some members of the World Trade Organization had pressured the country to become a member of UPOV. See Adhikari, R. and K. Adhikari. 2004. 'UPOV: Faulty Agreement and Coercive Practices.' In *Evolving Sui Generis Options for the Hindu-Kush Himalayas*, edited by R. Adhikari and K. Adhikari. Kathmandu: South Asia Watch on Trade, Economics and Environment, pages 71–82.

54 Winge, T., K. Adhikari, and R. Andersen. 2013. 'Advocacy for Farmers' Rights in Nepal.' In *Realising Farmers' Rights to Crop Genetic Resources: Success Stories and Best Practices*, edited by R. Andersen and T. Winge. Abingdon: Routledge, pages 181–194.

country.'[55] This *sui generis* option provided the basis on which Nepal started to conceptualise its own kind of plant variety rights system.

Following the formal accession of Nepal to the World Trade Organization in April 2004, the Nepali Ministry of Agriculture prepared the first draft of its plant variety rights law, which was entitled the *Draft Bill on Plant Variety Protection and Farmers' Rights*. This TRIPS-compliant legal framework encompassed a broader scope than standard models of intellectual property for plants, which typically only recognise the exclusive rights of plant breeders to produce, reproduce, and market the seeds of protected varieties. In so doing, the Nepali Bill included provisions to counterbalance the rights of breeders with the rights of farmers to save, use, exchange, and sell the seeds of protected plant varieties.

Despite its express objective to protect farmers' rights through the incorporation of UPOV-plus provisions, numerous actors criticised the initial draft of the Nepali Bill. Some civil society organisations argued that the conceptualisation of farmers' rights in the Bill was too vague. These groups were concerned that it was not clear whether the objective of the Bill was to protect plant varieties that farmers breed, or to protect all traditional varieties that farmers conserve and cultivate under diverse ecological and growing conditions.[56] Furthermore, critics suggested that the Bill should be revised to incorporate a more detailed understanding of the meaning, nature, and role of farmers' varieties.

10.4 The evolution of the farmers' varieties concept in Nepal

The concept of farmers' varieties was not formally recognised in Nepal before 2006. The first comprehensive institutional effort to embody this concept in law was when the Nepali Ministry of Agriculture formed a new drafting committee to revise the national system of seed regulation in 2007, which included the *Draft Bill on Plant Variety Protection and Farmers' Rights*.[57] The new drafting committee included representatives from multiple stakeholder groups, including: (1) officials from the Nepali Ministry of Agriculture, the Department of Agriculture, the Nepal Agricultural Research Council, and the National Seed Quality Control Centre; (2) seed traders affiliated with the Seed Entrepreneurs Association of Nepal; (3) legal experts from the Nepali Ministry of Law and the International Centre for Integrated

55 World Trade Organization. 2003. *Report of the Working Party on the Accession of Nepal to the World Trade Organisation*. WT/ACC/NPL/16. World Trade Organization. Accessed May 28 2019. www.wto.org/english/thewto_e/acc_e/a1_nepal_e.htm

56 This civil society group was led by the National Alliance for Food Security in Nepal and its key members such as South Asia Watch on Trade, Economics and Environment, Forum for Protection of Public Interest, and ActionAid Nepal. For a detailed analysis of the first version of the Nepali *Draft Bill on Plant Variety Protection and Farmers' Rights*, see Adhikari, K. 2004. 'A Commentary on Draft Bill on Plant Variety Protection and Farmers' Rights.' *The Rising Nepal*. November 9.

57 In addition to the revision of the *Draft Bill on Plant Variety Protection and Farmers' Rights*, this committee was mandated to provide suggestions to amend the 1988 *Seeds Act*, the 1997 *Seeds Regulations*, and the 2007 *Agricultural Biodiversity Policy*.

Mountain Development; and (4) civil society experts from non-governmental and community-based organisations such as Local Initiatives for Biodiversity, Research and Development (LIBIRD), South Asia Watch on Trade, Economics and Environment,[58] and the Forum for Protection of Public Interest.

Between 2007 and 2011, the new drafting committee compiled information on the experiences of different farming communities, and reviewed a number of local cases to explore how farmers in Nepal understand their plant varieties.[59] The committee members found that Nepali farmers often recognised their varieties as native and indigenous (*Raithane*), traditional (*Paramparagat*), or local (*Sthaniya*). For farmers, the categories of native, indigenous, and traditional all implied that these varieties were 'indigenous' to their lands, or that they were being cultivated and used in a particular geographical location for generations. Although local varieties shared a similar meaning, some of the farmers who interacted with the drafting committee members highlighted that local varieties could also be understood as varieties that were originally introduced to their areas from outside sources, but that naturally were adapted to, or were developed by farmers based on local growing conditions.[60]

The meanings of native, indigenous, traditional, and local varieties were discussed substantially in numerous drafting committee meetings. The committee members observed that Nepali breeders, government authorities, and scholars also used these concepts – in addition to the term 'landraces' – to refer to varieties belonging to specific local areas, or to local, indigenous, and farming communities.[61] Based on the review of the terms that farmers used to identify their varieties, members of the drafting committee started to explore whether the Bill to protect plant varieties could use the catch-all term 'farmers' varieties' to signify all of the categories that Nepali farmers had described.

After extensive debates about how to define farmers' varieties in the prospective Nepali plant variety rights regime, the committee members concluded that it would be problematic to establish protections in the form of intellectual property for native, indigenous, traditional, and local varieties. This is because it would be difficult for these

58 From 2007 to 2011, the author was also invited to be an expert member of the drafting committee that revised the *Draft Bill on Plant Variety Protection and Farmers' Rights*, in addition to the *Seed Act*, the *Seed Regulations*, and the *Agricultural Biodiversity Policy*. At that time, the author was Research Director at South Asia Watch on Trade, Economics and Environment.

59 The relevant cases and data on farmers' perceptions about their plant varieties were collected based on a review of existing literature, government reports, civil society reports, and workshops that were organised in various parts of Nepal by LIBIRD, and South Asia Watch on Trade, Economics and Environment.

60 Examples of these varieties include the hundreds of plant varieties that were released and/or registered under the 1988 *Seeds Act* of Nepal. Most of these plant varieties were bred from the 1960s to the 2000s by using parental lines provided by external agencies such as the CGIAR (Consultative Group for International Agricultural Research). See Joshi, et al., note 49.

61 See, for example, Wyss, R., I. Lopez Noriega, D. Gauchan, and D. Guenat. 2018. *Farmers' Access to Quality and Diverse Seed in Nepal: Implications for Seed Sector Development*. Rome: Bioversity International.

types of plant varieties to meet the criterion of novelty. Native, traditional, indigenous, and local varieties were known to many farmers, and had been cultivated, used, and sold for generations in multiple locations. Moreover, because these varieties were often characterised by genetic heterogeneity,[62] there were also concerns about whether they could meet the uniformity and stability requirements for plant variety protection.

The committee members also felt that defining the scope of farmers' varieties to include native, indigenous, traditional, and local varieties could complicate the implementation of a new access and benefit sharing regime that the Nepali Ministry of Forests had generated in the form of the *Draft Bill on Genetic Resources.* The committee members were aware that this CBD-compatible Bill included some protections for plant genetic resources that were owned and/or controlled by the State, private persons, farmers, and local and indigenous communities.[63] For example, the Genetic Resources Bill included provisions that would require all of the country's genetic resources to be inscribed in a national biodiversity register.[64] The Genetic Resources Bill also would require third parties to present evidence that they had obtained prior informed consent from owners to access their genetic resources, and that they had negotiated benefit sharing agreements with the relevant resource owners.[65]

Notwithstanding the complications surrounding the various meanings of the varietal categories, the drafting committee members were able to determine the best way forward by analysing the case of the *Pokhareli Jethobudho* rice variety. Until 2005, this variety was known only as a traditionally grown cultivar of the Pokhara valley. The variety was referred to as *Jethobudho*. However, in 2006, an improved version of *Jethobudho*, named *Pokhareli Jethobudho* obtained legal recognition as the first new variety to be bred expressly for commercialisation and registered under the *Seeds Act* by farmers in Nepal.[66]

When the drafting committee members reviewed the case of *Pokhareli Jethobudho* (which is discussed further in section 10.5), they took special note of the following three phenomena. First, in contrast to *Jethobudho* rice, *Pokhareli Jethobudho* was developed expressly to meet the requirements of distinctness, uniformity, and stability. Second, the improved *Pokhareli Jethobudho* variety was registered under the Nepali *Seeds Act* of 1988, and thus it had received legal endorsement to be commercialised in the country. Third, because the *Seeds Act*

62 For a detailed analysis of the genetic heterogeneity of landraces and farmers' varieties, see Cherfas, J. 2016. 'Technical Challenges in Identifying Farmers' Varieties.' In *Farmers' Crop Varieties and Farmers' Rights: Challenges in Taxonomy and Law*, edited by M. Halewood. New York: Routledge, pages 27–42.

63 *Draft Bill on Genetic Resources* of Nepal. Section 4.

64 Ibid, Section 6.

65 Ibid, Sections 7 and 20.

66 Van Etten, J., I. López Noriega, C. Fadda, and E. Thomas. 2017. 'The Contribution of Seed Systems to Crop and Tree Diversity in Sustainable Food Systems.' In *Mainstreaming Agrobiodiversity in Sustainable Food Systems: Scientific Foundations for An Agrobiodiversity Index.* Rome: Bioversity International.

was silent about the scope of proprietary rights for registered plant varieties, *Pokhareli Jethobudho* highlighted the need to protect farmer-improved varieties with some form of intellectual property.

The *Pokhareli Jethobudho* case prompted members of the drafting committee to revise the *Draft Bill on Plant Variety Protection and Farmers' Rights*, and to divide plant varieties into three categories. The new typology included 'new plant varieties,' 'farmers' varieties,' and 'local varieties.' According to the most recent version of the Bill (which has not been revised since 2011), new plant varieties are those which breeders register and that meet the criteria of novelty, distinctness, uniformity, and stability;[67] farmers' varieties are those which farmers register and that are distinct, uniform, and stable;[68] and local varieties are those which are under the knowledge and use of farmers, or that are available within the territory of Nepal as traditional varieties.[69] As discussed later, under this classification, *Jethobudho* could be considered a 'local variety' and *Pokhareli Jethobudho* a 'farmers' variety.'

For new plant varieties, the Nepali UPOV-plus Bill grants rights to breeders that mirror those provided in conventional plant breeders' rights regimes, such as the UPOV system. These include the right to produce, reproduce, export, import, and sell the seeds of protected plant varieties. However, in contrast to UPOV, the Nepali Bill explicitly states that farmers have the right to save, reuse, exchange, and sell (except in branded form) the seeds of breeders' new plant varieties.[70] According to the UPOV-plus Bill, Nepali farmers also have other rights in relation to the seeds of breeders' new plant varieties. These include: the right to receive compensation for crop losses if breeders supply substandard seeds or sell seeds using misleading or false information;[71] and the right to access the seeds of breeders' varieties if breeders fail to supply seeds in quantities sufficient to satisfy farmers' demand, or if breeders engage in anti-competitive practices to sell seeds.[72]

Furthermore, the Nepali UPOV-plus Bill recognises three specific rights that farmers can exercise once they protect their distinct, uniform, and stable varieties as farmers' varieties. Notably, the duration of these rights for farmers' varieties is unlimited. First, farmers have the right to register their varieties and to obtain a varietal ownership certificate.[73] Because the Bill does not specify the scope of ownership rights over farmers' varieties, it appears that this provision has been designed only to grant social and legal recognition, and not to recognise the exclusive right to produce, reproduce, and market the seeds of protected farmers' varieties. The second and third specific rights that the Bill grants to farmers are the

67 *Draft Bill on Plant Variety Protection and Farmers' Rights* of Nepal. 2011. Section 2(f).
68 Ibid, Section 2(l).
69 Ibid, Section 2(m).
70 Ibid, Section 27(1)(a).
71 Ibid, Section 27(1)(d).
72 Ibid, Section 27(1)(e).
73 Ibid, Section 27(2)(a).

right to provide prior informed consent if third parties seek to access farmers' varieties for commercial research or use;[74] and the right to know about any instances in which farmers' varieties would be accessed or used for bioprospecting.[75] Both of these rights are intended to operate as a means to enforce disclosure requirements for plant breeders, and to obligate breeders to share any benefits that are realised through the commercialisation of the plant varieties that they develop through the use of farmers' or local varieties.

The drafting committee members likely assumed that farmers' varieties (improved and distinct) would originate from the improvement of local varieties (source germplasm). Thus, the Nepali legal framework defines local varieties as those which are 'under the knowledge and use of farmers' or that are 'available within the territories of Nepal as traditional varieties.'[76] This definition implies that local varieties could be under the ownership or control of farmers or other actors (such as the State). However, the Bill does not explicitly recognise any rights that these actors may have in relation to local varieties. According to the drafting committee, the rationale for this lacuna was that rights related to local varieties would be protected under the access and benefit sharing principles of the *Draft Bill on Genetic Resources.* Meanwhile, the Plant Variety Protection Bill would regulate rights related to farmers' varieties (i.e., improved and distinct varieties).

Following the conceptualisations of farmers' varieties as improved and distinct varieties and local varieties as source germplasm, the Nepali government was prepared to implement the *Draft Bill on Plant Variety Protection and Farmers' Rights* before mid-2013. However, after Nepal and other least-developed member countries of the World Trade Organisation were granted an exemption from compliance with the TRIPS Agreement until July 2021,[77] the Nepali Ministry of Agriculture decided not to pursue the implementation of the plant variety rights law. In the meantime, important developments occurred that raise a number of questions and concerns in relation to the conceptualisation of farmers' varieties as intellectual property in Nepal. In an attempt to identify and discuss these questions and concerns, section 10.5 explores how the *Jethobudho* rice cultivar evolved to be recognised under the *Seeds Act* as the distinct, uniform, and stable *Pokhareli Jethobudho* variety.

74 Ibid, Section 27(2)(b).
75 Ibid, Section 27(2)(c).
76 Ibid, Section 2(m).
77 As a response to the special needs of least-developed member countries of the World Trade Organization, the transition period to protect intellectual property through national legislation has been extended twice by the Council for TRIPS, first in 2005 and again in 2013. For further details, see World Trade Organization. 2019. 'Responding to Least Developed Countries' Special Needs in Intellectual Property.' World Trade Organization. Accessed May 28 2019. www.wto.org/english/tratop_e/trips_e/ldc_e.htm

10.5 The historic evolution of Pokhareli Jethobudho as a commercial variety

Before *Pokhareli Jethobudho* was registered as a commercial variety in 2006, there existed a population of traditional rice cultivars known as simply *Jethobudho* in the Pokhara valley of Nepal. Despite its popularity as one of the oldest traditional varieties in the valley, in the 1990s Pokhareli farmers, who were growing *Jethobudho* at an altitude of 600 to 900 metres above sea level, expressed the concern that the rice had begun to underperform due to certain problems with its agronomic traits. According to Pokhareli farmers, these local cultivars were susceptible to lodging, and to insect pests and diseases, such as leaf and neck blast infection. Furthermore, the agronomic yield of *Jethobudho* was very low compared to other types of rice that farmers were growing in the Pokhara valley. Nevertheless, *Jethobudho* was still in high demand, mainly because it was indigenous to the Pokhara valley and local rice growers and consumers preferred *Jethobudho* due to its postharvest traits such as aroma, taste, softness, and other cooking qualities.

Because Pokhareli farmers remained interested in benefitting from the production of this local variety, in 1997 a group of national and international actors designed a participatory plant breeding project to improve *Jethobudho*. One of the key objectives of the project was to create a distinct, uniform, and stable version of *Jethobudho* and eventually to help Pokhareli farmers to register the improved *Jethobudho* variety under the Nepali seed certification system. Doing so was important for two main reasons. First, the 1988 *Seeds Act* of Nepal contains a requirement to test the distinctness, uniformity, and stability of plant varieties before a decision is made to release and register them for commercial production and sale in Nepal.[78] Second, no individual or organisation is allowed to sell or distribute the seeds of plant varieties that have not been released, registered or certified under the Nepali *Seeds Act*.[79] Although these provisions had minimal impact on customary farming practices of seed saving, exchange, and sale in Nepal,[80] it was possible that the seed law would prevent Pokhareli farmers from commercialising an improved *Jethobudho* variety in the future.

The process of improving *Jethobudho* was complicated. It involved substantial internal and external resources, including years of research in different farmers' fields in the Pokhara valley. Throughout the course of the project, Pokhareli farmers, breeders, extension workers, and community researchers actively were engaged in a series of participatory varietal research trials, which were conducted from 1998 to 2005 to evaluate and improve the agronomic and postharvest traits

78 *Seeds Act* of Nepal. 1988. Section 5(6).
79 Ibid, Sections 11(a) and 11(b).
80 At the time of the interviews and focus group discussions that I conducted with the Nepali seed authorities in November 2018, they revealed that there was no record of any legal initiative that to date had been undertaken to prevent customary farming practices of seed saving, exchange, use, or sale.

of *Jethobudho*.[81] The major partners of the project were: a Nepali not-for-profit community-based organisation (LIBIRD); an autonomous agricultural research organisation (the Nepal Agricultural Research Council); and a CGIAR Research Centre (Bioversity International).

The purpose of the project was to monitor the performance of all of the collected lines, and to select a set of lines that would contain improved and locally desired agronomic and postharvest traits. During the initial stage of these research trials, two sets of 338 lines of *Jethobudho* were collected from Pokhareli farmers. These farmers were from 11 different sites of the Pokhara valley: Satmuhane, Malmul, Sisuwa, Maidi, Khaste, Arghun, Rithepani, Kundhar Arba, Kamal Pokhari, Biruwa, and Fewa. In 2000, the project reached an agreement with local farmers to research the collected two sets of 338 lines in farmers' fields at the Malmul and Fewa sites, as well as in the Melapaten-based public research station of the Nepal Agricultural Research Council. In 2003, based on the preferences of local farmers, breeders, and consumers, the project members narrowed down the selection of *Jethobudho* accessions to six locally preferred lines, and also reached a consensus to promote *Jethobudho* as an improved composite variety of these six lines. Subsequently, the project mobilised five different farming communities to produce and distribute the seeds of the improved *Jethobudho* variety among a large group of Pokhareli farmers. The rationale for this decision was to evaluate how a broader community of farmers would assess and adopt the selected six lines of the variety.

The results were promising, given that a wider group of farmers expressed interest in growing the composite variety, not least because its cultivation led to an increase of grain yields from 2.4 tonnes per hectare in 1999 to 3.4 tonnes per hectare in 2005.[82] Compared to the local *Jethobudho* population, the composite variety also provided greater resilience to local growing conditions – including tolerance to blast disease and lodging – while maintaining favourable postharvest traits such as aroma and taste. The positive feedback from both farmers and consumers encouraged the initiators and partners of the participatory plant breeding project to submit an application to register the improved *Jethobudho* variety under the Nepali seed law.

Ultimately, after a favourable evaluation in 2006, the composite *Jethobudho* variety was registered as a multiline enhanced variety called *Pokhareli Jethobudho*. In accordance with the Nepali seed law, the decision to register *Pokhareli*

81 For a detailed analysis of the participatory research trails of Pokhareli Jethobudho, see Shrestha, P. K. 2016. 'Leveraging the Successful Participatory Improvement of Pokhareli Jethobudho for National Policy Development in Nepal.' In *Farmers' Crop Varieties and Farmers' Rights: Challenges in Taxonomy and Law*, edited by M. Halewood, 59–72. New York: Routledge; and Gyawali, S., B. R. Sthapit, B. Bhandari, J. Bajracharya, P. K. Shrestha, M. P. Upadhyay, and D. I. Jarvis. 2010. 'Participatory Crop Improvement and Formal Release of Jethobudho Rice Landrace in Nepal.' *Euphytica* 176 (1): 59–78.

82 This information is based on the data collected from the official records of the National Seed Quality Control Centre of Nepal (November 2018).

Jethobudho as a commercial multiline variety was made by the Variety Approval, Release and Registration Sub-Committee of the National Seed Board. Before making this decision, a technical team of the Sub-Committee had visited relevant farmers' fields to conduct a scientific evaluation of the variety. After the conclusion of this testing and a detailed review of the application for registration of the variety, the Sub-Committee confirmed that, compared to the traditionally grown *Jethobudho* rice, *Pokhareli Jethobudho* was preferred locally and met the criteria of distinctness, uniformity, and stability. Thus, its developers (owners) could legally commercialise the variety through the production and sale of improved seeds.

Following the legal recognition of *Pokhareli Jethobudho* as a commercial variety, farmers from the Fewa Phant of the Pokhara valley especially were pleased. These farmers were proud of the fact that their 'Fewa Seed-Producing Farmers' Group' – together with LIBIRD, the Nepal Agricultural Research Council, the Pokhara-based District Agriculture Development Office, and Bioversity International – were recognised as the legal owners of *Pokhareli Jethobudho*. In the words of a farmer from the Fewa Seed-Producing Farmers' Group: 'It is a priceless reward for our farming communities to be recognised as co-owners of Pokhareli Jethobudho and to make the first step towards the legal recognition of a traditionally grown variety in the national seed system.'[83]

Over time, the accomplishments of the Fewa Seed-Producing Farmers' Group were not limited to obtaining co-ownership of *Pokhareli Jethobudho*. Its members emerged as a vibrant group of local seed producers, who earned significant profits from the accelerating production and sale of the seeds of *Pokhareli Jethobudho*. Estimates suggest that from 2006 to 2016, members of the Fewa Seed-Producing Farmers' Group were able to increase the annual production of *Pokhareli Jethobudho* seeds from 3,425 kilograms to 10,000 kilograms. Over the same period of time, the per kilogram price of these seeds increased from NPR 35 to NPR 170.[84] The scale of these economic benefits was significant. Between 2010 and 2016, farmers were selling the seeds of *Pokhareli Jethobudho* at a price that was two to three times higher than the prices of the seeds of other locally sold rice varieties.

Despite the strong economic returns from the commercialisation of *Pokhareli Jethobudho*, in recent years tensions have arisen between members of the Fewa Seed-Producing Farmers' Group and other stakeholders. Particularly after 2016, a number of consumer-farmers and seed traders began to express concerns about the quality of the *Pokhareli Jethobudho* seeds that the Fewa Seed-Producing Farmers' Group provided. This is because the *Pokhareli Jethobudho* seeds that circulated in local markets were characterised by off-types to such an extent that consumer-farmers suffered

83 Personal interview with a farmer of the Fewa Seed-Producing Farmers' Group (November 2018).

84 Personal interviews with an official of LIBIRD and a farmer of the Fewa Seed-Producing Farmers' Group (November 2018).

from significant losses in grain production.[85] The reputation of the commercial variety began to deteriorate based on the poor seed quality.

Because *Pokhareli Jethobudho* is a legally registered variety in Nepal, in mid-2018 some of these consumer-farmers approached the Pokhara-based Agricultural Development Directorate to claim compensation for the losses caused by the substandard quality of *Pokhareli Jethobudho* seeds. At the time of the author's fieldwork in November 2018, and while the government officials of the Agricultural Development Directorate were planning to undertake a legal action to address farmers' complaints, another co-owner of *Pokhareli Jethobudho* – LIBIRD – had already stopped working with the Fewa Seed-Producing Farmers' Group.

From the registration of *Pokhareli Jethobudho* in 2006 until approximately 2016, LIBIRD had coordinated the maintenance of the breeder seed of the variety (the initial source of seed), thereby enabling the Fewa Seed-Producing Farmers' Group to produce foundation seed (the progeny of breeder seed and a pure seed stock to maintain the variety's genetic purity and identity). Following multiplication of foundation seed, the Fewa Seed-Producing Farmers' Group oversaw the production and circulation of 'truthfully-labelled' improved seeds. However, although the Nepali *Seeds Act* requires seed producers who use truthful labels to meet certain quality standards, the Fewa Seed-Producing Farmers' Group neglected this obligation.

According to the officials of the Agricultural Development Directorate and LIBIRD, members of the Fewa Seed-Producing Farmers' Group prioritised short-term gains, and thus they did not identify and remove off-type plants. Furthermore, seed traders asserted that members of the Fewa Seed-Producing Farmers' Group had tarnished their reputation in local seed markets after they failed to maintain the quality of *Pokhareli Jethobudho* seeds. In the words of one local seed trader: 'I do not want to do business with the Fewa Seed-Producing Farmers' Group. The seeds produced by their members contain off-types to such an extent that my clients do not want to purchase their seeds.'[86]

Recently, LIBIRD has begun to support farmers in other parts of the Pokhara valley to produce and sell *Pokhareli Jethobudho* seeds.[87] This new partnership between LIBIRD and local farmers from other areas also aims to expand the market for *Pokhareli Jethobudho* seeds from the Pokhara valley to other suitable regions of Nepal. The members of the Fewa Seed-Producing Farmers' Group – who continue to produce *Pokhareli Jethobudho* seeds – seem worried about LIBIRD's partnership with other farmers. Members of the Fewa Seed-Producing Farmers' Group fear that LIBIRD's new partnership with other farmers, coupled with widespread customary practices of seed saving and reproduction, will affect their ability to benefit exclusively from the production and sale of *Pokhareli Jethobudho* seeds.

85 Focus group discussions with government officials of the Pokhara-based Agricultural Development Directorate and the Ministry of Agriculture (November 2018).

86 Personal interviews with local seed traders in the Pokhara valley (November 2018).

87 Personal interview with an official from LIBIRD (November 2018).

The fear of the Fewa Seed-Producing Farmers' Group is largely justified. Because the Nepali *Seeds Act* is silent about the scope of any ownership rights granted for registered varieties, the legal recognition of *Pokhareli Jethobudho* did not empower these farmers or other owners of the variety to exclusively produce, reproduce, and sell *Pokhareli Jethobudho* seeds.[88] This issue is unlikely to be addressed by the current version of the Nepali *Draft Bill on Plant Variety Protection and Farmers' Rights*. Section 10.6 identifies and discusses a series of questions and concerns that the case of *Pokhareli Jethobudho* raises in relation to the conceptualisation of farmers' varieties as intellectual property in Nepal.

10.6 Questions and concerns that the *Pokhareli Jethobudho* case raises

At the time of the revision of the Nepali *Draft Bill on Plant Variety Protection and Farmers' Rights*, the analysis of the *Pokhareli Jethobudho* case played a significant role in how the drafting committee members conceptualised farmers' varieties as intellectual property. In particular, this case provided empirical evidence that farmers could improve local varieties to become distinct, uniform, and stable, and thus that varieties created through local breeding efforts could be registered for intellectual property protection as farmers' varieties. Despite this, several questions and concerns exist in relation to the conceptualisation of farmers' varieties as intellectual property, which lawmakers in Nepal should address before the country implements its UPOV-plus plant variety rights law.

10.6.1 Do farmers have the necessary resources to develop distinct, uniform, and stable varieties for intellectual property protection?

The Nepali *Draft Bill on Plant Variety Protection and Farmers' Rights* requires all farmers to meet the criteria of distinctness, uniformity, and stability to register their varieties as intellectual property. There is concern about whether Nepali farmers – the majority of whom are poor and depend on subsistence farming for their livelihoods – would be able to fulfil these requirements. The case of *Pokhareli Jethobudho* illustrates that in the absence of support from external actors and agencies, it would have been very challenging, if not impossible, for farmers in the Pokhara valley to manage and mobilise all of the resources that were required to conduct varietal selection trials, to improve *Jethobudho*'s agronomic and postharvest traits, and to develop an application for the legal registration of the variety.

In view of the constraints that many Nepali farmers face, the *Draft Bill on Plant Variety Protection and Farmers' Rights* enables farmers to register their varieties free of cost.[89] However, this may not be sufficient to incentivise farmers to protect

88 *Seeds Act* of Nepal. 1988. Section 5(6).
89 *Draft Bill on Plant Variety Protection and Farmers' Rights* of Nepal. 2011. Section 27(2)(a).

their varieties. As the *Pokhareli Jethobudho* case shows, there are many costs other than the registration fee that Nepali farmers must incur to develop distinct, uniform, and stable farmers' varieties. In recognition of the need to reduce farmers' financial, technical, and administrative burdens, the Bill also intends to relax the uniformity and stability standards of farmers' varieties.[90] Nonetheless, it is important to recall here that in the case of *Pokhareli Jethobudho*, the failure of members of the Fewa Seed-Producing Farmers' Group to remove off-type plants and to maintain the uniformity and overall quality of the variety led many consumer-farmers to suffer from significant losses in grain production. There are pragmatic reasons to argue why it might be important for the developers of farmers' varieties to strive for high uniformity and stability standards.

10.6.2 Who is eligible to obtain intellectual property for farmers' varieties?

In the *Draft Bill on Plant Variety Protection and Farmers' Rights*, a 'farmer' is defined as: (1) any individual, local community, or indigenous community who is engaged in farming or in the conservation and development of plant varieties; or (2) any institution that the 'farmer' has established as per the Bill or other pertinent laws of Nepal.[91] This definition of farmer implies that under the Bill, an improved traditional variety such as *Pokhareli Jethobudho* – even if it meets the criteria of distinctness, uniformity, and stability – would not qualify to be registered as a farmers' variety. This is mainly because the legal ownership of *Pokhareli Jethobudho* is shared between a seed-producing farmers' group and a group of non-farmer entities, that is, LIBIRD, the Nepal Agricultural Research Council, the District Agriculture Development Office, and Bioversity International.

Thus, for varieties such as *Pokhareli Jethobudho*, which are developed through the involvement of non-farmer entities in participatory breeding projects, registration as farmers' varieties would not be an option. This situation could be problematic for both Nepali farmers and the officials who implement the Bill. On the one hand, Nepali farmers frequently lack the necessary resources to breed and develop distinct, uniform, and stable varieties. On the other hand, the idea of shared ownership between farmer and non-farmer entities might not help in registering improved local varieties as farmers' varieties. In such cases, an alternative option would be to seek registration in the category of breeders' varieties. As discussed in subsection 10.6.3, this option is also fraught with certain complexities.

10.6.3 What complexities are involved in the registration of improved local varieties as breeders' varieties?

Pokhareli Jethobudho has been registered as a distinct, uniform, and stable breeders' variety under the Nepali *Seeds Act*. This implies that varieties such as

90 Ibid, 28(1)(a) and 28(1)(b).
91 Ibid, Section 2(k).

Pokhareli Jethobudho, a commercial variety derived from the improvement of locally cultivated *Jethobudho* rice, might also qualify to be registered as breeders' varieties under the *Draft Bill on Plant Variety Protection and Farmers' Rights*. However, this possibility is complicated by two main factors.

First, to be registered as breeders' varieties under the Bill, all improved local varieties (such as *Pokhareli Jethobudho*) are required to meet the criterion of novelty, in addition to the rigorous standards of uniformity and stability.[92] It is important to note here that the selected six lines of *Jethobudho* that were used to create *Pokhareli Jethobudho* were not generated through sophisticated breeding methods. These lines had been under cultivation and use in different sites of the Pokhara valley for decades, and they were selected to create the composite variety based on their agronomic and postharvest traits and local farmers' preferences.

It also should be noted that the Nepali seed authorities were lenient when they evaluated *Pokhareli Jethobudho* as a unique composite variety. They accepted the traits of the multiline variety as 'adequately uniform' and 'adequately reproducible in new plants in the subsequent years.' The seed authorities were flexible in their evaluation of *Pokhareli Jethobudho* because of a 2005 amendment to the 1997 *Seeds Regulations*, which enabled them to verify the traits of *Pokhareli Jethobudho* based on the traditional knowledge-based perception data that the applicant farmers provided in their variety registration application. Furthermore, the 2005 amendment also allowed the seed authorities to exempt farmers from the requirements of: (1) the submission of the variety's 'multiseason scientific data with statistical analysis'; and (2) the fulfilment of several other conditions, including 'the adoption of more formal breeding procedures.'[93]

Second, even if improved local varieties could meet the same rigorous standards that are required for the protection as breeders' varieties, the owners of these farmers' varieties would not be able to prevent Nepali farmers from saving, producing, reproducing, and selling the seeds of improved traditional varieties. This is because the right of consumer-farmers to save, produce, reproduce, and sell the seeds of breeders' varieties is guaranteed in the *Draft Bill on Plant Variety Protection and Farmers' Rights*. This would likely limit the prospective economic returns that developers of improved local varieties could expect. Indeed, the customary practices of saving, production, and reproduction of the seeds of *Pokhareli Jethobudho* have had a major impact on the economic benefits that the Fewa Seed-Producing Farmers' Group was able to reap.

92 Ibid, Section 5(1)(b).

93 For a detailed analysis of the 2005 amendment to the Nepali *Seeds Regulations* and a discussion of how the traits of Pokhareli Jethobudho were evaluated by the seed authorities, see Shrestha, P. K. 2016. 'Leveraging the Successful Participatory Improvement of Pokhareli Jethobudho for National Policy Development in Nepal.' In *Farmers' Crop Varieties and Farmers' Rights: Challenges in Taxonomy and Law*, edited by M. Halewood. New York: Routledge, pages 59–72, 69.

10.6.4 What are the obligations of the owners of farmers' varieties in relation to the use of local varieties?

At the initial stage of the participatory plant breeding project that developed *Pokhareli Jethobudho*, hundreds of Pokhareli farmers from 11 different sites were involved in the collection of the 338 lines of *Jethobudho*. Most of these farmers were also involved in the participatory varietal selection trials that were conducted from 1998 and 2005 in different farmers' fields at the selected sites. However, at the time of the preparation, submission, and approval of the application to register the variety, the seed-producing farmers from the Fewa Phant site were the only farmers to be recognised as joint owners of *Pokhareli Jethobudho*. No benefit sharing agreement was concluded with other farmers, who had provided hundreds of locally cultivated *Jethobudho* accessions from different sites and who were involved in the participatory varietal selection trials.

Members of the Fewa Seed-Producing Farmers' Group did contribute some of the six selected lines of *Jethobudho*, and they had the interest and capacity to produce and sell the seeds of the improved composite variety. Despite this, the failure to recognise farmers from other sites as co-owners of *Pokhareli Jethobudho*, and the lack of benefit sharing with them raises a number of legal questions and concerns. For example, because farmers' varieties will likely use local varieties as source germplasm, do the owners of farmers' varieties – as is the case with breeders of new varieties who use local varieties – have the obligation to seek prior informed consent from, and conclude access and benefit sharing agreements with, the providers of local varieties? If so, what models or options should be used to guide benefit sharing between the owners of farmers' varieties and the providers of local varieties? Should prior informed consent and access and benefit sharing agreements that are concluded between the owners of farmers' varieties and the providers of local varieties be regulated under the TRIPS-compatible national plant variety rights law, or under the CBD-compatible national access and benefit sharing law?

10.6.5 What kinds of exclusive rights do farmers need to commercialise their varieties?

The case of the Fewa Seed-Producing Farmers' Group suggests that in order to benefit fully from the commercialisation of farmers' varieties, the owners of these varieties require some exclusive rights to control the production, reproduction, and marketing of their seeds. Although the revised *Draft Bill on Plant Variety Protection and Farmers' Rights* recognises the right of farmers to register their varieties and to obtain an ownership certificate for an unlimited period, there is no provision that would substantiate the scope of farmers' ownership over their varieties. In effect, this means that the Bill does not grant any explicit, exclusive commercial rights to the owners of farmers' varieties.

Nevertheless, it could be argued that the *Draft Bill on Plant Variety Protection and Farmers' Rights* contains certain implicit exclusive rights to produce, reproduce, and commercialise the seeds of protected farmers' varieties. This is because the Bill does not recognise the rights of consumer-farmers to save, use, exchange, and sell the seeds of protected farmers' varieties, as is the case for protected breeders' varieties. However, it is unlikely that any implicit recognition of exclusive commercial rights over farmers' varieties actually would enable owners to exclude others from producing, reproducing, and marketing the seeds of protected farmers' varieties. This is evidenced in the case of *Pokhareli Jethobudho*, where LIBIRD – a joint owner of the variety – has collaborated with a local farmers' group that is not named as a co-owner of the variety to commercialise *Pokhareli Jethobudho*.

Furthermore, it is unclear why the Bill does not recognise the rights of consumer-farmers to save, use, exchange, and sell the seeds of protected farmers' varieties. This would seem to be an important provision to include, especially given that the Bill expressly recognises these rights of consumer-farmers in relation to all protected breeders' varieties. Even if the Bill were revised to recognise the rights of consumer-farmers to save, use, exchange, and sell the seeds of protected farmers' varieties, an additional concern would still be raised. That is, if consumer-farmers did have the right to save, use, exchange, and sell the seeds of all protected varieties, what incentives would the owners of farmers' varieties have to commercialise their varieties in local seed markets?

10.6.6 Should there be any protection period for farmers' varieties?

According to the *Seeds Act* and the *Seeds Regulations* of Nepal, the *Pokhareli Jethobudho* registration will remain perpetually valid, provided that the variety continues to meet the criteria of distinctness, uniformity, and stability, and that it does not demonstrate a significant decline in yield or production, for example, due to disease or poor adaptive capacity. To date, the Nepali government has used these criteria to deregister a total of 32 varieties of rice, wheat, and maize after they were found to be inappropriate for further commercialisation.[94] In contrast, under the *Draft Bill on Plant Variety Protection and Farmers' Rights*, there is no provision that would limit the period of protection for registered farmers' varieties. The fact that Nepali farmers' intellectual property rights over their varieties would ostensibly remain valid for an unlimited period of time is a unique feature of the Nepali Bill. The *sui generis* laws of India, Thailand, and Malaysia expressly limit the period of protection for farmers' varieties.

According to the members of the committee that revised the Bill, there were two related reasons why the protection period for farmers' varieties was not limited. The first relates to the fact that according to the standard logic of intellectual property, all protected varieties enter into the public domain after their period of

94 Focus group discussions with Nepali seed authorities (November 2018).

protection expires.[95] The second is explained by a provision in the Plant Treaty that obligates Nepal (and other Contracting Parties) to include in the Multilateral System all Annex 1 plant genetic materials that are in the public domain.[96] Based on these considerations, the drafting committee members did not want to create any legal arrangement that would obligate farmers to include their varieties in the public domain, or in the Multilateral System. Doing so would mean that farmers' varieties such as *Pokhareli Jethobudho* would be accessible to anyone, without restriction. Furthermore, any future benefits that might accrue from the commercial use of farmers' varieties that are included in the Multilateral System would flow directly to the multilateral fund of the Plant Treaty.

While lawmakers' concerns about the relationship between farmers' varieties and the public domain are justified, many questions remain unanswered about the unlimited period of protection that farmers' varieties would receive under the prospective Nepali plant variety rights regime. For instance, would farmers be able to, or be required to, maintain the distinctness, uniformity, and stability of their varieties for an unlimited period of time? If farmers' varieties fail to maintain these characteristics, would it be appropriate to revoke their intellectual property? These questions raise additional concerns that are associated with the rights of consumer-farmers to receive compensation and to access protected varieties through compulsory licensing.

10.6.7 Should the rights of consumer-farmers to receive compensation and to access protected varieties through compulsory licensing apply to farmers' varieties?

The *Pokhareli Jethobudho* case demonstrates that instances could occur in which farmers fail to maintain seed quality or to supply the seeds of registered varieties at a reasonable price. For example, members of the Fewa Seed-Producing Farmers' Group failed to maintain the quality of the seeds of *Pokhareli Jethobudho*. Furthermore, this Group was selling the seeds of *Pokhareli Jethobudho* at a price that was two to three times higher than the prices of the seeds of other locally marketed rice varieties. Although it is understandable that the quality of and demand for *Pokhareli Jethobudho* would be reflected in a premium price, at least some consumers believed that the price of the seeds of this variety was unreasonably high.

In November 2018, a member of the Fewa Seed-Producing Farmers' Group admitted that the Group was unable to evaluate systematically the market trends or the needs of consumer-farmers. Previously, members of the Fewa Seed-Producing

95 Correa, C. M. 2013. 'Plant Genetic Resources under the Management and Control of the Contracting Parties and in the Public Domain.' In *Crop Genetic Resources as a Global Commons: Challenges in International Law and Governance*, edited by Halewood, M., I. L. Noriega, and S. Louafi. Abingdon: Routledge, pages 177–186.

96 'The Multilateral System [...] shall include all plant genetic resources for food and agriculture listed in Annex I that are under the management and control of the Contracting Parties and in the public domain.' Plant Treaty. Article 11.2.

Farmers' Group had sold the seeds of *Pokhareli Jethobudho* at the price of NPR 170/kg to local seed traders, and then local seed traders had sold these seeds to consumer-farmers for NPR 220/kg. Because the price of the seeds of *Pokhareli Jethobudho* was extremely high, in some cases the local units of the Ministry of Agriculture provided subsidies to enable consumer-farmers to purchase the seeds of this variety.

In an attempt to address the potential adverse implications of these kinds of incidents, the Nepali Plant Variety Protection Bill recognises that all farmers have the right to receive compensation for crop losses if breeders supply substandard seeds or sell seeds using misleading or false information.[97] Furthermore, the Bill grants farmers the right to access the seeds of breeders' varieties if breeders fail to supply seeds in quantities sufficient to satisfy farmers' demand, or if breeders engage in anti-competitive practices to sell seeds.[98] Lastly, the Bill creates a mechanism of compulsory licensing to enable farmers to access the seeds of protected breeders' varieties. For example, under the circumstances of insufficient supply of seeds by breeders or breeders' involvement in anti-competitive practices, any person or institution can apply for and obtain a compulsory license to produce and sell the seeds of a protected breeders' plant variety.[99]

Despite these safeguards for farmers, it is important to note that under the Nepali *Draft Bill on Plant Variety Protection and Farmers' Rights* the right of compensation and the scheme of compulsory licensing apply only to breeders' varieties, and not to farmers' varieties. A relevant example of why the right of compensation also should apply to farmers' varieties is evidenced by the complaints that consumer-farmers voiced in relation to the supply of substandard seeds of *Pokhareli Jethobudho*. Likewise, an example of why the scheme of compulsory licensing also should apply to farmers' varieties is evidenced in LIBIRD's decision to stop working with the Fewa Seed-Producing Farmers' Group, and to help new groups of local farmers to produce and commercialise the seeds of *Pokhareli Jethobudho*.

10.7 Conclusion

The emergence of a new set of plant variety rights laws in countries such as India, Thailand, Malaysia, and Nepal have challenged the conventional way of thinking about intellectual property for plant varieties. These UPOV-plus and 'TRIPS-compliant' *sui generis* laws suggest that the meaning of intellectual property for plant varieties is not confined to the traditional ambit of plant breeders' rights, nor is it fixed. Rather, the concept of intellectual property for plant varieties is dynamic and adaptable to the needs of diverse countries and multiple stakeholders, including plant breeders and farmers. This is evident in how the UPOV-plus laws reconceptualise the notion of intellectual property for plant varieties. As with

97 *Draft Bill on Plant Variety Protection and Farmers' Rights* of Nepal. 2011. Section 27(1)(d).
98 Ibid, Section 27(1)(e).
99 Ibid, Section 23.

standard models of plant breeders' rights, these legal instruments offer protection for the new, distinct, uniform, and stable plant varieties that professional breeders develop. Furthermore, UPOV-plus regimes also grant intellectual property for other categories of plant varieties, including those that farmers regularly cultivate, use, and develop under diverse ecological and local growing conditions.

Despite the interest in UPOV-plus laws, to date scholars have paid scant attention to exploring the local needs and dynamics of the conceptualisation of farmers' varieties as intellectual property, let alone the implications of such protection. As discussed in this chapter, there exist numerous questions and concerns in relation to the conceptualisation of farmers' varieties as intellectual property. These questions and concerns range from whether farmers have the ability to leverage the necessary resources to develop and protect farmers' varieties as intellectual property, to the implications that participatory plant breeding programmes between farmers and non-farmer entities may have for obtaining intellectual property rights for locally bred varieties. Of equal importance are other questions and concerns, such as: should farmers' varieties be subject to any protection period, or should these varieties be in the public domain? What kinds of exclusive rights do farmers need to commercialise their varieties? What are the implications of consumer-farmers' rights to save, use, exchange, and sell the seeds of protected farmers' varieties? What are the access and benefit sharing obligations of the owners of farmers' varieties in cases where they use other farmers' local varieties as source germplasm? Lastly, should the rights of consumer-farmers to receive compensation and to access protected varieties through compulsory licensing apply to farmers' varieties?

The questions and concerns that the case of *Pokhareli Jethobudho* raises suggest that there is a need to move beyond the standard binaries that are so often applied to the protection of farmers' varieties. These dichotomisations hold that farmers' varieties should be protected either as exclusive property, or based on non-proprietary aims, including social recognition, unfettered exchange and circulation of plant varieties, and benefit sharing. To transcend this stalemate, this chapter argues that legal protections for farmers' varieties should be rooted in historical and emerging contexts that consider how local farmers perceive, undertake, and perform different roles, for example, as the conservers and suppliers of native, indigenous, traditional, and local varieties plant varieties, and as the breeders, producers, and consumers of farmer-bred plant varieties.[100] A deeper understanding of these kinds of local needs and dynamics of farmers' varietal use and breeding practices might help us better explain what it means to protect farmers' varieties as intellectual property.

100 For a comprehensive understanding of why historical aspects of farmers' seed management practices are important for lawmaking, see Chapman, S. 2018. 'To Make One's Name Famous: Varietal Innovation and Intellectual Property in The Gambia.' *American Ethnologist* 45 (4): 482–494.

Index

For Product Safety Concerns and Information please contact our EU
representative GPSR@taylorandfrancis.com
Taylor & Francis Verlag GmbH, Kaufingerstraße 24, 80331 München, Germany

www.ingramcontent.com/pod-product-compliance
Ingram Content Group UK Ltd.
Pitfield, Milton Keynes, MK11 3LW, UK
UKHW022026061126
477531UK00002B/53

* 9 7 8 0 3 6 7 1 8 0 9 9 7 *